Your Swiss bank book

Your Swiss bank book

Robert Kinsman

 1975

Dow Jones-Irwin, Inc.   Homewood, Illinois   60430

First Printing, July 1975

ISBN 0-87094-099-6
Library of Congress Catalog Card No. 75-7277

Printed in the United States of America

Preface

THIS BOOK was written to provide a factual and balanced reference source on Swiss banking. While much care has been taken to insure its accuracy, it is not intended to be minute in its detail about all Swiss banks. There are simply too many variations in a country with nearly 500 banks to capture them all as a photographer would an alpine scene, even if they never changed.

If you read this book carefully, you will know how and why the Swiss banking industry operates differently in many respects from other banking systems in the western world. You will know how to open an account in a Swiss bank and what services will be available to you. More importantly, you will understand the advantages and disadvantages of banking in Switzerland.

I hope that my efforts will help remove some of the mysteries surrounding Swiss banks and that this book will enhance your understanding of man's unique ability to protect and multiply his resources.

I am most grateful to literally scores of persons who have aided my research on Swiss banks and assisted me in uncovering the salient facts about them. I particularly wish to express my appreciation to the dozens of Swiss bankers, both in the United States and abroad, who have provided valuable insights into their industry but who, for reasons of their own or their bank's privacy, wish to remain anonymous. An exception comes through the kind assistance of Hans Mast, Executive Vice President of Swiss Credit Bank, who has been especially helpful in providing details and critical comments, and whose company on the many occasions we conversed was unfailingly charming, despite his busy schedule and the vagaries of the international telephone system.

My warmest thanks go also to Catherine Cashman and especially Linda Greenlee, who assisted in research and preparation of the manuscript far more than required by the call of duty or purse. Special thanks for technical assistance over the past several years to Harriet Collopy, head librarian, and Jane Ferdon, senior librarian, of the San Francisco Public Library, business branch. Finally, a special note of appreciation is due Peter Landau, editor of *Institutional Investor* magazine, who has shepherded my writing efforts from calamity to fulfillment over the past several years and who, unknowingly, whetted my appetite to undertake this book.

June 1975   ROBERT KINSMAN

Contents

one Introduction 1

two The Lore and the Lure 6

Sagas. The Pied Pipers. Media Intervention. Banks Do
Collapse. Investments. "Hot" Money.

three That "Mysterious Call of the Past" 39

Pillars. Reformation. War for Money. The Guilds and
Cottage Industries. The Cry of Revolution. The New
State. The Budding of Banking. The Federal Birth.
Neutrality. Conclusions.

four The Great Money Game 68

European Dodges. Marco Polos at the Border. Business
Favorites.

five In Gold They Trust 101

Provocateurs. An Inflation Hedge? Where and What.
Margins. Quotations. Why Use Futures?

six The Laundry List 149

The Currency Issue. Account Paperwork. The Savings
Idea. Securities. Private Banks. Investment Funds.
Stock Exchanges. Gold. Americans in Zurich. Perqs.

seven   Those Swiss Myths   184

Who's Passé? Two for the Seesaw. Dealing in Size.
Play Money. There's Gold in Those Francs. The Numbers
Game. The Great Ice Box.

eight   The Pros and Cons   213

Convenience, Costs, and Personality. The Drummer
Factor. Privacy. Judicial Assistance. Stability. Services.
Gold. Some Negatives.

nine   Swiss Bankers Talk   253

Technicalities.

ten   A Recession Shield   264

Index   273

Chapter one

Introduction

WHAT is so fascinating about Swiss banks? Why, when they are mentioned, do we immediately conjure up images of gnomes scurrying into caves with billions to hide, of darkly veiled secrecy surrounding illegal underworld money, of alpine remoteness and incredible money-management success? Why, indeed? Swiss banks are the subject of less fact and greater fantasy than any other financial medium in the world. Anyone willing to take the trouble, and a little time, can find out a great deal about them. But few people are inclined to travel to Switzerland expressly for that purpose.

I was, however, and discovered that facts about the Swiss banking system are simple enough to ascertain there — and also that the Swiss banks' reputation for secrecy is well deserved, if somewhat complex. Their reputation for money-management success is perhaps less well deserved. The banks' lure for money of all types — both legal and illegal — is also real, but is

1

heightened by troubles in the world outside their haven.

In fact, the more of an economical and political mess our world gets into, the more we have found need for the Swiss banks' measures of privacy, protection, and immutability. Recently, it has looked very much as if our interest in, and real need for, Swiss financial institutions were increasing.

U.S. citizens present a special case in their lack of knowledge about Swiss banks. We have rarely needed such information, and generally never cared much about it. The great majority of us have never held or used a foreign currency — a result of our geographic isolation. Among those who have, tourists make up the large bulk, a temporary interest factor if anything, and then only occasionally related to Switzerland. Even U.S. business interests — which only began their international gobbling in earnest a little over a decade ago — were increasing their overseas staffs notably just at the onset of the Great Money Game in 1967, when currencies began their most recent unreasoned gyrations.

Shortly after this point, we found the Congress actively engaged in investigations of American tax evasions and securities frauds through the Swiss banks. We heard about servicemen's club frauds linked with the same banks. We watched the machinations of the gold market and followed gyrating currencies, subjects which had rarely intrigued us before. And then we heard about the U.S. Bank Secrecy Act and its Big Brotherish designs on our private transfers of money. And rather suddenly, isolated America felt a solid need for information about those mysterious Swiss banks. Not just historical or anecdotal or biographical information, but cold facts on how to take advantage of the range of services the Swiss banks have to offer. Now that the United States finds its economic woes currently pressing our awareness of Swiss banks is concurrently awakening. Already it is estimated that some 150,000 Americans hold Swiss bank accounts.

I was motivated in 1972 by all of these factors to write the first "how-to" pamphlet on Swiss banks, "Everything You Always Wanted to Know about Swiss Banks." Now, with this new book, I am expanding and updating that information to show just how a Swiss bank account might be profitable to you, and revealing the methods and motivations of many holders of Swiss bank accounts. You will see how the Swiss banking system passively lures people (some, skimming along on the fine edges of the law, running risks of years in prison) to make use of its quiet, mist-shrouded services. The reasons are as basic as human nature, the banks' contributory influence noble in intent if not result, and our personal needs dynamic and compelling. It is time for the facts to balance the myths. Anyone who wishes to make rational decisions about the value of Swiss banks in terms of personal profits should be able to do so with realistic and not mistaken information.

Among the myths we will explore in leading you to "Your Swiss Bank Book" are a few very popular bits of folklore. For example, "You need a large amount of money to open a Swiss bank account." A large amount of money helps with many things these days, but you'll discover that it is hardly required to open a Swiss account.

Another favorite: "A numbered account at a Swiss bank is a guarantee of privacy of dealings in that account." There is a long list of persons who have believed that and learned the facts behind prison walls. Also, it is widely accepted that only the numbered account can gain the full force of Swiss bank secrecy. That is not true at all. Numbered accounts represent only a few percent, at most, of total Swiss bank accounts. But all Swiss accounts are equally protected under the bank secrecy law. That law makes no distinction between numbered and regular accounts.

Gold has held a great fascination for people of many countries, most recently Americans. It is generally believed that gold buyers can easily purchase gold bullion through Swiss banks, no matter the laws against it in their home countries. While that is believable, you should not go along with the idea that you can buy and store bullion in any size lots in your Swiss bank. Some business just isn't profitable, and with gold the banks will refuse to hold your bullion if it is not in sizable enough parcels. But you can *buy* virtually any size pieces.

Another myth that seems to be widely believed: If the Swiss franc is 100 percent backed by gold held by the Swiss government (which it is), one can redeem francs for gold at any time. Actually, no one can; and no one has been able to since the 30s. We'll see what good that gold "backing" really is.

Finally, the Swiss bank image of a cold, small, highly secretive, and unobtrusive institution could hardly be further from the truth, at least where the public banks are concerned. It may have been a fair image a few decades ago, but not now. The slick, huge, multicolored displays lining the windows of the major banks in the larger cities of Switzerland give as much lie to that worn image as do the public speaking efforts of many Swiss bankers around the world, the free concerts and educational programs offered by the banks for the public in Switzerland, and the occasionally offered drink of Scotch for a client in a banker's office.

With tourism one of Switzerland's leading industries, it is difficult to imagine why these myths persist. Certainly the major banks with their sizable public relations staffs or outside consultants have attempted to set the record straight. Perhaps the world of high finance must always hold a mystique for the average person. After all, not everyone can be in on "a billion dollar killing"—or it wouldn't be a killing. It is true that Swiss bankers have stood at the center of many such grand events. They like it there. They would not change that aspect of their world for anything. In fact, it is probably fair to say that one of the most misleading statements made about the Swiss came from one Andrew Shonfield in 1958 (it might have been partially true in that year; certainly not now):

"It is tough on the Swiss" he wrote, "that William Tell should be replaced in English folklore by this new image of a gnome at the end of a telephone line." It isn't tough on them at all. They wouldn't have it any other way. Permitting that fanciful image to persist is simply their way of compensating for the myths the rest of the world has built up around them.

Chapter two

The Lore and the Lure

THE DEVALUATION of the pound sterling in November 1967 heralded a new era of currency price swings, unknown in nearly a half century, and marked the beginning of the Great Money Game (the subject of Chapter Four). Since then, interest in and use of Swiss banks at first blossomed, and then exploded. By 1974, Swiss bankers said they were receiving thousands of requests a year from Americans for information about accounts; and over 150,000 U.S. citizens were estimated to hold Swiss bank accounts. Assets of the five largest public Swiss banks had nearly tripled in the decade through 1972, reaching over $40 billion by year's end 1973. Swiss banks were then handling an average of $2 billion worth of foreign exchange business *every day*. Deposits alone at the largest, Union Bank, more than doubled in the five years through 1973 when the bank held more than 1.3 million deposit accounts — in a country with a population of less than 7 million persons. And these figures exclude the investment portfolios being managed by all of the banks, which are omitted from public financial statements. One estimate of this most significant money corral

6

runs to $75 billion, well more than double the managed trust assets of all the banks in California, including the world's largest commercial bank, Bank of America. In short, the Swiss banks have grown to control an immense amount of wealth, and they are therefore intriguing a great number of people.

Why this interest in, and enormous growth of the Swiss banks? In addition to those peculiarly American interest factors noted in the previous chapter, the answer begins quite simply. With a reputation for both financial and political stability, Swiss banks became a natural refuge from the suddenly uncertain monetary environment and violence-prone world of the late 1960s. With a banking secrecy system of great fame and real advantage for both legally and illegally obtained funds, the usefulness of Swiss banks was redoubled. Add a handful of highly publicized scandals, reports about Mafia involvement, drug money, and folks like the Clifford Irvings, plus two devaluations of the "good as gold" dollar, and the Swiss "situation" inevitably became one of widespread fascination.

These "facts," however, exist in limbo. They are facts without embellishment. They lack trappings, decor, and circumstance. They are constantly confounded with myths and rumors, and reinforced by the urgings of money "gurus" to save ourselves through the medium of Swiss banks.

Sagas

Indeed, some of the true stories about Swiss banks are more startling than the rumors. For example, in one of the most embarrassing episodes in Swiss banking history, a bank in Basle, the principal commercial city of the country, situated in the northwest corner, on the Rhine river, went so far out on a limb in commodity contracts that in early 1970 it is reliably reported that the bank held contracts valued at 20 times its net worth. Moreover, the bank later failed in a highly publicized scandal in the summer of 1970. UCB, Basle, A. G., was the name. It is no more.

Sounds American, you say? Yes, in a way. It was principally owned by the Western Bancorporation of Los Angeles, also parent of the United California Bank. It was run by an American president, Paul Erdman, now a best selling (but convicted) author. The men involved directly with the commodity contracts were Swiss and German, however, and the bank was incorporated under Swiss law, making it entirely a Swiss entity and subject to all of that nation's statutes and regulations. Three key UCB, Basle, officials were convicted in late 1973, after more than three years of investigation (a large part of which two of the three spent in prison), of the Swiss equivalents of misappropriation of funds and falsification of documents and accounts. Western Bancorporation paid out nearly $50 million in claims, about half of which was settled by actual UCB, Basle assets remaining.

One of UCB, Basle's stockholders was the successful money man and author, George J. W. (Jerry) Goodman, better known by his pen name, "Adam Smith" of *Money Game* and *Supermoney* fame. He didn't find out about the troubles until, too late for remedial action, the bank's closing was revealed in *The Wall Street Journal*. Neither was he able to talk with top bank officials immediately after the collapse, nor sell his stock, nor fully discover what was happening, either through Switzerland or Los Angeles. In *Super-money*[1], Goodman quotes Erdman's wife as saying to him after he had inquired about her imprisoned husband (who had instigated Goodman's investment), ". . . this is not the United States. There is a long phrase . . . I don't know how to translate it . . . I think it means 'suspicion of crimes against a bank'. . . . In Switzerland this is very serious. More serious than murder." The crime turned out not to be, but you couldn't have proved that by any one of the officials in prison at the time. Erdman remained incarcerated in the 17th-century Basel prison for nearly a year during the initial investigation of the bank's demise. One of his codefendants, Rudolph Kummerli, resided there for three years before his trial. You see, habeas corpus doesn't exist in Switzerland, where the legal system is based on Roman, not Anglo-Saxon, law. This fact provides a most efficient basis for conducting investigations of alleged crimes. The prosecuting magistrate in the Swiss criminal system is also the judge who issues orders for bail in lieu of habeas corpus. If his prosecution project is best served by ignoring bail, so be it. All he needs do is renew a retention order every two weeks during the investigation. Thus the long repose for UCB, Basle, defendants.

Apparently, this practice was also handy in the case of one Julio Munoz who headed a financial empire that controlled two Swiss banks until 1964. He was jailed at that time after the banks collapsed under the weight of loans made to his other companies. Munoz

---

[1] "Adam Smith," *Supermoney* (New York: Random House, Inc., 1972).

was released a full decade later, in 1974, without ever having gone to trial, and only then after an action was brought against the Swiss attorney general to settle the case.

As grossly unfair as this may seem to any Anglo-Saxon, a Geneva attorney underscored the Swiss perspective to me. "No countries in the world," he explained, "have this odd thing, habeas corpus, except the Anglo-Saxons. Why should we?" Its lack, and the prosecution's granting of bail, serve the Swiss well.

Paul Erdman may just have the last laugh in his case, however. Writing his best selling novel *The Billion Dollar Sure Thing* while awaiting issuance of bail in the Basle lockup, he promptly skipped his delayed bail prior to his trial. Now residing in the United States, he is apparently feeling secure that his native country won't extradite him to Switzerland. However, his action has undoubtedly furthered the Swiss belief that correct legal concepts were better applied in the Munoz case than in the Erdman affair.

The facts of criminality in the case of the Clifford Irvings are more complex than in either the Erdman or Munoz debacles.

The Irvings, Edith and Clifford, involved in a proposed Howard Hughes biography for the McGraw-Hill Book Company of New York, committed a special crime against Swiss banks. As will be explained in detail in Chapter 6, Swiss law makes the revealing of any pertinent facts about a Swiss bank account punishable by *criminal* statute, much the same way as falsifying accounts was in the UCB case. Switzerland is one of the few countries in the world to so stifle the tongues of bank employees about their bank's business. This is one of the keystones of Swiss bank secrecy, and a not-so-minor thought that permeates the thinking of a Swiss banker whenever he speaks with anyone but his own colleagues.

The celebrated Irving case illustrates the sometimes fascinating application of the bank secrecy law in Switzerland. The Irvings, of course, didn't violate bank secrecy. They used it to fine advantage, for a time. But they did something worse. They defrauded a bank, and that itself was sufficient to force an opening in the fabled curtain of Swiss bank secrecy.

The scenario unfolded quietly enough. As was later revealed, on May 13, 1971, a blonde, long-haired woman about five-foot-three opened an ordinary bank account, numbered 320 496 at the Swiss Credit Bank's Paradeplatz main office in Zurich. She identified herself with a Swiss passport in the name of Helga R. Hughes and signed her opening deposit slip for SFr. 1,000 (paid in cash), "H. R. Hughes," matching the name and initials of billionaire Howard Hughes. In addition, she presented a check for $50,000 for collection.

On May 27, a woman of similar description opened an account at the Winterthur branch of Swiss Bank Corporation, using a West German I.D. card issued to one Hanna Rosenkranz. The family name was later revealed to be that of Edith Irving's former husband. So far, so good for the Irvings. During the balance of 1971, Mrs. "Hughes" made several deposits and withdrawals of substance at Swiss Credit Bank. To bank officials it was obviously a relatively sizable account.

Next, at Clifford Irving's insistence, three checks totalling $650,000 were made out by McGraw-Hill in payment for all rights to Howard Hughes' biography and presented for collection in favor of H. R. Hughes to Swiss Credit Bank's Zurich main office. The account number into which they were deposited was 320 496, in the name of H. R. Hughes.

In December 1971, Helga Hughes appeared at the same Swiss Credit Bank office and asked to withdraw the balance in her account. After withdrawing all but a small amount she took the proceeds, in more than 1,200 one-thousand franc notes, from the bank in an airline flight bag. Later that same day, Hanna Rosenkranz deposited $450,000 in her Winterthur Swiss Bank Corporation account to be managed in an investment portfolio by the bank.

Meanwhile, the legitimacy of the Irving biography of Hughes was in the midst of swirling controversy. In the course of it, Howard Hughes' attorneys asked for an affidavit from Swiss Credit Bank in Zurich that he *did not* have an account there. This caused some consternation at the bank. Swiss banking secrecy requires that the bank reveal no information whatsoever about any account. But was a request to reveal that there was *no account* considered the same as revealing information about a real account? The bank satisfied itself that the Hughes attorneys' request was legitimate. Then, after extensive consultation within the bank, it was agreed that the request was not a violation of banking secrecy in this case, and so advised Hughes' attorneys: Howard Hughes had no such account.

Now McGraw-Hill was in a fix. Its money had disappeared into an account made out in the name of H. R. Hughes at Swiss Credit Bank and they couldn't touch it, nor find out anything about who really held it. It belonged to an H. R. Hughes. But they had been told that

Howard Hughes had no account there. Swiss banking secrecy was now operating in favor of what McGraw-Hill knew was a fraud against them.

On January 19, 1972, a group of officials and attorneys from McGraw-Hill met with chief counsel Hegetschweiler of Swiss Credit Bank. Hegetschweiler confirmed the fact that Howard Hughes did not have an account at his bank. But then who opened the "H. R. Hughes" account which held their funds? Hegetschweiler demurred. "Private bank information," he said; to reveal it would be a violation of bank secrecy laws.

Fortunately for McGraw-Hill, little in this world is absolute, even in Switzerland. The company had one option and they took it: ask a Swiss court to compel the bank to reveal the true H. R. Hughes account holder. In a rare parting of the bank secrecy veil, the court agreed that there existed substantial evidence of fraudulent use of the bank account through falsification of the account papers. This, it was decided, was a crime committed primarily in Zurich which, according to standard practice, made it obligatory to reveal information about the account. The bank was directed to comply with McGraw-Hill's request. One Helga R. Hughes was named as holder of the account. Local journalists identified her as Edith Irving, and later Swiss Bank Corporation added the Hanna Rosenkranz twist to the matter. The Irvings were immediately charged with fraud, as well as falsification of bank documents, and subsequently jailed.

In the short-run analysis, Swiss bank secrecy acted to protect criminals, an argument critics often use in lambasting Swiss banking practice. But it later functioned to convict them, an ultimate justification for their system, argue the Swiss. In Switzerland, no one is in a great hurry for *final* justice. The morally right end justifies the means. And the means—in this case, bank secrecy—protects the account holder, a noble enough objective. Swiss bankers believe their handling of the Irving case was most sound.

However, a less sanguine view of the secrecy situation is offered by a U.S. SEC official familiar with Swiss banking practice. "Swiss bank secrecy can be pretty much what they want it to be," he told me. "If they want to divulge information they will find a way to do it." And there the argument rests.

The Pied Pipers

Who else uses Swiss bank accounts? Obviously, the Swiss aren't talking. The only estimates we have are the amorphous group of Americans noted previously and, by reputation, countless European and Middle-East users—all unnamed, of course.

We do know a bit more. Before their breakup, Liz and Richard Burton were reported to own an interest in a Swiss bank and lived in Gstaad; Actor William Holden lives in Saint-Prex, as does author Irwin Shaw. Sophia Loren and Deborah Kerr keep homes in the country, while Peter Ustinov resides at Vevey on Lac Léman, and Orson Welles at Klosters. These luminaries are hardly ignoring their neighbor banks. Ingrid Bergman once told me of problems her husband Lars Schmidt had with his Swiss account over recording errors, and the CIA has been shown to have used Swiss accounts in numerous foreign payments. Two

major U.S. corporations, Dow Chemical and Firestone
Tire, have established their own merchant banks. And
the list could go on to the last foreign worker in Zurich's
garbage department—one of the nearly 1 million
foreigners working in the country.

There is another whole cadre of Swiss account
holders who have a great deal in common but who are
largely unknown to each other. They are like spies in
a great international apparatus, all having the nature of
their business in common, but largely unaware of each
other's specific existence. This compartmentalized
group was enticed to the Swiss financial haven by the
newly prominent gurus of finance. They are the followers
of "The New Jeremiahs," as *Newsweek* magazine
dubbed a handful of the gurus in August 1974. These
"Jeremiahs" are believers in a collapsing world
financial structure. They see the Swiss bank as Salvation in the form of francs, gold, and privacy. They
have shown the way to followers through their private
letters, books, and seminars. Evidence has it that they
have substantially increased American use of Swiss
banks among their faithful.

One of the most prominent of the gurus, and one
featured in the *Newsweek* "Jeremiah" issue, is Dr. Harry
Schultz, lately of London, now of Amsterdam. He estimates that he has prompted at least 25,000 Swiss bank
accounts to be opened by readers of his *International
Harry Schultz Letter* and numerous books such as
Switzerland and Other Financial Havens. When
pressed on the accuracy of the number of devotees taking the Swiss bank step, he paused only a moment before rejoining "That's conservative."

Dr. Schultz has built his following over the past

decade of his peripatetic life, publishing his letter from Beverly Hills, Washington, Hong Kong, Switzerland, as well as London and Amsterdam, to name a few. He estimates "several thousand" current subscribers and then neither says more nor offers verification. That's *de rigueur* for a money guru. However, his success in attracting a crowd to his irregular International Monetary Seminars at ever-increasing prices is easily documented. "The Millionaire's Conference," as a Montreal newspaper dubbed his 1973 seminar in that city, enticed over 450 attendees at $600 apiece (plus air fares from around the globe). From their demeanor, plumage, and spending habits, the newspaper wasn't far wrong about their financial status. In addition, Schultz's readers spent another $15,000 on tapes and transcripts of the conference.

Schultz has built his largely American clan and led it to Switzerland with a monetary philosophy of inevitable doom, in which he strongly believes, expressed in an enigmatic shorthand style of writing. For example, consider this excerpt from the end of April 1974 issue of *The Harry Schultz Letter* (*HSL*):

> Adolf Volcker, 1 man, one man, put us into runaway inflation & destroyed the $. Well, this wk. I'm happy to tell U that HSL and Hslm's have checkmated Herr Volcker & the banking interests behind him. Our revelations of PAV selling US gold (vigorously denied by the Treasury) were brot to the attention of Congressman Patman (Texas) by many Hslm's & he investigated our revelations. He heads the powerful Congressional Banking Comm. The investigation led to pressures which resulted in the resignation of Volcker. But Patman ruffled a lot of feathers in his investigation & Volcker-booting. My top secret top echelon man in DC tells me money is coming into Texas "by the car-loads"

to get rid of Patman, to defeat him at the coming election. They think money can do it. Didn't the Committee to elect Nixon prove that? Well, they haven't reckoned with the power of hslm's & an aroused, well informed, readership.

Schultz also combines some of the best contacts and financial perception available in the topsy-turvy Great Money Game with frequent self-promotion. From the mid-March 1974 issue:

> Our mail is running at *1,000* ltrs a week. U can appreciate that I can't possibly reply to such a mountain. But I faithfully read every ltr & much *valuable* data comes from them. Plez keep writing. Just don't expect a reply.

Two weeks later:

> HSL membership count hit another alltime hi this wk. Thanks for your faith & welcome to new readers. . . .

And from the mid-July 1974 issue:

> *Every* mbr of hsl staff made separate trips to the continent last wk. A real go-go group. . . .

It all has paid off: First in devotion. His regularly quoted readers' comments border on those of true religious converts. From the mid-March 1974 issue:

> Dr. GC writes: "The education that HSL provides should be taught every college student as a course with exams and credits. It's bound to be worth more than sex education in the long run." Oh, Doctor, I wouldn't go that far.

Or from the early June 1974 issue:

> *Letter of the Month*
> Dear Dr. Schultz:
> In HSL 317, I was unequivocally appalled to read the statement: "Treasury & bank clique . . . are looking for new ways to block me, to actually stop HSL from being written

or getting to U." To those bureaucratic bastards my answer is: The value of HSL far exceeds the value of American citizenship. I would make a rapid departure if this totalitarian control materializes. Maybe a "man without a country," but with HSL, never a man without freedom.

Devoted follower . . .

And it has paid in money too. Schultz' devotees now pay $250 a year to read their master's words in *HSL*, and scrape together a fee of $1,000 per hour for private consultation.

Presumably this has also paid off in handsome profits for Schultz's faithful. He has quoted readers complimenting him on providing advice sufficient to "triple my money in 18 months" and "7 years of hsl made retirement come easy." Or is it all part of the pitch? There's no certain way of telling. I observed one man presenting Schultz with a 100-ounce silver bar at IMS, Montreal, "as a token of what you have done for my profits as a result of your letter." The bar was worth nearly $400 at the time, later over $600.

Modern financial gurus are anything but impoverished.

Schultz acquired a fascination for Swiss banks in the mid-60s when he says he saw "the coming wave" of economic difficulties in the withdrawal of silver backing to dollar notes and later gold backing through inconvertibility. He was "one of the first to realize that the dollar was in for demise and therefore one had to move funds from dollars into other stable currencies to protect and profit and avoid exchange controls." The Swiss franc was his principal candidate for the move, along with gold. He openly encouraged his devotees to use

Swiss accounts to buy gold "in the form legal for you." He says he has stopped short of telling Americans to buy gold illegally. Privately, he confides, "I don't ask people their nationality when they ask me for advice. I'm not their conscience."

Although American citizens may now (as of 1975) legally buy gold, the desperate search for reliable and profitable financial advice continues.

Schultz moved to Basle, Switzerland, for a short time in 1967 where he was a consultant to a Swiss bank on various market trends and writing. Writing? "When they wanted to write polite business letters," explains Schultz, "they constantly sounded like they were threatening to sue." Not unexpectedly, he has made, and still makes, favorable comments about Swiss bankers (he still has an office in Basle, and his *Letter* is printed and mailed from there). Most of the original comments about Swiss bankers remain pointed and valid. Witness this one, which time has modified, but which is still properly cautionary. It is from the February 1967 *HSL:*

> You must not conclude that every Swiss banker is a genius or a monetary expert. This myth is no more true than the one that goes "every American is rich" even tho many are . . . in both cases. I've found the same human frailties here as elsewhere—the most dangerous of which is that men generally do insist on speaking with seeming authority on subjects on which they are unqualified & unread & unexperienced. . . . *Most* Swiss bankers *are* good *commercial* bankers. . . . *Many* are good *merchant* bankers (perhaps the best in the world). *Some* are good financial *investment* bankers. Only very *few* are heavyweights in int'l *monetary* matters. They, like bankers elsewhere, subscribe

to a dozen US periodicals, from which comes most of their knowledge. But most don't even know the relationship of US gold to its currency or to its int'l debt. A majority sell gold bars but understand little about gold's significance. Some will ramble on about political risks in So. Afr. but admit to never having been off the continent. In short there are more bankers here than anywhere in the world, per capita. And they are virtually all *good* bankers, far above the world average. But they are each good in different areas. Almost none are a "walking Swiss Bank" as outsiders tend to view them.

Nevertheless, Schultz found Switzerland an impossible place personally. He left within three months of arrival. Swiss banks and bankers are immensely right in their philosophy when viewed from afar, but were "so deadly dull' up close, he says. "The Swiss are rigid, narrow-minded, insular, the most unimaginative people on the face of the earth," he opines. But Schultz quickly adds, "that all may be very good in a banker. He won't take risks." A guru can't be too negative while inciting readers to open 25,000 Swiss bank accounts.

Since the 1967 sojourn, his orders to followers to trade gold and foreign currencies and suggestions of Swiss bank usefulness have come with machine-gun rapidity. He also calls the shots in every letter on a dozen stock markets around the world, picking a handful of stocks for trading (both long and short), usually in the U.S. or South African markets. From my personal observation, while picking some losers, he has called many correct turns. He is now one of the most widely quoted of the financial gurus.

Another guru with an apparently steadily increasing following has been investment counselor Harry Browne, who first gained fame with a 1970 overreaction to a developing likelihood titled *How to Profit from the Coming Devaluation.* By the time his second book, *You Can Profit from a Monetary Crisis,* hit the best seller lists in spring 1974, Browne had not only joined the ranks of the personally wealthy, but the monetary crises he dangled before readers had been dramatically changed in nature through the daily minor adjustments of floating currency rates.

The 41-year-old Browne, who sports a beard (and is reported to have been in debt by nearly $15,000 from silver commodity contract losses in 1967[2]), holds to the conviction that there will be full-scale bankruptcy of business, blood in the streets, and, withal, more than a dozen ways to make a bundle while the millennium is coming. Though Browne has made several clear predictive errors (many of which he admits and rationalizes in *You Can Profit from a Monetary Crisis*), including the one that the dollar devaluation would immediately release another Great Depression, he insists that, though not always right, he is certain. "The biggest problem in predicting events," he says, "is putting a time scale on them." The rest, we are given to believe, is easy.

These difficulties notwithstanding, Browne has been a prime proponent of Swiss banks and still is.

This guru builds his case for gold, Swiss francs, Swiss banks, and a "retreat" home, in much the same

---

[2] Charles Foley, London *Sunday Observer*, August 18, 1974, p. 13.

way as Schultz. (Schultz doesn't worry about the "retreat.") After explaining in *You Can Profit* . . . that governments are the most dangerous entities in inflationary times, thereby clutching at the coattails of current popular mistrust of politicians, however blameworthy they may actually be, Browne insists this is because of governmental interference with free market forces. "Since governmental powers have expanded tremendously since the 1930's, the next depression should be by far the worst in the history of the U.S.," he says. "It isn't that politicians are necessarily determined to wreck the economy," he explains, "it's just that they're opposed as anyone else to changing employment . . . *their* employment. And pressure from academic and government economists is universally in favor of greater governmental intervention. Anyone concerned about his job is bound to bow to such pressure."

"But," he goes on, "the greatest danger of all is that the government will rely upon inflation as a tool of salvation. With only 3% gold backing now [to money supply in the United States], it's unlikely that it would take much more inflation to bring about *runaway inflation*.

"And that's the worst kind of depression."

Two chapters later, he points out the salvation: ". . . a currency like the Swiss franc offers a very small downside risk and a very high upside potential." And further, ". . . I'll recommend gold and silver for even the most conservative investors. But if safety is your object, and you can only do one thing, I'd recommend that you put all your savings in a Swiss bank in Swiss francs."

Hardly an equivocation there, even for the special needs of elderly widows and orphans. And well over a quarter million Americans have read that. But Browne will only admit to occasional predictive errors, not uncertainty, as he said.

It is this certainty in the incredibly complex Great Money Game that causes most economists to find fault in the writings of the financial gurus. Unfortunately, most economists have taken the complexities into account and produced both uncertainty *and* errors. Thus the popularity of the gurus.

In his push for Swiss banks in *You Can Profit. . . ,* Browne devotes only 22 pages to details of services available from them. For a quick once-over, this is sound. But we must remember that these banks are one of the principal means Browne recommends for survival in the next depression. Thus, those few pages become critical, even bolstered as they are, by additional chapters on gold and Swiss francs.

It is also worth noting that Browne lists a handful of Swiss banks with his personal recommendations. One is Union Bank of Switzerland. More than one of this bank's officials have told me they are quite embarrassed by this identification. Why? "Too much paperwork; thousands of letters to answer for little business, and frankly," one official explained, "we would rather not be identified with Mr. Browne's conclusions."

Another bank which has not objected to identification in Browne's book is the tiny Foreign Commerce Bank of Zurich and Geneva, which he also recommends with favorable comment. It is associated with the Deak–Perera organization in New York, a major money exchange firm across the United States.

Both Schultz and Browne were antedated in their Swiss bank call to the cloth by a third popular and successful financial guru, James Dines. Dines, of New York, who has been the author and publisher of *The Dines Letter* since 1961, has been crying out for gold and Swiss accounts for most of the past decade. Again with Dines, as in the cases of Schultz and Browne, the golden metal provided the lure to the Swiss vaults. Early readers of *The Dines Letter* who were touted onto American South African, Ltd. stock (a gold mining company stock) would have had their purchase rewarded with a 15-fold increase in their stake by 1974—although the great bulk of the gain came only after a faith-testing wait of a dozen years.

For almost as many years, Dines has been advising clients to get enough money out of the United States and into a Swiss bank via francs or gold coins so that they can travel overseas for five years' time. He foresees the coming of the economic apocalypse and warns against it in his letter virtually every week—a prediction which, if not prescient so far, is certainly consistent. His summer 1974 forecasts suggest the event for 1975 — but no later than mid-1976. The five-year expense money in a Swiss bank reflects his outside guesstimate of the duration of the collapse.

How and when will it come?

The Dines Letter said in 1974 that it "has never been more bearish." It sees an ultimate explosion in the current inflation cycle, a convulsion which Dines predicts will turn the public against itself. As he wrote on May 17, 1974:

> It is helpful to reflect on how really dangerous the human
> beings around you are capable of being, particularly in those
> days when religion has been replaced by opium derivatives
> as the new "opium of the people." Never forget that Himmler
> was a chicken farmer before Hitler made him head of the
> dreaded Gestapo. Similarly, don't think for one minute that
> just because the world is sunny and nice now that it cannot
> quickly degenerate into an unpleasant period.

And then the inevitable pitch, "While we cannot escape
our destiny, perhaps *The Dines Letter* can anticipate
it, and thereby help you survive it a bit better."

Whether any of the financial gurus of the current
era are the new Jeremiahs or simply popular guessers
is not the important point. With a debt to Marshall
McLuhan, their medium is their message: the expensive, privately circulated word. Yet with Schultz's
"millionaire's conference" and his dozen books, and
with Browne's move onto best seller lists, their word is
now being widely read, heard, and observed, probably
by the most influential minority in the country, the portion capable of the widest range of monetary choices.

Because of the dramatic form of the gurus' urgings,
the size of their audience, and the real monetary bind
of the world at present, it seems safe to assume that the
popularity of Swiss banks has been increased measur-
ably by their efforts. The result may not have been over-
whelming in numbers of sizable new bank accounts,
and it is likely overshadowed by the number of fasci-
nated inquiries to the banks. But as worldwide infla-
tionary/recessionary forces move more in the direction
of the gurus' predictions, it is a safe bet that gold and
Swiss banks will find increasing numbers of converts.
(See also "The Drummer Factor" in Chapter 8.)

Media Intervention

It is likely, based on my experience with the news media, that broad press reporting of the Swiss bank phenomena will increase as it becomes "newsworthy" —i.e., too late for the general public to do anything about it. Most news reports about Swiss banks over recent years have been confined to the financial press and comments about specific events such as the congressional hearings on secret accounts, 1968–70. Magazines such as *Forbes, Business Week, Institutional Investor*, as well as *The Wall Street Journal* and *Barron's*, have clearly added to the popularity of Swiss banks among their specialized audience, or at least to the fascination with them. But the U.S. mass media have generally left the subject alone unless a scandal of the Irvings' proportion broke. An exception which caused a significant stir in Switzerland was the spring 1974, NBC-TV documentary, "If That's A Gnome, This Must Be Zurich." It left many viewers with the impression that the Swiss drink too much as a result of psychological hangups, and leave all their dirty work to foreigners. Swiss bankers felt it eminently unfair—and I agree with them.

European radio/TV has been onto the Swiss bank scent for many years, of course, although often in an uninformed way.

"By 1964," wrote one author, "a stock in trade of London TV coverage of any important politico-economic event . . . was a live banker on tap in Zurich, whose invariable and very reasonable response to the breathless question, 'And what do they make of that in Zurich?' was, 'Well, how do you see it in London?'"³

European electronic media won't do that again, but with satellite TV coverage now common, American broadcasters could become blissfully tempted if the subject of Swiss banks becomes "hot" in the U.S. mass media.

A point of further public interest at the mass-media level could arise from the monetary strictures in which many international banks were finding themselves in 1974. After the collapse of four German banks, the receivership of a handful of merchant banks in Britain, the San Diego First National and Franklin Bank demise in the United States, and the foreign exchange losses running over $50 million at Union Bank of Switzerland and $76 million at the Swiss unit of Britain's Lloyd's Bank, plus the problems of International Credit Bank of Geneva, the failure of any widely known Swiss bank could bring the mass media out in droves.

Banks Do Collapse

While it seems inconceivable that any *major* Swiss bank could fall, there have been cases in the past decade where small private banks, usually financing personal empires, have collapsed.

The myth of Swiss bank solvency was put to rest for the first time since the depression when the two banks owned by Munoz financial interests, Banque Genevois d'Epargne et de Credit and Schweizerische Spar und Kreditbank were closed in 1964 for overextending their

---

³ Fred Hirsch, *Money International* (Garden City, N.Y.: Doubleday, 1969).

resources. At about the same time, the interesting case of the Arab Commercial Bank of Geneva arose.

Mohammed Khider, leader of the Algerian Nationalists in early Gaullist days, had become treasurer of the Algerian Provisional government after its establishment in 1961, and, as such, was responsible for governmental funds. He deposited these in the Arab Commercial Bank of Geneva, in government-controlled accounts. By September 1962, however, when Ahmed Ben Bella came to power, Khider had managed to transfer most of these funds to his own accounts at the same bank, an amount of some SFr. 43 million. Upon discovery of the loss, Ben Bella's government brought action in Geneva to recover the funds under Swiss criminal statutes. A search warrant prompted the scandal: The accounts were missing. The bank was then closed.

Next, Algeria brought a separate action to recover the funds, wherever they existed, under the theory that the bankers had a "duty of care" to know with whose money an account holder was acting. A lower Swiss court upheld this argument, but before the funds could be unfrozen, the matter was appealed to the Swiss Supreme Court. In July 1974 that court reversed the lower court ruling, holding in part, that to require such a duty was a violation of bank secrecy laws. Meanwhile, the only man who held access to the proper accounts, Khider himself, had been assassinated in Spain. Subsequently, the bank was reopened and depositors, who had a decade hiatus in the use of their funds, will now be paid off. Algeria is out SFr. 43 million.

An especially mysterious bank demise was that of

the $7 million Bank Germann in Basle in spring 1967. Its doors were closed after the sudden and secrecy-wrapped death of its founder, international financier, Walter Germann. It was closed, "in the interest of our clients" according to a spokesman. Seven weeks after his death, the *Wall Street Journal* was reporting, "American investigators still don't know how and where he died. Was it a heart attack at Klosters, a popular ski resort not far from St. Moritz, as his family announced? Did he slash his wrists or shoot himself, as some newspapers reported? Or did he die in his office at Basle, as was also reported? 'We're working on it through channels,' says one U.S. government attorney, 'and it's frustrating as hell. We haven't been able to establish anything to our satisfaction.' The U.S. official had good reason for his curiosity. Germann had his fingers in a good many pies—primarily abroad."

The pies included banks, juke boxes, "dry cleaning," investment trusts, and reported links to corporate shells for both U.S. tax evasion and stock manipulations. A year earlier, Germann had been called before a federal grand jury convened by New York district attorney Robert Morgenthau to investigate tax evasion and stock manipulation through foreign banks. After four appearances with little relevant testimony, Germann was asked to return to Switzerland and obtain appropriate papers to prompt his memory. He never came back. Upon his death in 1967, he was reported to have owed some $200,000 to the U.S. court in contempt citations for refuge behind the Swiss bank secrecy veil. Speculation at the time, including that in the *Wall Street Journal* article, suggested that because of the grand jury proceedings, Bank Germann sustained a substantial overflow of deposits as "hot money" fled the revelations of further testimony. Bank officials had little choice but to close the doors. As a postscript, Germann was reportedly "seen" in South America well after his death. The fact or fancy of that report was never established.

It makes sense to remember, in light of the above bank cases, the comment of a leading Swiss banker, Chairman Felix W. Schulthess of Swiss Credit Bank: ". . . Swiss banks have fended off statutory controls by disciplining themselves under 'gentlemen's agreements.' But the preamble," he added, "does not define the term 'gentlemen.'"[4]

The above cases should not suggest weakness per se in the Swiss banking system. Quite the opposite: Behind the closed doors of banking secrecy a great deal can be done to protect banks in difficulty, *if* the banking authorities believe there is real danger to confidence in the banking system. Quite clearly, the demise of a few small banks under manipulative or fraudulent circumstances have not prompted this emotion from the Swiss banking establishment. This should give potential account holders an important suggestion: consider only the larger and/or most reputable of the Swiss banks for your funds, or be prepared to risk the vagaries of time and distance to utilize your capital if serious difficulties develop. Inquiries through major international banks other than Swiss, and some homework spent in reading changes in balance sheets or profit/ loss accounts of the Swiss bank in question, is time well spent.

---

[4] Ibid.

Investments

Another widely held bit of lore about Swiss banks is that some genius exists on the part of Swiss bankers in investment portfolio management. This idea deserves an early burial. The Swiss moneymen are hardly super-human. Their handful of investment blemishes is not glaring, but neither are they a rarity. Moreover, by year-end 1974, overall Swiss bank public investment performance was looking as dour as that of most United States financial institutions. (See Swiss Bank Mutual Fund Performance Tables, pp. 240–42). The record reminds us that having Swiss banks invest in securities or real estate for you puts your money at risk as with any investment you might make through an American, British, or German bank or broker. There are no guarantees.

Probably the most widely reported of these invest-ment lapses was the floating of $59 million in notes to several Swiss financial institutions including leading banks in April 1970. It involved a company which was one of the first American firms to list its shares on the Zurich Bourse some years earlier. The firm was also due to file bankruptcy within two months of the place-ment of the 1970 notes: the Penn Central. The notes were placed by a leading international financial con-cern, Ufitec, Zurich, and would have provided annual yields at maturity of around 10 percent on a discount basis, as they carried no interest coupons. But how did the Swiss lapse, especially with the risk sign of high non-cash yield?

One Zurich banker was quoted as saying, "Every-body makes mistakes. Even the careful man has tumbled downstairs." Nobody's perfect, in other words. A more direct explanation came from another Swiss banker. ". . . we Swiss have weaknesses, and one is . . . well, call it investment loyalty, or tradition. Buying Penn Central seemed natural, even though the issue manager cautioned us that this was a high risk situation. We went into it with our eyes open. Nobody could even dream that the Penn Central would go bankrupt."[5]

For many years Wall Street traders have been of the opinion, apparently gathered through direct experience, that Swiss banks are so conservative and relatively slow to move in the market, that "difficult situations" can often be unloaded on them, sometimes at prices well away from the best available on a given day in New York. Certainly, the Swiss banks' investment portfolios were severely shocked in the market break of 1969–70 (and again in 1973–74). Like everyone else, they were heavily invested in the New York market after the great market of 1967–68. They were, in many cases, even slower to unload than their American counterparts. As *Institutional Investor* magazine put it in December 1971, "The harsh object lessons of the collapse of the American stock market in 1969–70 were distressing to all European investors. . . ." The author added, "stunned by the lack of follow-up research on many of the stocks they had been sold, they quickly came to resent Wall Street. . . ." ("They" refers to Swiss and other European financial institutions.) One prime result was a drastic cutback on the number of U.S. brokers the Swiss banks would do business with, and a concurrent strengthening of their own analytical

---

[5] Ray Vicker, *Those Swiss Money Men* (New York: Charles Scribner's Sons, 1973).

staffs. Even with this, the Swiss are watching about 15 stock markets a day worldwide—many a great distance away. While they will clearly emphasize their strengths in such undertakings, a truly international view with ability to diversify from country to country, this also means they don't have true depth of analysis in most major markets. A bank might have one analyst covering all of Asia and Australia, for example. And there are other problems.

Until recently at least, the execution of orders on certain foreign stock exchanges left something to be desired. While watching the opening order executions on a U.S. regional stock exchange in 1973, I asked one floor broker who regularly dealt with the U.S. subsidiary of a Swiss bank, how the foreign orders were pointing that day, bullish or bearish. The general market was opening strongly higher.

"They're all sell," he shot back, hurrying to a post to execute one.

"Then why execute on the opening today with a strong market?" I asked, trying to sound like I knew something about the business.

"Market's strong all right," the broker replied, "but they always execute on the opening. That way they can see the printed price in the paper and know if we're screwing 'em."

That might sound sensibly cautious to the unitiated, since the *Wall Street Journal* does print opening prices daily. But in a strong market there might well be a higher sale price to be obtained later in the day. The price obviously depends upon the stock itself. But why not wait until later to find out, with a stop order in at the opening for protection? The broker later explained that the opening execution was an almost invariable practice for this firm. Since that time I have asked several Swiss bank traders if the practice continues, and they have said that it doesn't. Usually. That it did, or might, suggests there is something to that Wall Street opinion about Swiss bankers being a bit sluggish in their trading practices.

"Hot" Money

Another piece of lore which has made wide rounds as part of the public image of Swiss banks, is that there is a great deal of illegal money in the country. We will deal with this subject in some detail in Chapter Four; however, it should be pointed out now that the Swiss bankers entertain no subject with less humor than the charge of harboring illegal funds. An incident in 1973 illustrates.

As is often the practice in magazine publishing, the senior editor at a magazine's home office will decide on artwork to accompany an article done by a writer away from that office. This was the case in an article which I did for a New York financial magazine in 1973.

Without my knowledge, until it was in print, the article was accompanied by a cartoon that distorted a portion of a Swiss banker's quotation more than it should have been. The cartoon showed a Swiss bank teller with one hand out to accept money, the other hand over his eyes. The implication therein of blind acceptance of all money under the caption, "We don't care where the money comes from or how it gets here," is entirely contrary to fact, as it was only part of the quote and excluded my balancing comment. The balance read,

" 'But we do *hate* to invest illegal money.' He meant illegally *gotten* money as opposed to money taken away from a country extra-legally, usually tax avoidance money." It went on, "If you told the Swiss it was illegally gotten, or they somehow found out, they wouldn't take your business."

After the cartoon appeared without full text, one Swiss banker contact of some duration revealed his sensitivity to the illegal money matter by refusing to return my calls for a period of some two years, despite my explanations to his bank colleagues.

As I point out in Chapter 6, the issue revolves around a peculiarly Swiss distinction between money illegally obtained in another country and money avoiding taxation by another country. Since tax *avoidance* is merely an administrative matter under Switzerland's tax system, it is not a criminal act, compared with other acts of tax fraud that are criminal acts. Swiss bankers would not knowingly cooperate in handling the latter. To lump both kinds of funds together is to combine black and white in the Swiss mind. But they are, of course, both black in the minds of U.S. tax authorities.

Swiss Credit Bank's Dr. Hans Mast makes the point concisely: "The most important question about bank secrecy to Americans," he observed, "is the tax matter. But that is the problem of our foreign customer, not our bank's problem. This is a matter of tax laws which have nothing to do with bank laws in Switzerland." He added, "If a proposal is made to change the tax laws in Switzerland, no one will agree. No one wants to give further reaching power to the government." It can hardly be argued that it is a Swiss bank's job to police another nation's laws, especially when they differ from Swiss laws. "Besides, liars have short legs," adds

Mast with a smile, quoting a favorite Swiss saying advancing the idea that criminals usually get caught. In this day and age, it is naïve to think that such would be a general rule, as much as it is to believe that the "FBI always gets its man." But it is not naïve to think the catching should be left up to law enforcement in the nation where the crime is committed, not in a foreign one.

Despite this, and mindful of the criticism they have received from countries like the United States which have different criminal laws, Swiss bankers have supported ratification of the Mutual Assistance Treaty between the United States and Switzerland, which takes some steps toward reconciling the different legal systems where they both must deal with organized crime. However, as a spokesman for the U.S. Embassy in Berne explained, the treaty does not deal with legal differences over tax evasion matters for the average citizen.

And the treaty is hardly unanimously favored in Switzerland. One banker explained, "From our standpoint, the U.S. need for this assistance is based on weakness of U.S. laws. Why should a gangster, a real criminal, have to be prosecuted under *tax* laws?" The explanation that other laws couldn't reach many of the multilayered and creative tactics of organized gangsters, only brought his comment, "Then you see, your laws are too weak."

Swiss bankers will, in fact, go to greater lengths than their American counterparts to determine the correct legal form of deposits, especially if large. I have seen a Swiss bank require several carefully notarized verifications that funds belonged to the persons who claimed them, under proper legal authorization, that these persons were empowered to deposit the funds in the given bank, and that the persons' identities were factual. This is more than required for a similar U.S. account. I do doubt if they ran a security check on the persons involved, but I've never heard of an American bank doing so either.

There are, of course, banks which will be more lenient with questionable deposits than others. The perfectly logical point is often made that it is very difficult to know where money comes from, usually with the wry observation that "money doesn't smell." However, this point is sometimes weakened by an obvious inclination to take in all comers. One Swiss banker at a small public bank told me, "Often clients don't want to explain where money comes from. Is it the responsibility of the bank to check? Is it the responsibility of a business executive to check his clients? Either we accept or we refuse a client,'' he went on, "and if we refuse he will be accepted by another of 100 banks."

If a Swiss banker gives you the latter reasoning, you probably don't have to worry too much about your *bona fides* past the top layer of paper work.

Such are the vagaries of Swiss banks. They simply cannot be a monolithic block of diligence, honesty, hard work, and utter secrecy. Arguments that Swiss banks are generally blind accepters of illegal funds are just as specious as arguments that Swiss banks can't collapse or that Swiss bankers never harbor funds which have been illegally obtained under Swiss law. It should come as little surprise at this point in the book, that Swiss bankers have their own notions of ethics. They are also a little cold and fishy-eyed, perhaps. But then, aren't most bankers? It is the lore of Swiss banking which has built an image not wholly correct, and which I have subjected to some factual tests. The lure remains primarily the banking secrecy system; and one might still fairly say that it *attracts* all forms of funds, legal and illegal.

If you wish to test the philosophy and stringencies of Swiss banking, you may be able to do more than simply open an account; you might open a Swiss bank. A Geneva-based Swiss attorney explained to me that one can occasionally buy an existing charter of a Swiss bank for as little as SFr. 250,000, and bring the capital of the bank up to the level of SFr. 2 million. Of course, you'll have to obtain the prior permission of the Swiss Banking Commission, and they'll need to know a bit more than name, address, and whether you'll accept mail at that address or not. The bank will have to remain a Swiss legal entity, be Swiss controlled through a majority of its board of directors, and be subject to all the regulations, peer pressures and methods of doing business in Switzerland. This, of course, includes privacy practices. But you may thus initiate your own Swiss bank "lore and lure," and imprint your own crest on your Swiss bankbook.

It will, in this context, be especially important to recognize that the Swiss have considered privacy a grave matter for far deeper reasons and a longer period than the American legal conscience has fretted over illegal funds buried in Swiss vaults. Switzerland's impressive history plays the lead role on this stage.

Chapter three

That *"Mysterious Call of the Past"*

TRAVELING THROUGH Switzerland you can feel the touch of the country's past everywhere. A stroll down Zurich's modern Limmatquai or through the hilly winding streets of Geneva's "old town" brings an immediate impression of a long history. On one hand is the great 16th-century Grossmünster Protestant Church looming from a hillside above the shop-packed Zurich street. On another hand is St. Peter's Catholic Cathedral, begun in 1150 and commanding the full hilltop of old Geneva. Castles like Visconti or Parpan quickly remind one of the depth of the Swiss past. Statues from Rousseau to Voltaire and Zwingli, fountains and town halls of Renaissance, Reformation, and revolutionary times abound.

But there are few of these monuments, memorials, or even museums which fully reveal how significant the troubled history of Switzerland is to its people's current thinking—thinking about such diverse issues as personal freedoms, a weak central government, or even bank secrecy. The historical influence is not surprising. Most nations with extensive histories borrow much from their past, but do not memorialize the nuances or difficulties of that past. Thus, without delving into the compelling pattern of life which has gone into forging this unusual nation over the past seven centuries, one does not easily discover how deeply the Swiss people have been conditioned to many current beliefs and fears.

Protestant and Catholic churches standing virtually side by side in many cities obscure the profound impact that religious strife between the two faiths had in forging the current tolerance for all types of personal beliefs. In Berne, the moderately imposing nature of the federal government buildings conceals the fact that out of the seven centuries of Swiss national history, a federal government of any kind has existed for only slightly more than one, and that the country became a potent economic force in Europe before even becoming a federal state. The high visibility of the Swiss army around the countryside correctly suggests that it is comprised of nearly all able-bodied men in the nation, either in reserves or on active duty. But this masks the fact that it has existed for 150 years for purely defensive purposes, while during the preceding five centuries Swiss soldiers were the most readily available and feared mercenaries in other nations' wars.

These hidden facts have shaped the Swiss psyche and conditioned its attitudes toward all issues. Without a knowledge of how the shaping took place, you may find Swiss banking practices confusing and the importance of bank secrecy nearly unfathomable. To clarify these matters, we undertake a short journey through Swiss history.

Pillars

A most powerful support of Swiss banking is the 700-year tradition of belief in individual freedom and personal independence within the Swiss nation. From the fabled trials of 13th-century folk hero William Tell, across the tumultuous chasm of five centuries where the beliefs were nearly lost, to the past century and a half of resolute political neutrality, Switzerland has maintained the longest and deepest tradition of such freedoms in the world. To be sure, this was not accomplished without periodic leaps backward, even to virtual serfdom in the pit of the 17th and 18th centuries. But the beliefs surged to new strengths by the mid-19th century, and today they are at the crest of one of the longest surges, unbroken since 1848. It is now difficult to imagine a more pervading, more encompassing, and more deeply believed concept in any country than that of personal freedom in Switzerland. It has been the rallying cry for Swiss public opinion in numerous religious conflicts, during the period of physical encirclement by the Axis powers in World War II, and in the center of recent parliamentary debate over the proposed Swiss-American Mutual Assistance Treaty. It has been equally a pillar of Swiss bank privacy, a vindication for the country's reputation as a political refuge, and a justification for execution of spies during World War II. It is at least partially responsible for the country developing as an important economic power in the 19th century.

About the time Marco Polo commenced his wanderings to the Far East, and shortly before Dante had completed his *Divine Comedy*, the Swiss union was born.

The union was conceived during a continuing struggle of three cantons, Uri, Schwyz, and Nidwalden, against the tyranny of the Hapsburgs to the east. The three formed what they termed "The Treaty of Everlasting Alliance" in 1291, which for that age was a remarkable statement of determination to become masters in their own house, eschew foreign domination, and most importantly, to establish a respect for law. Two paragraphs of the treaty, signed 76 years after the Magna Carta, and still on aging display in the canton of Schwyz, set forth these principles concisely:

> The people of the valley of Uri, the community of the valley of Schwyz, and the community of Nidwalden, seeing the malice of the times, have solemnly agreed and bound themselves by oath to aid and defend each other with all their might and main, with their lives and their property, both within and without their boundaries, each at his own expense, against every enemy whatever who shall attempt to molest them, either singly or collectively.
>
> . . . we have unanimously decreed that we will accept no judge in our valleys who shall have obtained his office for a price. . . . Every difference among the confederates shall be decided by their wisest men; and whoever shall reject their award shall be compelled by the other confederates.

Thus were the principles of Swiss independence and law founded in clear agreement on the Rütli Meadow near Lake Lucerne. But they were to undergo severe tests and substantial reversals before becoming accepted as national ideals.

Historians are now generally agreed that the William Tell legend is a mixture of fact and fable. Whether Tell existed as an individual is in doubt; whether someone actually was compelled to shoot an apple from his son's head as punishment for not having saluted the hat-on-staff of the Hapsburg governor, and after killing the man, escaped with communal aid, is problematical. However, the actions are given general historical documentation as believable of the people bound by the Everlasting Alliance. The Tell legend simply idealizes the principles of resistance to foreign oppression and the cooperation between individual and community common to those days. It is the "right" story for the era, no matter its accuracy. Through its later revival in the Schiller drama of 1804 and the Rossini opera of 1829, the Tell legend came to epitomize the Alliance and became the first conditioner of the Swiss mentality.

Reformation

By the year 1420, the Alliance had become the basis for full political independence of the three cantons plus their important northern neighbor, Zurich. After settlement of the first Swiss civil war in 1450, less than two decades after the burning of Joan of Arc at Rouen, France, the Alliance had become a burgeoning confederation. But only burgeoning. Its form and substance was, as yet, weak.

Historians do agree that by the middle of the 15th century the confederation had achieved important powers vis-à-vis the neighboring Hapsburg empire and the kingdom of France. Victories in the Burgundy war of 1476 and the Swabian war of 1499 had increased Swiss fighting prestige to the degree that European rulers began to compete for the services of Swiss soldiers. And by 1501 the Swiss confederation was comprised of thirteen allied cantons. However, the loose Alliance was not strong enough, nor sufficiently unified against the outside world to become a potent nation. Religious strife had begun earlier in Switzerland than the rest of Europe.[1] It complicated the unity matter, and, combined with the growing mercenary drain and a lack of natural exportable resources, kept the confederation in a largely untenable political position.

During the 16th century the confederation grew as a refuge of persecuted Protestants, a breeding ground of strong Catholic counter-Reformation action, and became the greatest provider of mercenary soldiers in Europe. The St. Bartholomew's Day massacre in France in 1572 saw several thousand Protestants killed, and in its wake over 2,300 Huguenot families found safety in Geneva. The city of refuge gave them immediate assistance, providing more than two-thirds of the Huguenots with permanent shelter, despite the fact that this group comprised nearly half the existing population of the city. There were also numerous Protestant exoduses to Basle and Zurich at this time, from the Catholic influences of Locarno in Tessin. This flight was a follow-through to the great religious reforms of John Calvin, who died in 1560 having made Geneva "the citadel of the Protestant faith."

However, strong Catholic pressures from the Italian states and France had led to deep religious division within the confederation. As in so much of the history of Europe of that time, the ideals of personal freedom which were at one with the principles of Christianity, were fought over fiercely in details of practice. In

---

[1] George Thürer, *Free and Swiss* (London: Oswald Wolff, 1970).

Switzerland, this rending marked the beginning of a religious strife which was to last until 1848, nearly 300 years later. The Swiss psyche was receiving its second conditioning.

Because of the resulting disunity, the Swiss confederation was initially required to accept neutrality more by domestic impotence than real belief. The confederation remained officially neutral through the Thirty Years War in Germany, but was too weak to enforce its neutrality, which was often violated by the belligerents as a result. The Peace of Westphalia in 1648 gave the confederation status as a country, real independence from the Hapsburg Empire, and the name Schweis (Schwyz), which was to endure until the mid-18th century. But its founding principles were to decline under the brutality of the age.

War for Money

During the three centuries beginning in 1291, the confederation had seen more than two million of its men under arms, a great drain of strength into the mercenary forces of neighboring empires. Historians have noted, "It was probably easier to keep men in the army than get them out."[2] This fact sapped both unifying will and national blood until well after the French Revolution. The neutrality of 1648 only meant that the Swiss could no longer offer their soldiers to one side. They could, and did, feed all buyers.

With these mercenaries in increasing demand, espe-

---

[2] E. Bonjour, H. S. Offler, and G. R. Potter, *A Short History of Switzerland* (Oxford: The Clarendon Press, 1952).

cially by France, but also by Austria, Holland, Venice, and Spain, the export of blood became considerable. On many occasions too, Swiss men fought each other under the banners of different nations. In a Flanders battle during the War of the Spanish Succession, for example, a "French" Swiss regiment and a "Dutch" Swiss regiment nearly annihilated each other.

But if the export of blood was great, so was the import of money, especially to Berne, paid for the mercenaries' services. A part of the confederacy, led by Berne, became wealthy on it. And so the evils grew upon themselves and came close to obliterating the principles of Rütli Meadow in the process. Frequent peasant uprisings, beginning in 1653, religious battles in the Villmergen wars of 1656 and 1712, plus deep class divisions became common. During the 17th and 18th centuries, the Age of Absolutism, the confederacy was seeing its most inglorious hours. By the French Revolution of 1798, after almost a century of clamor for an end to the exportation of mercenary blood, a Zurich pastor was still able to charge that the blood shed in French military service alone by the Swiss was sufficient to fill a navigable canal from Basle to Paris, and that with the money paid for the men, a wide road from Paris to Basle could be paved.[3]

And yet, the disaster could not truly end until the country found something equally profitable to export while feeding and occupying its men in more peaceful pursuits at home. It was to find it in the local manufacture of imported goods for later resale abroad. Production of goods for export was to be made a virtue out

---
[3] Lorenz Stucki, *The Secret Empire: The Success Story of Switzerland* (New York: Herder and Herder, 1971).

of necessity. The mercenary practice was to become the mother of Swiss international trade.

The Guilds and Cottage Industries

Young Swiss mercenaries, many of whom became wealthy emigrants, soon came to know the world around them and made extensive contacts in it. During those times, even more than now, having a Dutch, French, or German contact to be cultivated as a future local representative, was the soundest of business methodology. Meanwhile, in the guild-run Swiss cities of Geneva, Zurich, and Basle, export trades had become established by what appears to be a natural Swiss inclination to do business beyond local borders. The first exports were gold watches and clocks, as well as silk, ornaments, and other luxury items. These were exported in quantity to the new foreign mercenary contacts. Gradually, true cottage industries run by Swiss country peasants were able to grow, nurtured by lower costs, freedom to expand with cheap labor, and lack of the guilds' strict constraints. The peasant industry was textiles, principally cotton. It became Switzerland's leading industry by the 17th century, and remained so until the second half of the 19th century. The rigid, narrow, and inbred guild industries did grow, of course, but could not leap ahead as the peasant textile industry did. How could one step up production of watches in a guild city, for example, when one of few occasions to enter or notably expand a business came upon its inheritance from a father or father-in-law after having served half of a lifetime in the patriarch's employ? In fact, the guild industries were actually an impediment to progress in industrial growth for a long time.

The Cry of Revolution

The growth of true industry, international from the outset, and born of necessity, had begun amid the decay of the old Switzerland. It was a decay which was hastened by the writings of many, but most notably Jean Jacques Rousseau in Geneva, culminating in his famous *Social Contract* of 1762. As it became the bible of the French Revolution it pre-empted similar fervor in Geneva and environs. Tyranny and corruption were by now rife; revolts sprang up and were quickly quashed, usually through execution of the leaders. The *ancien régime* was being tested and found wanting in Switzerland as in France. Swiss leaders had forgotten all about William Tell and the Rütli Meadow.

The Berne-led confederation was so close to aristocratic France in outlook that it quickly expelled an English diplomat on one occasion at the mere suggestion from Paris. It produced gold watches, silk, and embroidery on demand for the court and the wealthy surrounding King Louis XIV. At the beginning of 1798 it was to welcome Napoleon Bonaparte with a royal fete on his march through Switzerland to Germany. Almost without noticing it, the Swiss found themselves in the midst of occupation by the French legions. What resistance there was, once organized, collapsed shortly. And the old confederacy gave way to a unitary centralized state enforced by French bayonets: the Helvetic Republic.

The armies of the revolution proclaimed equality, freedom, and the elimination of class privileges, including that of ruling cantons over the countryside areas (another onerous practice of the mercenary period). But these noble changes were seriously breached in practice; the revolution became a new subjugation by the revolutionary armies. This, in turn, rapidly degenerated into new uprisings against the Helvetic government; and, upon removal of most of Napoleon's troops in 1802, brawls flared up between factions favoring strong central government on one hand and federalist (essentially the old confederacy) on the other. Napoleon mediated the situation in 1803, favoring resumption of authoritarian government. But the peace was soon lost in new internal bickering when the old guard resumed its discrimination of city versus countryside, added new peasant land taxes, and re-enforced the rule of the guilds.

Meanwhile, economic difficulties grew as the once burgeoning export markets were unable to be satisfied by industry which had been plundered during the French occupation. Foreign markets were lost as the introduction of cheap English machine-spun cotton gained the Swiss place. By 1805, most of the Swiss weavers were idle; an estimated 25 percent of the population of 1.7 million lived off the textile industry. However, the catastrophe was soon to give way to another necessity-born trend. Now required to produce fabric at low unit cost to compete with the English threads, the enterprising Swiss imported a few of the English mechanical weaving machines, copied them, and established a new industry on top of the old. The manufacture of machinery grew as an industry of its own, and the export of "mule," or spinning jenny machines, became the foundation block of a new Swiss move into international commerce. The Swiss were aided considerably by an eight-year French blockade of English goods from the European markets. It was the time of the victorious march of the machine, the first impetus to a rising class of capitalists in Switzerland.

As seen over seven centuries of Swiss history, industrialization took place very rapidly. The sweep from the peak of the mercenary era to the collapse of the Helvetic Republic and the emergence of true industrial capacity had taken little more than a century.

The New State

By the time of the Congress of Vienna in 1815, after Napoleon's defeat in Russia and at Waterloo, the former again spilling Swiss blood, Switzerland had become the second most "industrialized" country in Europe, behind only England. When that Congress unified Switzerland with 22 cantons, increased by 9 from the 17th century, and guaranteed neutrality, the form was to endure to the present day. The European powers recognized the country's position at the crossroads of Europe, central to both east-west and north-south routes of commerce and war. It was in the great powers self-interest to do so. Recognition of this situation was a blanket of security for Switzerland, and probably worth more than the written guarantee, and it laid the groundwork for a reinstitution of the principles of individual freedom and cooperation within the community, although these were to be argued over in detail for another 33 years.

The Congress of Vienna had occurred at a propitious moment. The industrial growth of Switzerland was well underway, embryonic capitalism was flourishing; in addition, the draining use of national manpower in mercenary causes was ending, and there was a clear moderating of religious antagonism (this to flare on one more dramatic occasion). All of the ingredients which had been absent for four centuries in proper combination to revive the principles of the Everlasting Alliance were now present again. The final format for a centralized state was still lacking, but the means for unity had been provided by the times and the Congress of Vienna. International trade was now drawing the diversity of Switzerland together and making the country grow. From this point on, all ingredients mutually increased the value of each other. Swiss thinking was receiving its most important conditioning.

The Budding of Banking

It was during the period from the mid-18th into the 19th century that Swiss banking began in earnest. It was initiated, as was so much industry then, by private families who were primarily merchants and manufacturers doing a small amount of banking on the side.

Of those private banks in existence today, Rahn & Bodmer was the first, beginning in Zurich in 1750, and joined shortly thereafter in 1755, by Leu & Compt., functioning as a Zurich city bank, and later transformed into a private institution, ultimately to become the

Bank Leu. In 1759, Orelli Im Thalhof was founded. As the turn of the century and revolution approached, La Roche & Co. of Basle (1787), Ferrier, Lullin & Co. (1795), Hentsch & Co. (1796), and Lombard, Odier & Co. (1798), all of Geneva, had joined the banking establishment. One of today's major private banks, Pictet & Co., joined the roster in 1805, followed by Dreyfus Sohne & Co. (1823), and A. Sarasin & Co. (1841). With the addition of numerous smaller private banks throughout the 19th century, concluding with Julius Bär & Co. in 1890 and J. Vontobel, a latecomer in 1924, the modern private banking establishment was complete. It was to become the ground floor in the mobilization of funds for growth of the Swiss economy.

Foreign banks also contributed notably to the growing need for capital by the blooming Swiss industry. In development of the early Swiss railways, two large French banks played a significant part, financing a large portion of railway development from 1830–60: Credit Mobilier and Rothschild. But it was not until 1856 that the first public Swiss bank was to be promoted.

In order to participate in the financing of railway enterprises in Switzerland, a credit bank in Leipzig, Germany, attempted to open a subsidiary in Zurich. But Zurich authorities preferred a domestic bank for the purpose, with a large share (50 percent), or 7.5 million francs, of the capital subscribed by the Leipzig bank. The balance was set aside for former Zurich government president and railway director, Alfred Escher, plus the cantonal government of Zurich, and some 3 million francs were sold to the public. Apparently inspired by the exciting concept of owning a piece of a new bank to be involved with railway financing and not unmindful of the fact that the great French railway financier, Credit Mobilier, had paid a dividend in the previous year of 40.7 percent, the Swiss public grabbed for the shares immediately. By the third and last subscription day, over 70 times the available capital for the new bank was subscribed; 442,500 people had paid in the required 10 percent of the subscription price. A total of 215 million francs had to be returned to disappointed prospective shareholders, but the Swiss Credit Bank—one of today's "Big Three" banks—was launched and modern capitalism was truly underway.

Savings and mortgage banks had already flourished, usually without government funding, by the 1860s. With the founding of Schweizerische Volksbank in 1869, government banks became prominent in the mobilization of the "small man's" savings as well.

The two other major Swiss banks of the present day were formed through mergers of local banks near the turn of the century. In 1895, Basle Bankverein (founded in 1872) joined with Zurich Bankverein and two other banks to become the Swiss Bank Corporation, and in 1912 the Winterthur Bank and the Toggenburg Bank merged into the Union Bank of Switzerland.

Along with the growth of industry, railroads, and people's capitalism, came a logical demand for insurance of risks taken in all areas of enterprise. The founding of many insurance firms had to follow, including the now giant Zurich Accident in 1870 and the world's largest reinsurance firm, Swiss Re-Insurance in 1863.

The commodity in trade of all of these financial

institutions, ordinary money, went through this same general period in a state of disarray. In 1848, there were no fewer than 319 different coins in use in Switzerland, many of them of foreign denomination. And the bank note situation was no better: every bank was allowed to print its own notes, guaranteed only by its ability to redeem them, thus limiting the value of the notes as items of trade largely to the given locality of the issuing bank. By 1881, after three decades of proof of reliability of the issuing banks, but coupled with monumental confusion in usage, the federal republic took over supervision of the notes, standardized them, and made them redeemable by all issuing banks. From a value of about 93 million francs in 1880, bank notes in circulation increased to 243 million francs by 1907, but were still simply "vouchers for coinage," the substitutes for real money in coins. Since many of the coins, by then all franc-denominated, were actually of foreign issue (e.g., 87 percent of the 5-franc coins were of either French or Italian imprint), the public could not know the true backing of its paper money. In 1907, the paper money was finally placed under the jurisdiction of the new Swiss National Bank and guaranteed by the federal government to be as reliable as the republic itself, and with a viable gold backing.

The now century-old neutrality of the country, its rapid growth of industry and finance, plus a nationally guaranteed currency, combined to produce both a tremendous growth in capital within Switzerland itself, and to make the nation a capital-exporting country as well. Foreigners came to invest heavily in Switzerland, and the Swiss reinvested heavily outside. This was truly a phenomenon of Switzerland, and of very few other nations, and remains a fact today. Through the export of high-priced goods to the rest of the world and the yield on this paid-in capital when reinvested, plus the old habits of savings thrift and frugality even among the very rich, the country itself came to function as a giant bank. The important tie between banking, work ethics, and success had been forged. "It is useless to think of banking *in* Switzerland." it has been said, "Switzerland *is* a bank."

The Federal Birth

As we have pointed out, the formulation of Swiss industrial capitalism catapulted the country into international trade before a true federal state had come into existence. We have seen that this formative gap was largely a result of the great religious conflicts of the previous several centuries and the attendant uneven growth of the country. By the early 1800s, the interior Catholic cantons of Switzerland had little or no industry and were controlled by priests with Roman Catholic ideology. They evidenced a great dislike for the worldly success and material orientation of the industrialized Protestant cantons. Following a liberal overthrow of the old guard in most of the Protestant cantons in 1830, strong measures of oppression of the Roman church were undertaken, greatly offending the Catholics. They banded together under the leadership of the pro-Catholic government of Lucerne, which had twice been the object of liberal armed overthrow itself. In 1843, a secret alliance was concluded by six Catholic cantons (interestingly including all three of the original

Everlasting Alliance cantons), to protect their interests against the inroads of liberal domination of the confederacy. Named the Sonderbund, the alliance neither remained secret long, nor did it mitigate any of the anti-ecclesiastical feelings of the other cantons. The result, after four years of increasing tension, was yet another civil war in the confederacy, pitting the underdog Sonderbund against the liberal cantons. Fortunately, it lasted only 26 days, with a loss of less than 130 lives. But a liberal Protestant victory was had, and within the still aristocratically ruled Europe this fused much liberal thought into action. Within a year revolutions had broken out in France, Austria, and Germany, preventing intervention by those governments in Switzerland on the side of the conservative losers. The result was a liberal-proposed new federal constitution for Switzerland which, through the wisdom of the victors in the Sonderbund War, neither repressed nor ignored the desires of the minority. It was approved with a near two-thirds vote of the people in June 1848.

For the first time, Switzerland had an executive arm of government: a Federal Council to be seated in Berne, with internal stability (its seven federal members were unremovable for three years), but also with very limited powers. Only control over foreign treaties, the postal system, customs, and tariffs was permitted. The latter brought another important innovation: abolition of a centuries-old system of intercanton tariffs and tolls, making the country a unified economic region for the first time. Furthermore, the Council was to ensure that minority rights were bolstered against the majority, and rural cantons protected against domination by the cities.

The concept of national unity in diversity, with continuing strength for local cantons, now had a unifying central government, patterned after the principles long out of practice since the Everlasting Alliance. The ideals sought through the travail of the mercenary and Reformation/Counterreformation period were being achieved under a new federal state. The process had taken 557 years.

In the 25 years following the first constitution, a growing liberal trend was clearly evidenced in Swiss politics. More and more rights were granted to the people through both federal state and individual initiatives. The liberalism was fully evidenced by a major revision of the Zurich cantonal constitution in 1869, allowing the first direct election of nearly all officials, a referendum process on new laws, and the right of initiative for legislation. Most of these rights were adopted into the federal constitution revision just five years later. By the turn of the century, with the strong backing of workers' leaders, the government had acquired a majority share in the railway network and further legislated the rights of the public over private individuals.

This was, of course, the great period of social change throughout Europe. Switzerland became the site of both Karl Marx's First (1866) and Second (1867) Internationale's and the burgeoning of socialist thought. The affect of Marx's thinking and that of worker leftists in Switzerland was to grow for the next half-century as old religious and class struggles were being transformed into worker/capitalist dichotomies. But the evolution under the expanding state was now largely peaceful.

Perhaps the greatest post-constitution social strain

in Switzerland occurred at the end of World War I. The economic consequences of the war hit even the neutral Swiss workers, especially in contrast to many in the entrepreneurial ranks who had made large war profits. Worker movements had grown, helped by socialist and neo-Communist forces. With the expectation of a great demonstration in Zurich for the celebration of the anniversary of the Russian Revolution in November 1918, the city was put under military control. In reaction, a general strike was called for November 11. It ended the following day without severe incident, but only after the expulsion of the Soviet legation and agreement by the National Assembly to debate demands of the strikers. However, the Assembly agreed only to approve and institute proposed reforms democratically. While strike leaders were then imprisoned four to six months, a majority of their demands were later enacted by the Assembly including election of the Federal Council by proportional representation, a 48-hour work-week, and regulation of working conditions in public transportation. Thus, a national disaster was averted in a now characteristically Swiss way: hard-headed pragmatism with democratic debate of popular reforms. The lawbreakers could not go unpunished; their demands did not go unrecognized. This was the pattern of the Swiss political process from 1848. It continues to this day.

Neutrality

The final binding threads of the fabric of Swiss history concern principally the state's role from World

War I in protecting the great growth of its economy and the trappings of that growth for its people. It is a role which revolves around the central issue of political neutrality, and the difficulty of maintaining it against the immense pressures of 20th-century world politics.

The first national consideration of the importance of the neutrality issue came during heated argument over joining the League of Nations in 1920. Those in favor of participation pointed out that formation of the League was evidence of the international communities' acceptance of principles congruent with those of the Swiss confederacy, and should therefore be backed by the nation. The argument against joining hung on the point that the League was not truly worldwide, and therefore might foster counterorganizations or political divisions in the future. If this could happen, should neutral Switzerland take sides in advance? The split of the cantonal vote, $10\frac{1}{2}$ in favor, $10\frac{1}{2}$ against League membership, revealed the tightness of the issue. But a late reporting canton, the mountainous Grisons, did cast the decision: Switzerland would join. The popular vote had been 415,000 yes, 323,000 no. Geneva then became the home of the League, and its Palais de Nations stands as a still-used reminder of Swiss participation. However, the neutrality issue was to become more complicated in succeeding years.

In 1933, privacy for individuals and refuge for them and their money joined the neutrality principle in Swiss debate via a flight of capital from the new Nazi powers in neighboring Germany. As will be noted in Chapter 8, the efforts of Gestapo agents to discover German funds sequestered in Switzerland prompted the National Council to enforce the strict banking privacy principle as an expansion of neutrality beliefs by placing violations of banking secrecy under criminal penalties. It was an affirmation of the freedom to be neutral in Switzerland, but increased this potential for citizens of any nation, too. It is seen by some as an offer of neutrality and refuge for anyone's money regardless of its owner's citizenship. This is the heart of the now 40-year-old debate over the propriety of bank secrecy enforcement.

In 1935, the League of Nations voted economic sanctions against Italy which member states were bound to observe. The Swiss had made a condition of their entry into the League that they would not be bound under economic, but only political sanctions. Italy was one of the country's most important trading partners, and blood ties were common especially in the canton of Ticino. Once again the neutrality issue became a national debate. For three years Switzerland tried halfway measures to balance neutrality demands for trade with League wishes for sanctions.

In 1938, the impossibility of the conflict was forced to a head when the National Council decided on a policy of strict neutrality with continued trade. Economics and the neutrality principle had won out over the League. With the immense pressures of Hitler's Germany developing on the country, it is little surprise they did. Indeed, it was the Nazi threat which now caused another variation on the neutrality theme.

Nazi Germany in the late 1930s was engaged in both a public and covert campaign to soften up the Swiss Confederacy. Through Goebbel's propaganda measures, through formation of pro-Nazi societies in Switzerland, and through the inclinations of a bored youth, in addition to certain social climbers in society, the campaign appeared headed for the usual end: an armed attack. Shortly before the German invasion of Poland in September 1939, the Swiss Federal Council took a series of defensive steps. Army reserves were called, emergency powers granted the government, and a Federal General was appointed, the first commander-in-chief of the army since 1918. General Henri Guisan immediately ordered general mobilization. Swiss neutrality was taking an obviously defensive turn. The German border was only 29 miles from Zurich.

Isolated after the fall of France in 1940, Switzerland had acquired the distinction of becoming the only democracy remaining in continental Europe. By May 1940, Switzerland had a half-million men under arms, but was still hardly a match for the multimillion man German hoard. Still defiant of the threat, the Federal Council would now declare, "Any reports disseminated by radio, leaflet or other means which seek to cast doubts on the determination of the Federal Council and army to resist aggression should be regarded as enemy propaganda lies. Switzerland will resist to the utmost with all means at its command."[4]

As the European war progressed, the intensity of pressures on Switzerland grew. Plans were developed and advanced for a last resort interior defense of the confederacy in the high alpine country due to its believed impregnability. The border cantons were to be sacrificed ultimately if a major Nazi advance was undertaken.

It was in 1943, at the height of internal fears for

---

[4] Thürer, *Free and Swiss.*

safety and amid the propaganda and fifth column activities of the Nazis that the nation found a new strength from an ancient inspiration. General Guisan took the extraordinary and perhaps overly dramatic step of calling his senior officers to a conference at the famous Rütli Meadow, the site of the signing of the 1291 Everlasting Alliance. He arranged the conference for the purpose, as he put it, of hearing "the mysterious call of the past," and to draw for the nation a new understanding from it. The result was predictable, if even stronger than hoped. A great upsurge in national morale and personal popularity for Guisan was widely expressed and well recorded in the press of the day. A gap of nearly 700 years from the alliance was suddenly bridged. The principles of 1291 were, in 1943, to be recalled in a new will to resist foreign oppression. The shame of the 1798 overrun of the confederacy by Napoleon was to be obliterated within two years time.

While the resistance in Switzerland was increasing, so was the danger. Both peaked in early 1944. During the previous year Hitler had become increasingly preoccupied with Allied successes in Africa, the bombing of German cities, a new Russian front turning notable losses, and Allied progress up the Italian peninsula. With Switzerland providing the major access route for supplies to Italy, which were in constantly greater demand, the Führer was deeply distressed. As Italy verged on collapse, Hitler's needs for continued supply lines and communications reached a critical juncture. He worried whether they were as well served by an open route through neutral Switzerland as they would be by a route through a conquered land.

Swiss intelligence reported a Nazi invasion of the confederacy was imminent. Again it was General Guisan who rose to the occasion, and again with a conference. This was not called for inspiration, however, but rather to convince his potential opponent of Swiss determination. He met with German General Walter Schellenberg to make the case.

Historians believe it is likely that Guisan actually did not convince Schellenberg of the inadvisability of an invasion, or that if he truly did, the case was not made to Hitler. But the eventual result was as satisfactory as if he had. Hitler demurred, reportedly with displeasure about the Swiss "hedgehog" of mountain defenses. Probably equally important was his growing belief that the Saint Gotthard Pass was usable so long as Switzerland remained neutral; destruction of it by the Swiss in event of a Nazi invasion became a foregone conclusion in Germany. That risk may have been critical in Hitler's lack of an invasion decision.

Whether this "nonevent" came from an active or a passive decision on Hitler's part is unimportant to its effect on Swiss neutrality. By not invading, Hitler opted for permitting neutrality over capture of the country. And with that clear, the neutrality issue was vindicated in Swiss history.

The true value of neutrality to the Swiss can scarcely be overestimated. It is perhaps best summed up by the following:

> Swiss neutrality is not for the occasion, but forever. It affords other states an element of certainty in a shifting international scene, as the experience of centuries shows. Precisely because Switzerland has declared her neutrality perpetual, and because therefore her attitude to other

countries does not alter amid the flux of international relations, she cannot be accused of trimming her sails to the wind for her own profit.[5]

This may have overstated the case as far as other nations are concerned, but not for the historically conditioned Swiss mind.

Conclusions

The place of the federal state in Swiss history has clearly been a unique one. It was a full two centuries after the state was codified in law — and five and a half centuries after its modest beginnings as a defensive alliance — before a federal government existed. And yet, it is only at the time of the emergence of the federal state that we are able to recognize the main ingredients which make up the modern Swiss psyche. The federal state's formation coincided with an end to religious strife, the virtual end of mercenary export, and the beginnings of industrialization and capitalism. These factors would naturally tie together in the Swiss mind, and to understand the Swiss and their banking system, it will be useful to think of them as having done so. At the same time, the founding of the state marks a clear division between early Swiss history and the country's period of great growth, making it a logical point of focus.

It was largely the human cost of the mercenary period, and the economic conditions within Switzerland which it fostered, that brought about the initial burst of international trade and industrialization of the country.

---

[5] Bonjour, Offler, and Potter, *A Short History of Switzerland.*

This, in turn, after the invasion by Napoleon, helped to reduce religious battling, and that promoted evolution of the state into a form which was both cooperative with and protective of economic effort.

The banking system of the nation grew apace with economic activity, as would be expected, but especially through expansion of individual capitalism. Its maturation within the short period of less than a century also coincided with the growth of individual rights under the new federal state. It was thus natural that banking principles were closely tied to both religious and other freedoms, along with deep beliefs in governmental protection of those freedoms. In addition, this was the period when the old artisan ethics of hard work, frugality, and thrift were most prominent in achieving economic success.

One hundred and fifty years of avoiding the ravages of war and pursuing the accumulation of wealth has culminated in what the Swiss believe is a great national achievement. The freedoms of thought, expression, and work under a subdued government have combined to make the Swiss nation flourish.

When a Swiss talks about the need for privacy and the right to do as he wishes with as little government interference as possible, he is merely synthesizing those factors which have made his tiny country a major presence in the world economy. If banking privacy has been one of those factors (and it has since early days), then it is to be protected in the same way that any other ingredient of success must be. One does not easily reject the methods of gaining prosperity. In the Swiss mind, to tamper with any of them is to threaten them all.

While most Americans and a good many other people in the world would agree with the principles of the Swiss, they often argue that it is in their practice that problems arise. For example, why should the Swiss legislate (some ask) a temptation to separate a foreign citizen from the nationality of his money, and thereby foist banking secrecy on the rest of the world?

"Because we must export to live," reply the Swiss, "and we can't protect our own money in Switzerland without protecting that of the people with whom we do business." Certainly no one forces the rest of the world to buy Swiss products, whether they be watches, chemicals, cheese, or banking. If the rest of the world lived with this concept, argue the Swiss, it probably wouldn't need to come to the alpine nation for privacy.

But why then, some might moralize, encourage criminals to hide their ill-gotten gains? To which the Swiss reply, "Which encourages criminals more, a place to keep their money or the ways available to get it in the first place? Besides, the Swiss aren't the only bankers with secrecy." Indeed, it is difficult to imagine a racketeer thinking about a secret place for his booty *before* thinking about how people will buy drugs, prostitution, or a numbers game.

Doesn't Swiss banking secrecy make the criminal's hiding job easier? Probably. But are the Swiss to be blamed more than the bankers in Mexico, Luxembourg, Belgium, Lebanon, Hong Kong, or New York, all of which have sufficient measures of privacy to attract criminal funds? Moreover, if Swiss bank secrecy is such a handy criminal refuge, why isn't Switzerland a hotbed of crime, instead of the possessor of one of the lowest crime rates in the world? Quite possibly because the Swiss moral and ethical beliefs (which include bank privacy) are too strong, and honest business with the rest of the world too good.

These answers will hardly put the matter to rest, but they represent the historically honed logic of the Swiss. Whether it is "correct" for you is a personal decision, and providing facts for such decisions is what this book is all about.

Chapter four

The Great Money Game

By LATE 1973 the Great Money Game of floating foreign currency rates had developed two distinct playing areas. One, as we've noted earlier, was formed with the devaluation of the pound sterling in 1967. The principal players there became the huge international banks, including the Swiss, and multinational corporations, which had taken to swinging ape-like and in tandem from currency to currency, crushing one here, breaking off another there, and soaring with still another. This segment of the Game involved enormous sums of money, equally enormous risks, and, to the surprise of many players, some shocking losses. Press coverage of this arena was restrained, except for major events, for most of the period—especially subsequent to the last dollar devaluation in February 1973. Americans were, therefore, largely curious spectators. But not all of them.

The second area, enveloped largely by darkness since 1970, involved the small man, the not-so-wealthy, essentially unsophisticated, individual dodger of securities regulations, tax laws, and business ethics. He too was playing in the Great Money Game, but doing so only within the framework set up by "the big boys" away from their arena, and using different chips, markers, and stakes. Where the giants played by legal rules, the individual dodger toyed with illegalities, both outright and borderline. Media coverage of this side of the Game has been virtually non-existent since its inception amid the bursting affluence of mid-60s America.

Swiss banks have found themselves playing on both fields.

Largely because of public confusion over, and curiosity about, the big money side of the Game, radio and TV talk shows around the country were giving it more than usual attention by early 1973. With my booklet on Swiss banks having been published in December 1972, I was invited to be a guest on several of the talk shows in San Francisco and Los Angeles. During one show, after more than an hour of discussion, explanation, and conversation with the show's host and listeners, the host was summing up. As he concluded, he turned to me and said with a smile, "Well now, when you get right down to it, besides illegalities, a Swiss bank hasn't got that much to offer us, has it?" He had earlier suggested a similar belief about his own alleged Swiss account.

"No," I replied, "not much . . . unless you want to protect your money, or increase its profitability, or insure privacy from Big Brother government, or travel outside the United States, or do business internationally, or just improve your peace of mind!"

In retrospect, we were both looking at the same glass;

he thought it half empty, I thought it half full. The host had focused on the obvious points: The then low Swiss interest rates, slow motion withdrawal terms, and inconvenience. I was stressing the need for capital protection, new hedges against inflation, and putting blinders on the snooping eyes of government. We both made our points, I think. However, the show's host had ruled out "illegalities" in his question to me. We weren't going to become involved in telling listeners how to do things outside the law.

Nevertheless, these dodges do provide some of the most interesting and illuminating information about Swiss banks, revealing much of the lure of the Swiss secrecy system and the lengths to which some persons will go to take advantage of it. We will explore the illegality temptation with the understanding that by "illegalities" we mean violations of national laws in countries other than Switzerland.

It is important, before undertaking an explanation of a few of these creative methods of money hiding, that you are aware that it is not my intent to recommend or otherwise suggest in any way that domestic laws be violated to take advantage of Swiss bank secrecy. Quite the contrary, I strongly recommend against such ideas on both ethical and practical grounds. Many people have taken these steps already, however, since thoughts about hiding money are hardly new.

This chapter, therefore, is primarily a report of recent history. In addition, this chronicle should reveal to you that it is almost invariably the creativity of the money hider which accomplishes the task, not the guile of Swiss bankers, nor their cooperation in planning legal deviations. Moreover, this bit of recent history should suggest the universality of the idea of money-burying among people of almost any country.

We have already touched upon a few of the more famous cases in which Swiss bank secrecy had been abused. The Irvings, Herr Germann, and UCB, Basle, all belong on one side or the other of this coin. It is also true that similar advantages have been taken of banks in every nation with some form of bank secrecy, and this excludes few countries. Deviations through Switzerland have just received more attention.

The glaring light of publicity fell on American attempts to circumvent tax, securities, and corporate laws through secret foreign accounts during congressional hearings in 1968 through March 1970. During the latter phase of these hearings, which were called to decide the merits of Representative Patman's Foreign Bank Secrecy and Bank Records bill, some of the more creative money movements came out.

Robert M. Morgenthau, then U.S. Attorney for the southern District of New York, and the prime witness at the hearings, issued the call to the colors for the government on December 4, 1969, before the Patman committee. "The illegal use of secret accounts became so prevalent," he said, "that when I was here last December I could conservatively estimate that deposits in foreign secret bank accounts held for illegal purposes had a value in the hundreds of millions of dollars." He went on to describe the efforts of his office in tracking down such illegalities through investigation of "thousands of transactions," the resulting indictments of over 75 persons, and the referral to the Internal Revenue Service of dozens of additional cases. Yet, he added, "for each case we prosecuted there

were roughly six cases where we had specific information that a crime had been committed but we were
unable to prosecute either because we lacked the resources to complete the investigation or because the
evidence we had was inadmissible in court." He concluded, "For each potential case we uncovered, there
were literally thousands of other cases of criminal conduct cloaked by secret foreign accounts which were not
even touched by our investigations."

Both electronic and print media covered portions of
the hearings extensively, an exception to the otherwise
dim publicity given this aspect of the Great Money
Game. The public apparently found the ideas covered
provocative. As one Swiss banker observed, "Every
time there is a fuss like this in the U.S., we get dozens
of letters from U.S. citizens asking to open accounts."
More recent flaps have evoked responses in the
thousands.

Not only do most Swiss bankers have similar ex-
periences, but they generally agree with another banker
who told me, "the tighter the exchange controls or restrictions in a given country, the more people want to
get money out." He cited Germany in the 30s and Italy
in the 60s–early 70s as prime examples.

It is not difficult, in this light, to believe that while the
Foreign Bank Secrecy bill (enacted into law in 1970
and court tested through 1974) will make it easier for
the U.S. government to trace illegal fund flows out of
the country, it might well have some reverse effect
by inducing more citizens to *consider* sending money
abroad. This is especially likely if a seemingly innocuous proposal made by Senator Bentsen of Texas
during the Democratic Party reply to the Nixon administration's Economic Report of July 1974 gains any

following. "We should simply place restrictions on the outflow of dollars from this country . . . ," he offered, without embellishment. As though the old Interest Equalization Tax, curbs on business investment abroad, or the $5,000 declaration requirement for cash carried abroad weren't already restrictions. Should the Senator prevail in Congress with something more stringent than past or existing curbs, and if the Swiss bankers know whereof they speak, private money movement from the United States could become *vox populi* in the Great Money Game.

Meanwhile, the Currency and Foreign Transactions Reporting Act (Public Law 91–508)*, as the final law was titled in 1970, gives the government some important new tools in tracking down any escaping or illegally obtained funds. Your bank now has on microfilm any check you've written over $100 (many banks had such records prior to the act, but weren't obliged to furnish the evidence to the government as is now required). Your bank must also automatically advise the U.S. Treasury of any transfer in or out of the country of $10,000 in cash or greater, and both you and your bank (where it is involved) must declare any amount of $5,000 or more being sent or carried to or from the U.S. no matter whether it is by check, securities, or cash. You are also required to check the relevant box on tax form 1040 if you hold of have signature power over any foreign bank account. With the noose this tight around a prospective money hider's checkbook, the creativity of players in the Great Money Game will likely have to become *more* devious than in the days of the Patman hearings.

---

* Commonly called the "U.S. Bank Secrecy Act," and so referred to throughout this book.

During those hearings, Mr. Morgenthau provided details of selected cases in which his office was involved. Among the cases he noted in brief, was one where an indictment was filed against the executive vice president of Realty Equities Corp. and a consultant to the company, on an "insider" trading case. Morgenthau noted that through a series of transactions, "an opportunity became available to Realty Equities to repurchase a note with warrants attached, at a price substantially below its fair market value. This opportunity was not utilized for the benefit of the corporation," he went on, "but instead, the indictment charges, the note was purchased by a Swiss bank for the benefit of the consultant. The purchase was for $531,250; very shortly thereafter, the note was sold for $988,542 — a quick profit of $450,000." The consultant had been trying to cover the transaction through Swiss bank secrecy.

The Orowitz case was one of the more famous of the late 60s bank secrecy cases, since it involved an official of the then $1.5 billion General Development Corporation. The company was organized, according to one report,[1] by a former associate of gangland boss Meyer Lansky, one Lou Chesler, to "build and sell houses on the installment plan." He brought investors into the company including Michael Coppola, alleged longtime Mafia numbers boss of New York City, Gardner Cowles, then the publisher of *Look* magazine, and Max Orowitz, who became treasurer and a director of the firm. The action revolved around Orowitz, who in 1960 had some $500,000 worth of the corporation's convertible bonds

[1] Leslie Waller, *The Swiss Bank Connection* (New York: New American Library, 1972).

delivered to him personally from the Union Bank of Switzerland's account at Chase Manhattan Bank. He initially used the bonds to secure bank loans for himself, and later sold $250,000 principal amount without filing the required insider report with the Securities and Exchange Commission. His profit was claimed to be some $100,000.[2] Orowitz was convicted under the seemingly minor failure to report his insider sale, but the real question which was never answered was, "how and for what reason these bonds had been held in the Swiss bank under the control of the Treasurer of the corporation."[3] The implication was that illegal, privileged dealings might have been the reason, but that bank secrecy prevented any discovery; only the misstep over SEC insider rules permitted his conviction.

Morgenthau also revealed to the committee another and more dramatic case of securities fraud, this one involving a group of Liechtenstein Anstalts. Four such trusts, all holding Swiss bank accounts, were involved in the promotion of an unregistered, over-the-counter stock in the United States. All trusts were American-owned, it later developed, even though the apparent head of the trusts was a Swiss lawyer, a common practice. Morgenthau said that one of the American owners, a man with a criminal record who had previously been enjoined from trading stocks in his own name, bought some 750,000 worthless shares from an American company at a nominal price in the name of his Liechtenstein trust. "At the time," Morgenthau re-

---

[2] Ibid.

[3] Report of Hearings of the House Banking Committee on December 4 and 10, 1969, and March 2 and 10, 1970.

lated, "the trust had assets of $20.80." The amount paid by the promoter was not revealed. What do you pay for worthless stock? As it turned out, it became "worth" a great deal.

The stock's price was then run up to over $16 per share, in part through a strong buy recommendation by an investment advisory service. This organization later was shown to hold an interest in another of the Liechtenstein trusts, and its Swiss account became a recipient of part of the proceeds of the transactions. The promoter now caused the trust to sell the shares through American brokerage firms which transmitted the proceeds of sale to Swiss banks at which the trust had accounts. The American was able to realize a profit of more than $4 million by this share float, before the stock involved plunged to under $1 per share in the U.S. OTC market. Morgenthau added his opinion that the deal was compromised only when the insiders to the plan divulged its workings; Swiss bank secrecy would have protected the conspirators had they not "talked."

Widespread abuses of the Federal Reserve Board's stock purchase margin rules were perpetrated by public investors and stockbrokers, according to Morgenthau. During the great market of 1967–68, such violations were both popular and highly profitable. However, the result was a number of convictions for such activity, including the conviction and fining of the brokerage firm of Coggeshall and Hicks, a member of the New York and American Stock Exchanges, plus five of the firm's officials in 1969. Moreover, a grand jury indicted a Swiss bank, the Arzi Bank of Zurich, for the same violations, prompting a guilty plea from the bank, the first occasion under which a Swiss bank answered criminal charges in the United States. Its motives in so doing have not been explained; one can only guess that it may have been the lesser of two evils. In any event, shortly thereafter, the powerful Swiss Bankers Association directed member banks not to accept securities orders from Americans in violation of Federal Reserve margin regulations. With this weight of powerful peers and the collapse of the U.S. stock market subsequently, margin credit violations of U.S. laws in Switzerland have fallen precipitously, at least for the time being. What a new bull market might bring, especially in the popular, highly leveraged, options field, is anyone's guess.

Another area of illegality brought to light was one which received a good deal of attention in the public press over the past few years: The use of Swiss accounts for transferring drug traffic funds. One of these cases involved a Panamanian Corporation with offices in Geneva, called the "Me Too Corporation."

The two defendants in the case were convicted in November 1969 on facts arising out of heroin smuggling operations in June 1968, in which some $950,000 was sent to a Swiss account of the "Me Too Corporation."

"First," Morgenthau testified, "couriers delivered $800,000 in cash to two money exchange houses in New York City. From there the money was forwarded to the secret Swiss account of the 'Me Too Corporation.'" (Morgenthau did not detail the method of transfer. A bank draft or cashier's check drawn on a bank connected either by business or with legal ties to the exchange house would have sufficed; a draft from the exchange firm itself, if sufficiently known at the Swiss bank, would have done even better.) Morgenthau went on:

> While the appearance of unknown persons with large sums of money might have been questioned by the money exchanges, an official of the Swiss bank had previously advised them about the expected delivery of funds. Thus, because of their substantial business connection with the bank, the exchanges accepted these transactions as a professional courtesy.
>
> The other $150,000 in currency was deposited in the account of a South American brokerage firm with the First National City Bank in New York City. On the instructions of an authorized signatory of the account, a check for $150,000 was drawn on the First National City Bank and mailed to the Swiss bank for the account of "Me Too Corporation." *Although there was no evidence in either of these cases that the money exchanges, or the New York bank or the Swiss bank had any knowledge of the underlying narcotics transactions, the vital part they played in the heroin traffic is unmistakable.* (Italics mine.)

It all seems so simple. Secrecy closes off one end of the transaction, and an illegal act the other—the pattern of almost every illegality involving Swiss (or for that matter, any other country's) bank secrecy. If the illegal mind is creative enough, there is little that the various banks or brokers actually transferring funds can do to discover the illegality behind the transaction. As Morgenthau finally rested his argument, "each of these cases has involved countless man-hours spent piecing together thousands of documents and other disjointed sources of information: in short, proportionately far more investigative work than virtually every other type of prosecution [in his office]." His conclusion: "I feel that where criminals have made such extraordinary efforts to cover their tracks, we must respond with equal vigor to uncover them." His comment about criminals' "extraordinary efforts" is pertinent to our discussion. There have been, with few exceptions, no charges leveled at Swiss banks for "masterminding" illegal operations. In any event, Mr. Morgenthau and others were persuasive. The Currency and Foreign Transactions Reporting Act was the result.

A second great arena of fraud through the use of Swiss banks involves the escape from that ubiquitous harrier of all citizens, taxes. Testimony before the Patman congressional committee by the then Commissioner of Internal Revenue, Randolph W. Thrower, on December 10, 1969, cracked the multifaceted stone of tax evasion, avoidance, and fraud.

"[W]e cannot but be alarmed," reported Thrower, "at the apparently accelerating utilization of secret accounts in foreign banks in tax evasion schemes. These practices have been widely publicized and have been utilized both by members of organized crime and by business and professional people." Among the evidence he cited, omitting names and exact details, apparently for legal reasons, were:

1. Racketeer Money. The IRS stated it had "indications" that the funds allegedly used in two cases were the subject's own money which he "borrowed." One was in partial payment of $425,000 for a "well-known" hotel and gambling casino: $275,000 came from a foreign bank secrecy check and an ostensibly outside source. In a later instance, an internationally known

American figure, who the IRS claimed was an associate of major American racketeers, claimed that he paid interest by check at the rate of 10 percent on approximately $2 million assertedly borrowed from a Swiss bank. In both cases the funds were believed sent to Switzerland out of the individuals' own incomes. No taxes had been paid on these earnings and in the cases noted, tax deductions were then being claimed on interest paid themselves.

2. Currency Dealings. The IRS, Mr. Thrower indicated, had located individuals who appeared to have little reason to be dealing in the amount of funds they were. One case involved an apparently covert operation in which deposits of large sums of U.S. dollars with New York City banks were credited to the account of foreign secrecy banks. The people making the deposits said they were acting on instructions from unknown principals in South America, Israel, Switzerland, Belgium, and other countries. They claimed they knew nothing of the transactions underlying the money transfers. They were apparently dummies in a money-running scheme.

3. Personal Accounts. Mr. Thrower pointed out that an American controlling stockholder of a corporation in the commodity business directed the company to pay a foreign citizen amounts identified as business expenses. Upon his subsequent bankruptcy, it was discovered that these funds had been forwarded by the foreign citizen to a numbered bank account controlled by the American in the name of a relative.

In another case, Thrower reported the establishment

of a dummy corporation to receive commission income earned by the principal, which was later transferred to a foreign secrecy bank, allowing not only the nonreporting of the income, but, also, the dividends and capital gains on investment of these funds by the foreign bank. An additional case, which resulted in an indictment against two salesmen, occurred when it was discovered that they had established a foreign corporation, wholly controlled by themselves, to receive about 75 percent of their American commission income per year: $750,000. They had represented that the corporation had earned these commissions, not themselves. The corporation's Swiss account prevented the IRS from discovering the amounts of any legitimate foreign income.

4. Dodging Tax Collection. Thrower stated there had been cases discovered where individuals converted assets to cash and fled the country upon an audit by the IRS, but before the assessed taxes and penalties could be collected; one involved a $100,000 deposit with a U.S. bank, subsequently transferred to a Swiss bank; another, some $500,000 which disappeared into a Swiss repository after the man involved had served a three-year prison sentence for tax evasion, but prior to his payment of assessments.

The foregoing IRS cases seem exceptionally simple. It appears from Mr. Thrower's comments in the committee hearing record that barely minimal attempts at disguise were used by the conspirators beyond the first level of paper work. This has indeed not been so in the majority of money-hiding cases. With the more creative cases, the complexities begin.

European Dodges

Perhaps one of the more involuted of illegal profit making ventures utilizing a Swiss bank came to light in London during the summer and fall of 1974. This remarkable operation involved several persons, plus a list of firms stretching from London to Hong Kong, Geneva, and Liechtenstein. As the case also involves a peculiarity of British foreign exchange funds, it requires a few words of background.

British exchange control regulations, administered by the Bank of England on behalf of Her Majesty's Treasury, require that United Kingdom residents purchase foreign securities only with currency which has already been invested in foreign securities by other United Kingdom residents. The currency, known as "investment currency," arises from the previous sale of foreign securities by residents and forms an enormous investment pool. The size of the pool of securities and currency was estimated at some $11 billion in 1974. Because the demand for investment currency exceeds the supply, there exists a premium on it compared with the official foreign exchange rate available to United Kingdom residents for current transactions. By October 1974, this premium for "investment dollars" had risen to 54 percent *above* the official pound/dollar exchange rate. Thus, anyone devising a plan to pass off normal foreign currency for sale as investment currency could make a sizable profit. This was the essence of the case at hand.

Enter John Charles Stanley, a London accountant who immigrated from Czechoslovakia in the early

1950s, and who in 1970, in association with three other individuals, developed plans. One circuit in their plans shorted out in 1972, but only after developing an alleged profit of about $450,000 in option dealings in a wide range of U.S., European, and Japanese stocks. Mr. Stanley was tried and fined £5,000. Two companies concerned were fined £300,000 each. The second circuit, which was established shortly before the first developed difficulties, and thereby ran a bit longer, provides us with some clear details.

Stanley had established a company in 1971 called Unitex Capital Fund (U.K.), Ltd. as a securities broker-dealer. It later became eligible to be an authorized depositary, one of the formalities required for banks/brokers who wish to deal in pool funds for the purchase of foreign securities.

A second company was also established in London in 1971, named Hoadford Securities, engaged in the business of foreign stock options, principally those initiated by a Liechtenstein Anstalt named Carihuela Investments. The plan went as follows:

A Hong Kong firm named Ampo Trading apparently bought option contracts on numerous U.S. stocks on 10 percent margin from Cariheula of Liechtenstein. The contracts, covering stocks such as American Century Mortgage Investors, Biodynamics, Geon Industries, and several giants including Western Union, Gillette, Magnavox, and General Foods, were then assigned to Hoadford in London at fair market value, about $2.4 million. Hoadford paid the investment currency premium on the share of the assignment it put up, 10 percent of the total value.

Hoadford then exercised the options through the investment pool via Unitex, and immediately sold the stock underlying the options through the Interol Bank in Geneva. Hoadford then sold the proceeds back to the investment pool for "normal" pounds sterling, resulting in a gain via the dollar premium between investment and normal currencies of about $220,000.

The odd fact which caught the eyes of British Treasury officials, who were put onto the gambit by the large amount of funds flowing through the two small London securities firms, Hoadford and Unitex, was the existence of the same date on all of the trades from Liechtenstein to Hong Kong to London to Geneva and back to London. Even more intriguing was another slip which turned up: Ampo Trading and Carihuela of Liechtenstein were using the same typewriter on the paper work covering the trades, a remarkable feat, especially on the same day.

Poor Mr. Stanley was tried and fined another £2,000. Hoadford and Unitex were each fined £70,000.

Such cases appear to be rare in the United Kingdom. About 400 violations of Exchange Control are unearthed every year, and about 40 prosecuted. Apparently few Swiss accounts held by Britons are discovered.

Admittedly, the Swiss bank role in the Hoadford case seems superfluous. The schemes were complex enough that Swiss bank secrecy need not have been involved, especially since the Exchange Control violations occurred in the United Kingdom, and also in light of the gross flaws in the option dates and typewriter print. Nevertheless, a Swiss bank was brought in, apparently as a final cover for the traces. At the same time, it was made clear in evidence before the British courts, that the Swiss bank had no knowledge of the falsity of the exercise, and probably would have had difficulty in discovering any crime as it saw only a small part, and that legitimate, of the paper work.

More recently a sensation of sorts swept the financial and diplomatic communities in London and Berne, based on the efforts of someone in Her Majesty's Government to uncover a group of suspected Swiss accounts held by residents of the United Kingdom.

In March 1972, London newspapers were banner headlining an attempted bribery of Swiss bank officials in Geneva in the amount of £50,000 to obtain information about certain British citizens' bank accounts. In the United Kingdom, citizens are permitted to hold foreign accounts only if they have the approval of the Treasury, and then abide by regulations regarding repatriation of funds in the accounts. The alleged Swiss accounts, which the Treasury never admitted having discovered, apparently didn't meet one or another of the regulations. A certain amount of the story has been confirmed.

1. The actual funds which were involved in the alleged bribery attempt were reliably reported to have been in the £500 range, not £50,000.
2. The first Secretary of the British Embassy in Berne was removed from Switzerland at the time of the difficulty as a result of "a row between the two governments over how the information had been obtained." The Foreign Office would not admit the transfer was caused by a bribery attempt.
3. The Treasury's Senior Exchange Control enforcement officer, Mr. Stanley Little, was declared

persona non grata in Switzerland and advised he would be arrested if he should go to that country.

4. Two employees of a Geneva bank were arrested for violations of the Banking Act by the Swiss government and specifically charged with giving secret information to a foreign government.

The usual questions in Parliament came as a follow-up to the story, occurring on March 21, 1972. They are a collective masterpiece of distinction in fair play, despite the allegation of bribery.

Mr. Arthur Lewis asked the Chancellor of the Exchequer whether he will list the provisions of statutes and regulations which limit the rights of British citizens to open and hold numbered accounts in foreign banks.

Mr. Arthur Lewis asked the Chancellor of the Exchequer what actions he has taken to ascertain from the Swiss banks the numbered accounts of British citizens; with what results; and at what cost:

MR. HIGGINS: Under the Exchange Control Act, 1947, United Kingdom residents are required to offer for sale to an authorized dealer any foreign currency which they are entitled to sell, unless they have Treasury consent to retain it, and they therefore require such consent in order to hold foreign currency in bank accounts here and abroad.

It is a duty of the Treasury under the Exchange Control Act to take steps to secure compliance with and detect evasion of the provisions of that Act. It is not usual to give details of such investigations.

Mr. Arthur Lewis asked the Chancellor of the Exchequer whether he will give details of the duties and salary of Mr. Stanley Little, head of the Treasury's Exchange Control Enforcement Branch; what recent visits and activities he has had in connection with investigations into numbered accounts held by British citizens in Switzerland; and whether he will make a statement.

MR. HIGGINS: Mr. Little is the Senior Enforcement Officer in the Treasury responsible for suspected exchange control offences. His salary is £2,988 per annum. It is not usual to give details of investigations.

Mr. Arthur Lewis asked the Chancellor of the Exchequer whether he will initiate discussions with the Swiss Government to ascertain to what extent they will, on request from Her Majesty's Government or the Inland Revenue Department, supply details of numbered banking accounts held by British citizens.

MR. HIGGINS: I have noted the honorable Member's suggestion.

In its own way the foregoing exchange demonstrates another point about privacy: not only the Swiss find it useful. And there the bribery case rests.

Marco Polos at the Border

Certainly, the existence of large-scale currency outflows from Italy to Switzerland during the late 60s and early 70s is well known. A Lugano banker told me that on many days during the peak of the currency crises of 1971–73, long lines of Italians carrying suitcases full of lira formed every morning prior to the opening of most of the 39 banks in the small Swiss city. Fifteen miles from the Italian border, Lugano has the largest bank per capita ratio known: a full bank branch for every 800 inhabitants of the city and suburbs. What is more, the major banks in the Lugano area, canton of Ticino, have shown enormous growth during recent years as shown by the following table for five large banks which tend to be "average man's" banks.

Ticino Bank Growth (balance sheet totals in millions of Swiss francs, excluding branches of Big Three banks)

	12/67		12/72	*Increase of:* (as percentage)
Banca di Roma per la Svizzera	825.7		1,440.0	75
Banca del Gottardo.....................	403.0	(3/68)	1,013.0	152
Corner Banca............................	152.4		225.3	48
Banca del Sempione..................	60.2		182.4	201
Banca Prealpina.......................	32.9		83.6	64
Total.............................	1,474.2		3,944.3	108

How they grew is most interesting.

When I raised the question of veracity of the Italian Communist newspaper, *L'Unita,* with two local journalists and an American lawyer in Rome during August 1973, there was no hesitation from them. "Their facts are usually correct," responded one writer, "it's the conclusions they draw which get pushed in odd ways."

I was inquiring about a story I had first heard from a Swiss banker in Lugano regarding a pair of spaghetti manufacturers who had been caught smuggling a large amount of money into Switzerland on a train at the border town of Chiasso. The Swiss banker told me that the Italian press had carried the story in mid-May 1973. Curious, I made a few inquiries and was pointed towards *L'Unita* by a helpful reporter with *Corriere della Sera* in Rome, who discovered that the story had initially broken in *L'Unita.* Going directly to the newspaper's offices near the University in Rome, I bought a copy of each of the four issues developing the story — at twice the newsstand price, despite the fact that they were three months old. No capitalist money gain worries there.

The money-running story unfolded somewhat differently from the previous reports I'd heard, as translated by the American attorney, but was nonetheless intriguing. While the facts are believed to be correct as reported in *L'Unita*, the allegations of devious acts on the part of the perpetrators are still unproven. In fact, it was a lack of official governmental action which provoked the discoverers of the incident to break the story to the press. Since our interest here is in methods of utilizing Swiss bank secrecy to circumvent currency restrictions, the lack of proof of a crime in this case is not significant. Moreover, the method used to get around currency control laws could even be legal, according to the attorney in Rome.

According to *L'Unita*, very shortly after 10 A.M. on January 13, 1972, aboard the Milan–Zurich morning train, border guards and customs inspectors at Chiasso, Switzerland, came across an envelope in a man's suitcase, marked "24 hours." Its owner, Peter Barilla, one of the heads of a pasta empire in Bologna, was contently ensconced in the train's first-class section reading a newspaper. The contents of his envelope were destined to shatter bank and government officials on the Italian side of the border, while drawing reactions ranging from amusement to modest concern in Switzerland.

The first document in the envelope revealed that Barilla and his brother Robert held sizable bank accounts outside Italy; later estimated at over 30 billion lira, the equivalent of about $50 million at the time. Much of the money was in Swiss bank accounts, including $10 million in one account at the London branch of Union Bank of Switzerland. If it weren't for the strict Italian exchange controls over the amounts that citizens could take out of the country (then about $850 per trip), plus strong government propaganda efforts to halt the outflow of money in general, this would have been only a routine, if sizable, discovery. But because of the long lines at the doors of Swiss banks in Lugano most mornings, this document took on rather serious trappings. It was one thing to get a few hundred or even thousands of dollars worth of lira out of the country; quite another when the figure ran in the millions.

Barilla wasn't carrying any notable amount of cash with him that January morning. Nevertheless, on the strength of the envelope's contents, he was taken from the train, photographed, and released. Interestingly enough, it was about 16 months after the envelope's discovery before the Italian press obtained the story, apparently tipped off by irritated customs agents who had investigated the case and become angry at the lack of prosecution. But the important question was, how did the Barillas obtain the $50 million deposited in Swiss banks? Either, it would appear, they had earned it outside Italy legally but illegally not reported it within, or they had gotten the funds out in some creative way. Revealed in the next document in the "24 hours" envelope was the apparent Barilla method: a *fiduciaria*. For our purposes, knowledge of the process reveals one way in which many people could be transmitting funds from Italy or any tight exchange control country. For wealthy Italians it is a method of legally winking at the currency controls.

A *fiduciaria* in Italy is something of a cross between a trust agreement and an investment company. It is intended to be used as a vehicle for general investments by groups of individuals or families with sizable sources of funds within the country. It can invest funds directly outside of Italy, and can hold foreign funds out of the country when they were legally acquired there. In short, it can do much of what individuals can't. The function of a *fiduciaria*, in this case, appears to have been to keep certain funds outside Italy while bringing others in — all obscured from the prying eyes of the authorities.

The probable Barilla *fiduciaria* was revealed by a letter in the "24 hours" envelope from a Dr. M. Lauchli of Basle, Switzerland, who had apparently acted as a middleman and caretaker of the foreign accounts for the Barillas. The letter referred to a trip taken by Lauchli to Parma, Italy (near the Barilla pasta empire in Bologna), "for the investment of a fiduciary account deposit, care of Union Bank of Switzerland, in London, in the amount of SFr. 30,082,500" in 1971. It went on to discuss the interest payments made to the account from that time to the date of the letter in November 1971, and the separation of the funds into accounts for Barilla and his brother. However, no exact details of any *fiduciaria* actions were revealed by the letter.

According to the American attorney in Rome, one possible scenario emerges as likely. An investment *fiduciaria* could have been established in Italy and, with only small funding, have opened bank accounts there and in Switzerland through the good offices of one of the many Italian banks with branches in Switzerland. A Swiss account could have been initially funded in size by a loan from the bank's Italian branch, if no immediate source of foreign capital was available, but in anticipation that such a source would exist shortly. The Swiss deposit could then have been placed in other Swiss banks by a middleman such as Lauchli.

The next step, according to the American attorney, would have been the acquisition of new capital outside Italy, by holders of the *fiduciaria*, in order to repay the Italian bank's loan. *L'Unita* discovered one possible source in this case: the Barilla empire had been sold to W. R. Grace & Company, New York, in February 1971 for some $60 million in cash, stock, and notes. The proceeds of the sale could have been deposited in the *fiduciaria*'s account, which, after repayment of the Italian bank loan, might have left a substantial balance in the Swiss bank. The loan would probably have been repaid with an amount larger than the loan balance, a common *fiduciaria* practice, in order to have the excess funds handled as normal *fiduciaria* investments in Italy. The funds remaining in Switzerland could then have been safely transferred by the *fiduciaria*'s holders into their own names. With the closeout of the bank loan and the initial Swiss account, no record would remain on the *fiduciaria*'s books of any funds outside Italy. The holders would then have funds both inside and outside their country with little reason for the authorities to question the reason for either. Clearly, it is a neat scenario.

The lack of prosecution in the case suggests the *fiduciaria* device, which was perfectly legal, was the probable loophole through which Italian exchange controls or taxes were obviated. In fact, none of the funds need ever have come into Italy, leaving only questions of possible tax liability for the authorities to decide.

The reasons behind the lack of prosecution in this case may be more complicated, however. A Swiss attorney in Geneva familiar with banking practices told me that there is some reason to believe the major Italian banks are given the unofficial blessing of the Italian central bank to arrange such "legal" money transfers outside the country. This, the attorney suggested, could occur during favorable economic periods, so that when the government wishes to tighten the economy and dampen inflationary forces, there will be funds which could flow back into Italy, attracted presumably by higher interest rates and favorable investment opportunities. In 1974, however, the Italian government imposed restrictive measures on the *inflow* of lira to the country (having had little success with outflow controls), so that this theory holds little potential now. It might have been operative in the late 60s and even by 1970–71 when the Barilla case took place. Customs inspectors, of course, would not have been aware of any such policy.

One point which emerges from the whole Italian economic situation, perhaps illuminated by the "Affair Barilla" (as *L'Unita* dubbed it), as well as the earlier long lines at the Lugano banks and growth of their assets, is the truth of the previously mentioned Swiss banker's opinion that tight exchange controls only heighten the interest of citizens in removing their funds from the country issuing the controls. With the Italian economy in a stagnant and strife-torn state since the late 1960s, the effort at control there has been notable.

During the same European trip in which I ran across the Barilla case, I also discovered the network of middlemen that crisscrosses Europe like an invisible rough-spun cloth. These are the men that Dr. Franz Pick refers to as the source of "hand payments" or private transfers of money around the world. Each handles a relatively insignificant amount, but the sum total can be truly enormous. Middlemen range on the upper end of the scale from persons functioning as Lauchli did (his true occupation wasn't revealed in the Barilla story), to average traveling businessmen and private individuals. Finding them doesn't appear to be difficult. Almost anyone dealing in the European financial world knows someone, often several people, who will handle money transfers for you when prevented from accomplishing movement yourself. This occurs most often, as we've noted, in tight exchange control countries, where ordinary money brokers like the *agenti di combi* in Italy are tempted to run a night shift. I found these middlemen were known to such diverse sources as a former CIA agent turned stockbroker in London, a mutual fund sales manager in Germany, a private investment counselor in Lugano, and a former U.S. Army colonel in Italy. Their stories about the middlemen's activity range from the simple to the bizarre. All suggest the general practice is common.

The simplest is the "walk away" money transfer, exemplified by these events which I came across in London, with names and places changed for obvious reasons.

In the course of a dinner party in fashionable Hampstead in London, the English host was taken aside by a close English friend of many years' standing, and asked whether a certain German businessman also attending the party might be interested in performing a small service. A modest transfer of some funds abroad, perhaps. Discretion and suggestion were the deepest parts of the conversation. The host's friend had become aware that the host had known the German gentleman for some period of time; was it eight years, yes? It was nine on some reflection. The host wouldn't feel put out? Not in the least; he could determine the German's interest straightaway. After all, he'd recalled telling his friend about a similar personal transaction a few months previously.

By the end of the party on a Saturday evening in August, the host suggested his friend give the German businessman, Dr. Rathmunn, a call at his hotel early Monday morning. The doctor was leaving for Zurich on Tuesday. And yes, it had been a friendship of nine years and completely trustworthy.

After a quiet meeting at The Barley Mow pub just off Grosvenor Square on Monday evening, where arrangements were completed, Dr. Rathmunn left with a packet in his locked briefcase containing 250 £20 notes, a sum which no British citizen could dare carry out against the £25 traveling limit. A German, however, had only its location to be concerned with. There were other business papers in the same briefcase worth more than the £5,000 of this Englishman. Dr. Rathmunn was aboard the 6:30 A.M. Swissair flight to Zurich the next morning.

The key ingredient of the money transfer, a trusted third party, had played his introductory role. The middleman was due to return the same week to London on business. The Englishman now had to trust the word of his host's friend, even though he had been given a receipt for the funds by Dr. Rathmunn. It was hardly enforceable, but rather a gesture of intent.

The arrangements, I was told, turned out well. By

the following weekend, the Englishman had a Swiss bank deposit slip which required only the return of the two signature cards to verify, along with a signed "Statement of Conditions" required by the bank. The deposit slip read SFr. 30,200.

The German businessman had an additional SFr. 5,000 in his pocket for his trouble, a bit less than 15 percent of the funds handled, and rather high for this sort of transaction. But then, it was a last-minute undertaking. In any event, 15 percent wasn't too difficult to recover in the world of an exploding Swiss franc/pound sterling exchange rate. Within one year the Swiss franc had climbed 24 percent. Satisfied business partners all around included the Swiss bank which had acquired a new deposit at no effort, and with no concern about the source of the deposit. Dr. Rathmunn had been doing business with the bank for more than two decades.

And so the rough-spun webbing of the hand payments system flourishes without any notice, crossing borders and passing through exchange control systems like flies through bars of an old prison. Occasionally someone gets caught, like the son of a partner of one of Geneva's oldest private banks. He was picked up in Sweden leaving that tight exchange control nation on a middleman transfer and was jailed for a year. But this is all part of a much larger network of fund transfers which make use of banking privacy in most countries of Europe, through the Middle East and on to Hong Kong. Luxembourg's bank secrecy has been highly publicized on several occasions, and Brussels has a solid reputation in this regard as well. But Switzerland is still the center of this money flight plan, and will likely remain so. It is a passive business for Swiss bankers. None of the foregoing cases illustrates any active desire on the part of the Swiss to induce a foreign citizen to violate his country's laws. But if one wishes to do so, they believe it is none of their business to be your keeper nor an international policeman. And in the apparently great majority of the cases, the Swiss weren't even allowed to come close to the truth of the devious dealings.

Business Favorites

The Great Money Game is played, as we have pointed out, quite legally in many instances. In the United States this occurs most often in the business world, certainly when our largest banks and corporations make their moves. But individuals and smaller businesses have some legal gambits, too. They are provided through the Foreign Investors Tax Act of 1966 and the general provisions of the Internal Revenue codes, the former tempting some to establish foreign trusts, the latter inducing creation of many of those foreign corporations recently under scrutiny by Congress. Interestingly, in most of these legal tax avoidance efforts, Swiss banks need play no part whatsoever. They will assist in the establishment of either a trust or foreign corporation, if asked, however; and do so through one of the numerous tax havens outside Switzerland.

The list of these havens begins with Switzerland's next door neighbor, Liechtenstein, and includes Andorra, Anguilla, the Bahamas, the Cayman Islands, Malta, the Netherlands Antilles, the New Hebrides, Panama, and Pitcairn Island.

An American businessman would need to spend less than $1,000 in legal fees to establish his tax haven foreign corporation, thus enabling him to undertake foreign business. If his tax haven-headquartered firm were selling voodoo dolls, for example, in other foreign countries, the profits made would not be taxable in the United States, nor in the proper tax haven where the firm was incorporated. Then all that remains is for the American owner of that firm to be able to make use of the untaxed corporate profits. If the owner lives abroad, there is no United States tax problem. If you, as the owner, are a U.S. resident, the array of banks in the tax haven itself, or your Swiss bank, can lend a hand. Just obtain a loan guaranteed by the profits and assets of the foreign company, or borrow directly from your firm. The loan does not represent U.S. taxable income, and the proceeds from it can be used for either business or personal purposes. What is more, a legal reduction in your estate is possible also by borrowing a given amount per year; your estate could accrue a sizeable loan liability in the United States, but your heirs could have just as sizeable assets remaining in the foreign corporation.

This legal tax angle is well recognized by the IRS. Further, several rock musicians and successful authors, even those in prison such as Soledad Brother George Jackson and San Quentin Six defendant Fleeta Drumgo, are known to have made use of the tax haven corporation.

One variation on this perfectly direct method of saving taxes complicates it with illegalities. It is, nevertheless, a favorite with some international businessmen:

double invoice. Where it involves a Swiss bank, double invoice is virtually impossible to detect, and the bankers have no way of suspecting it either. It is as simple as it is ingenious.

If a Dutch toy windmill manufacturer, as an example, is doing important business with a British wholesaler to the toy trade in the United Kingdom, and knows his buyer well enough to broach the subject of the "problem he is having with high taxes these days," a plan to get around the tax impact can be readily laid on. The Dutchman obtains the Britisher's agreement to pay for goods received against two invoices for each shipment. The larger invoice is paid directly to the Dutch firm in the normal way against shipment or sight of goods. The second invoice, usually the smaller one, calls for payment directly to the bank account of the Dutch toy maker in Switzerland. Since the funds for this invoice never flow through the Netherlands, and the Dutchman retains only the one invoice which reflects the goods shipped (albeit at a lower unit charge than normal), there can be little question from tax authorities in Holland. The British wholesaler has solid invoices to back up his payments, and the Swiss bank isn't interested in looking into the reason for payments reaching every account in their bank. (And the payment is legitimate anyway.) Only a suspicious taxman in Holland who obtains cooperation of British Inland Revenue to investigate the wholesaler's invoices in the United Kingdom could have any chance of detecting the tax avoidance. What is more, the double invoice system can be worked without the payer being aware that any taxes are being evaded. Payments to

Swiss accounts are very common these days; the buyer of goods has no reason to act as policeman any more than the Swiss do.

Thus, the routes and motivations for movement of money into the Swiss financial havens are as numerous as the airmail stamps, suitcases, or courier pouches which take funds there. What you might wish to have done with your funds once they have moved behind the secrecy veil, is the subject of the balance of this book. It comes with the continued admonition that illegalities are no way to begin your use of Swiss banks. It comes also with the observation that the most popular investment excursion through Switzerland in 1973–74 has been made by persons who believe there is some truth to the old Swiss proverb, "For gold even the devil dances."

Chapter five

In Gold They Trust

AN ADVERTISING MESSAGE printed adjacent to the postmark on a letter arriving from South Africa's Chamber of Mines could not have been more timely when I received it in early November 1974. It pungently expressed the money world's attitude toward the yellow metal: "GOLD IS MONEY YOU CAN TRUST" announced the red headline next to the Johannesburg imprint. South Africa's message was then being heeded by Swiss portfolio managers, London gold bullion dealers, British citizens in their new rush for the Kruger Rand, and Americans who were anticipating gold legalization in 1975. Gold bullion reached $190.25 per troy ounce in London two days later, and $195.25 per ounce, the record London fixing, before year's end.

Framed on a wall in the office of a partner of London's important gold and silver dealer, Mocatta, Goldsmid, is the "golden rule": "He who has the gold makes the rules."

It is in gold, not God, that many have recently trusted. Too many monies have recently displayed their weak knees. Gold has substituted as a refuge for savings and insurance against the vagaries of the future.

Interest in gold was never greater. Nearly 40 percent of 1973's world production of 1,400 metric tons went into investment and speculation, marking the first net gain in this demand since 1968. With the late buying surge in 1974, it will probably weigh in at a similar level, despite earlier forecasts of a modest decline.[1] The record market price reflected an 87 percent gain from year-end 1973, and a leap of 79 percent from the 1974 reaction low set in July, much in anticipation of American gold legalization in 1975. These price runs reveal the already high volatility in the gold market.

Gold clauses are being prepared for legal contracts to protect their value for the first time since the 1930s.[2] Gold coins are being snapped up all over the world in record numbers. South Africa will more than double its 1973 level of 30.1 metric tons of gold used for coins in 1975. Austria, Hungary, Mexico, and Great Britain are only the most prominent countries to have begun re-striking old gold coins with their original dates. Most others with early issues have done likewise. The U.S. government, under pressure from skeptics, even opened Fort Knox to a news media congressional tour in October 1974 to prove America still had some gold in reserve.

And yet, more than a few Americans have wondered what all the fuss is about. Gold is a "barbarous relic" we've been told, first by John Maynard Keynes, then by

---

[1] Peter D. Fells, *Gold 1974* (London: Consolidated Gold Fields, Ltd., 1974).

[2] R. A. Wormser and D. L. Kemmerer, "Restoring Gold Clauses in Contracts," *American Bar Association Journal*, August 1974.

nearly every Treasury Secretary or Undersecretary since Franklin Roosevelt's first administration, when we were also told we could no longer own it. In its common forms, jewelry, timepieces, and tooth fillings, gold has all but priced itself out of the market. Consolidated Gold Fields estimates that total fabrication and industrial demand in 1974 will barely match that of 1973, with declines in jewelry and dentistry being offset by increases in the electronics industry. And, of course, Americans have never been visited with any calamity sufficient to make gold an emergency commodity of exchange.

As might be suspected, the world's passionate interest in gold is not new. The rush for gold is nearly 6,000 years old. It was being written about and coveted before the Egyptians built the pyramids. Its value as a gift coined the phrase "rich as Croesus," after a fifth century B.C. king of Lydia who gave 7,500 pounds of gold for the building of a temple to Apollo at Delphi. Julius Caesar acquired his fortune in gold through conquest of the Spanish provinces.

Its value as a bribe to the potentates on the frontiers of the Roman Empire collapsed at the same time as the empire itself. The yellow wonder was a prime factor in the early success of the Swiss watch industry, the springboard for fortune hunters during the great gold rushes of the 19th century, the key issue in the bitterly fought U.S. presidential election of 1896, and a condition of intense maneuvering between central bankers of Europe and the United States from 1927 through 1933.[3]

---

[3] Stephen V. O. Clarke, "Central Bank Cooperation, 1924–31," Federal Reserve Bank of New York, 1968.

The ebb and flow of the passion for gold runs like a brilliant thread through the entire recorded history of Western civilization, and much of the Far East, as well. No other metal, nor any precious stone, has captured the imagination of people for as long. This fact has also caused the greatest problems with gold today. If it were not for this almost timeless reverence for the precious metal, it would have been disposed of as an object of monetary affection within the past 40 years. Few traditions have withstood the collective destructive pressures of as many governments as has gold. With the legalization of ownership for Americans in 1975, the pernicious forces will have again retreated, at least a short distance. With the early 1975 French revaluation of gold reserves to a free market-related price the withdrawal was extended. Money printing presses will continue to have some form of gold regulator, albeit not the "economic vote" of pre-1933 when dollars could be exchanged for gold at a fixed price. But the battle between the gold monetarists and free-spending politicians goes on. The history of gold remains the fulcrum about which the believers in and destroyers of gold pivot.

Everyone knows what gold is, and yet few of us have ever touched it in its purest form, bullion bars. Most of us will have purchased gold in some form during our lifetimes, but do we really understand much about this heavy metal which has both caused and ended wars, knocked more men off balance than has love (according to Victorian Prime Minister Benjamin Disraeli), and literally killed thousands in pursuit of it for their fortunes? Why has this metal been so controversial over the centuries as to evoke from Pliny, "how innocent, how blessed, how luxurious life would even be if we did not crave anything deeper than the surface of the earth . . . in brief, if we were satisfied by what is around us. . . . Gold is grubbed up . . . man has learned to challenge nature. . . . Would that it could be wholly banished from our lives," and yet equally motivate King Ferdinand of Spain to write his men in South America, "Get gold, humanely if you can, but at all hazards get gold"?

The biblical book of Proverbs could question, "How better is the search for wisdom than the search for gold?" And French President Charles de Gaulle could emphatically insist, "There can be no other criterion, no other standard than gold. Yes, gold which never changes, which can be shaped into ingots, bars, coins, which has no nationality and which is eternally and universally accepted as the unalterable fiduciary value par excellence." And yet, more persons have likely gained their sum total of knowledge about gold from the film *Goldfinger* than from owning even a 10-gram bar.

We still must wonder, why all the fascination with gold? Was economist Robert Triffin of Yale talking sense when he observed, "nobody could ever have conceived of a more absurd waste of human resources than to dig gold in distant corners of the earth for the sole purpose of transporting it and reburying it immediately afterwards in other deep holes, especially excavated to receive it and heavily guarded to protect it"?[4] The answers to those questions must be carefully sought. Gold is a sometimes illusory substance.

---

[4] Robert Triffin, *Gold and the Dollar Crisis* (New Haven, Conn.: Yale University Press, 1961).

First, and allowing for some preference differential, gold is the most beautiful of all metals. It has an unusual softness of texture in bullion form, while shining in soft light with a marvelous luster, almost a liquid sheen that steadily glows. In polished pure form it has a dazzling brilliance. In alloy with silver it can be nearly the color of platinum; in alloy with copper, a luminous reddish hue.

Gold is virtually indestructible. Gold coins 200 years old found on the ocean floor are as bright as the day they were minted. It cannot tarnish, like silver, unless heavily alloyed with another metal. It cannot rust like iron. It will not corrode as does copper. It can neither laminate nor flake. In fact, it combines in nature with few other elements at all, including oxygen, nor as a primary element is it the product of combining other elements, much to the unending dismay of the medieval alchemists. One chemical with which gold will marry is cyanide in solution, which now provides the principal means of extracting South African gold from its rock ore.

As a function of both gold's indestructibility and desirability, it is estimated that nearly 90 percent of the gold unearthed in the past 6,000 years is still in existence today: nearly 3 billion ounces or almost 94,000 tons. All of that mined in the past five centuries, about 60,000 tons, would fill a room less than 55 feet on a side, or about equal in volume to twice the airspace in an average home.

Gold is also one of the most workable of metals. It can be wrought into an almost endless variety of shapes, from sharply angular to gracefully curving sculpture, from absorbing the tiniest details of artistry to filling every crevice and cranny in a tooth cavity. This work-ability arises out of gold's impressive malleability and ductility. One ounce has been beaten into a sheet covering more than 100 square feet and to a thinness 1,000 times less than that of ordinary paper. Another ounce of it can be drawn into a thread 50 miles long. Its heat-reflective capability has prompted its use in numerous space projects, including the umbilical cord tethering Major White to his spacecraft in man's first space walk.

Gold's electromagnetic reflective qualities have spawned paints now used for shielding electronic circuitry from random interference. At the same time, its electrical conductivity has made it commonplace in high reliability electronic circuitry. New uses are being found for gold annually, many as fallout from the U.S. space program.

These factors of beauty, permanence, reliability, and workability have given gold properties unique in total comparison to any metal. They are sufficient alone to prompt a demand for the metal which is significant if not explosive. Aggregate demand from industry, jewelry fabricators, coin and medallion imprinters, and dentistry absorbed about 60 percent of the total 1973 supplies.[5]

The fact is that gold has always been scarce and difficult to obtain. While gold has been discovered in quantity on all the five major continents of the world, demand for it over broad periods has usually exceeded supply with only temporary exceptions. The Egyptian, and later Roman, treasury stocks apparently never sur-

---

[5] Fells, *Gold 1974.*

passed 250 tons at their peaks.[6] This did not prevent both civilizations from being conquered, in part to obtain their then enormous supplies. In the 1970s, more than twice that amount is being absorbed by private hoarders *every year,* and still represents only about one third of the annual world production.

The causal point in gold's scarcity is the difficulty in obtaining it from the earth. Only in surface alluvial deposits, as in the cases of the California, Yukon, and Australian gold rushes, is it relatively easy to separate from its ancient earthly residence. The retrieval method used in all cases, as with the early Egyptians on the upper Nile, was the same: panning.

But the world's richest deposits, those in the reefs of South Africa, are hidden in immensely protective storehouses nearly two billion years old. Buried as they are two to two and a half miles beneath the surface, a trip to the richest veins resembles nothing so much as a legendary trip to Hell.[7]

Visitors who have deposited their clothing in exchange for a pair of white overalls to both discourage souvenir hunting and allow for washing recovery of particles that attach themselves to pant-legs and sleeves, find themselves in a gallery or tunnel soaked by humidity and natural rock temperatures above 100° F. Even extensive air conditioning leaves the body dripping as it combines with moisture from the dust control water sprays. Noise from the compressed air

---

[6] C. V. H. Sutherland, *Gold, Its Beauty, Power and Allure* (London: Thames and Hudson, 1959).

[7] Timothy Green, *The World of Gold* (New York: Walker & Company, 1968).

drills carving solid rock raises conversation to a shouting level.

The actual gold veins are contained in 40-inch high tunnels called *stopes*, partially covered with pools of warm water springing up from the dust control water. In most South African mines, the gold is held within a conglomerate of white pebbles and is all but invisible to the unaided eye. A magnification of two times is usually required to see even the largest flecks. The miners drill away a ton of ore, ship it to the surface, mill it to a fine powder, and subject it to the cyanide solution to recover $1/4$ or $1/2$ ounce, on the average, of the yellow metal. The richest mines obtain only about $1 1/2$ ounces per ton of ore. In the process of gaining the minute amount of gold from each ton of ore, some 500 lives are lost per year in underground accidents in South African mines. About 32 million ounces are still refined there in an ambitious year, but this has been declining steadily since 1970. The scarcity of gold is real and the production slowdown painfully obvious. The insertion of these factors into the gold market has caused more than tiny twitches in that skittish world, especially at the time of announced withholding of supplies, as occurred in early November 1974, by the Reserve Bank of South Africa.

But what of new supplies? Surely the high prices have given impetus to mining companies to explore and recover previously unprofitable sources? Consolidated Gold Fields' David Lloyd-Jacob stated, in 1974:

> I don't see any new production from mines coming for six or seven years. It takes that long in South Africa to come to

production in a new mine. And I don't see that number of
new mines on the horizon even at that time distance. There
is a possibility that in North America that some of the closer
to surface deposits now being investigated might come into
production in two to three years time. But there is nothing
very major now in the stocks that we hear of.[8]

His conclusion: "I continue to believe that output of
gold in five years time will be no higher than it is now,
more or less whatever the gold price is in the interval."

Mr. Lloyd-Jacob's reasoning is pragmatic. "Worldwide, mining companies are finding it extremely difficult to justify new gold projects at over $100 gold
[price]. The only thing that has happened in recent
months to change the forecast in the upward direction
is continued inflation. The $60–90 project price of last
fall [1973] has risen, maybe up to 9 percent higher, in
reflection of the increase in costs which beset us all."
Even this is not a one-way street. He postulated:

> A worrying thing has occurred, which might tend to off-
> set the rise [in project price]. With the move upward in the
> gold price, a number of fabricators have reduced their long
> term purchase intentions. A new gold mine has to be look-
> ing to a firm demand from six or seven years time to, say, 37
> years time. That means that one cannot rely on, for purposes
> of planning new mines, speculative or investment demand.
> One has to look to steady fabrication to support the mines'
> own cash position. . . . A number of mining firms will be
> much more interested in looking for gold because of the
> upside potential they have seen. . . . But I do not believe
> any major companies are looking for $100–$120 gold at the
> moment.[9]

---

[8] Dr. Harry Schultz and Kinsman Media Corporation, International
Monetary Seminar: Update 1974, San Francisco, April 1974.
[9] Ibid.

With the free market gold price remaining above the $120 level for the greater part of 1974, the project price for new mines could move somewhat higher. But Mr. Lloyd-Jacob's new production time horizon of six to seven years remains valid. This settles the gold price issue squarely in the realm of psychology. How much money will be pumped into the gold market for speculative or investment demand?

Provocateurs

Diodorus Siculus, writing in the first century B.C. set the condition of gold both for antiquity and the future. "Nature herself makes it clear that the production of gold is laborious, the guarding of it difficult, the zest for it very great, and its use balanced between pleasure and pain."

Egyptian gold objects made their first appearance around 3200 B.C., following the first prescribed legal value of the metal which occurred several centuries earlier under King Menes who ordered 14-gram gold bars produced under his imprimatur and with his name stamped thereon. The fineness of these bars was of uncertain measure, varying between 80 percent and 95 percent gold alloyed with silver. It marked the first attempt to set a standard for gold usage, felicitous as it was. From this point throughout the history of the Egyptian civilization, gold was an artifact of reknown. Many pharaohs' tombs were heavily laced with the metal, including that of Tutankhamen which was discovered in 1925 A.D., but dated from the 14th century B.C. It contained the most incredible array of gold artistry, its weight estimated at nearly a ton, including the third, innermost coffin which was solid, beaten gold $2\frac{1}{2}$ to 3 millimeters thick.

The yellow metal was also an important basis for the success of Egyptian ambitions: ". . . no doubt there was a close connection between the natural wealth of Egypt and the great power and continuity of Egyptian culture," Sutherland was to write. "A large store of wealth in the form of an imperishable metal which was especially prized for its ornamental value and easy working properties inevitably opened up the markets of neighboring peoples . . ." From this came a rapidly developing spread of gold over the Mediterranean.

Crete acquired great stores of gold between the 20th and 10th centuries B.C., as did the Phoenicians by the 12th century. Sutherland further observed that ". . . in a civilization which lacked its own supply of gold special efforts were made to acquire it from elsewhere as soon as the factors of either trade or conquest made it possible to do so." Mediterranean peoples found both methods propitious.

The Queen of Sheba made a gift of 120 talents of gold, some 6,500 pounds, to King Solomon, aware apparently of his fondness for the metal which lavishly adorned his palace and many personal effects, and which was the principal component of court wine goblets. The biblical book of Exodus describes grand adornments of the Tabernacle with the precious metal.

By 650 B.C., King Croesus had introduced his coinage system, in fact a bimetallic structure based on a gold to silver ratio of 1:10. His tiny oddly shaped gold coins became common tender not only in Lydia, but in the nations with whom it traded.

Persia's failure to subdue Greece in the first decade
of the fifth century forced the surrender to Greece of a
million ounces of gold, the opening flow of the metal
onto the European continent. The then silver-oriented
Greek city-states, previously relatively poor, began
their search for gold. Alexander the Great's eastward
conquests in the fourth century B.C. were accomplished
with the accompaniment of an expert mining engineer.

With the beginning of this gold movement into
Greece came the first gold ownership by the common
people, principally via coinage. This previously un-
heard of phenomenon marked the true beginning of
public interest in gold, although it initially developed
slowly and largely as a result of exploitation of conquered lands. The trade method of obtaining gold was
not favorable for Greece because of her states' previous
dependence upon silver and its unfavorable exchange
ratio for gold in the Greek world, of about 3:1.

It was in Greece—and, to some extent, among the
Etruscans in Italy—that development of intricate and
ornate jewelry was seen from the fifth century B.C. At
this point, however, Italy was notably poorer than
Greece, being without even significant silver, and
utilizing mainly bronze for fabrication until the third
century B.C. It was then that the first silver coin of
Rome, the denarius, was developed and circulated.

The Romans were not long in eyeing the fabulous
gold wealth of their Mediterranean neighbors. Roman
stocks were estimated at less than 1,000 pounds at the
outset of the Punic Wars with the rich Carthaginians.
By the end of the last Punic War in 150 B.C. Roman gold
stocks had soared to 17,500 pounds, despite the heavy
costs of virtually ceaseless wars for two and a half

centuries.[10] By the first century before Christ, Rome had been transformed from a nation of relatively plain life-style to one of luxurious standards where gold could become the private property of any person of substance. By the reign of Caesar Augustus, gold coins were available to anyone, where they had previously been issued on only four occasions in the history of the state. The epoch of military expansion of Rome had become measurable in terms of wealth, and gold was the principal standard.

The largest single hoard of gold captured by the Roman legions was taken by Emperor Trajan in Dacia. It totaled nearly 500,000 pounds, and marked the peak of the Roman treasury stockpile.

The third century A.D. saw a sharp inflation in the Roman world, ultimately debasing the silver coinage and prompting a decline in gold coinage as well, with an attendant decrease in the quality of minting. Abruptly in the first half of the fourth century, however, gold coins began to be issued in huge quantities, probably as a result of increased tributes and taxes paid by subject peoples. The new coins, including the weighty Roman emperor medallions, were used in large measure to bribe governors and subsidize their expenditures at a dozen places across the frontiers of the empire. When their conquering drive failed, the Romans turned to gold as a substitute in holding the peace. This sufficed until the middle of the fifth century when the frontiers burst, the empire was crushed, and its gold dispersed by the new conquerors. The center of gravity of the gold world was ready to

---

[10] Sutherland, *Gold, Its Beauty, Power and Allure.*

shift toward the East. Byzantium came forth as the next principal holder of the metal, although it had far less than Rome. Constant wars with Persia finally sapped even that empire's strength until it eclipsed into the darkness of the Middle Ages.

In the 16th century, gold again became a focus of conquering armies as Spain, through the urgings of King Ferdinand, acquired large stores of it in South America and Mexico.

By the end of the 18th century, with several new discoveries in the Ural Mountains, Russia became the world's predominant gold producer. This position grew to the point where in 1847 the country was producing 60 percent of all the world's newly-mined gold. While Russia was at the peak of its production, the history of gold took a turn which was to profoundly affect its subsequent use. The passion for gold became a public affair. For the first time since Roman days, gold was no longer to be the purview of governments and their armies alone.

The first great gold rush which involved the common man, occurred at Sutter's Mill near the joining of the American and Sacramento Rivers in California in 1848. On a January afternoon a Swiss carpenter named John Marshall discovered gold traces in the tail run of the mill. His find was to initiate the greatest rush for the metal ever known. By 1852, there were an estimated 100,000 men working the fields, including not only Californians and Spaniards from Mexico, but also an estimated 25,000 Frenchmen and 20,000 Chinese. The California yield that year alone was $81 million.

The U.S. Mint was the first to take advantage of the new gold, minting coins in such profusion that silver coins became scarce overnight. Still, some 20 percent of the California gold flowed overseas. Reserves in the Bank of England increased 56 percent to over $50 million between 1848 and 1852. The Bank of France fared even better, increasing its reserves from just over $8.5 million in 1848 to more than $60 million in four years.

Before the California rush had faded, gold was discovered in Australia in 1851, and the population crush began there all over again. The gold mined in the state of Victoria alone topped $25 million in the single year of 1856. Most of this gold, produced under stricter state control than in California, found its way to Her Majesty's Treasury in London, substantially aiding the growth of that city as an important financial center. Two of the present London gold market's five members were founded during this period, Pixley & Able (now Sharps, Pixley), and Samuel Montagu's.

Following the California and Australian rushes, which were of short duration because of the surface, alluvial nature of the deposits, came a series of secondary rushes. The most productive of these was that of the Comstock Lode near Virginia City, Nevada. A discovery on the island of New Zealand found 7,000 men working there within a year. Literally hundreds of rumors of new finds were run to the ground by gold-hungry populaces. Some were planted for the simple purpose of driving the crowds out of cities such as San Francisco. Others, including one about an alleged find in Queensland, Australia, sent an estimated 10,000 men packing before the earliest arrivals could communicate their failure.

A man familiar with rumors discovered the world's

largest field, but ironically, it was to become an illusion for potential gold panners.

Former Australian miner George Harrison discovered gold on a farm in the Witwatersrand of South Africa in 1886. But instead of alluvial gold, in an "outcropping" he found a conglomerate of white pebbles, showing only minute traces of gold, and unfortunately requiring extensive crushing to yield its tiny treasure. Gold nuggets were nowhere to be found.

As a consequence of the difficulty in obtaining gold from its ore, extensive capital had to be employed before any mining could take place. Each new South African mine required in excess of $1 million capital before bringing out its first ounce of gold. This was not to be an average person's game in South Africa. The capital did come, and quickly, from the largest, closest source: the men who had only recently made their fortunes in diamonds at Kimberley in the same country. The investors included Hermann Eckstein, Cecil Rhodes, Charles Rudd, and the Barnato brothers.

The early mines extracted only about 65 percent of the gold in the ore, using a mercury coating on copper plates to adhere the gold. It was a highly inefficient process, and by 1890 South African gold appeared to have economically peaked out. South Africa would have to await word of a new chemical extraction process invented in Scotland three years earlier. It was the mid-1890s before the cyanide process was to be extensively used in South Africa, but its results were dramatic. In 1898, South Africa topped the United States in total gold production, some 4 million ounces. In every year since 1901 (the mines were closed during the Boer War), South Africa has provided more than a quarter of the world's gold production. By 1974, the figure was over 65 percent. But, because it lacked the capital, the public had not been able to take advantage of its best bet: South African gold has been a corporate / government bonanza.

One more gold rush for the ordinary individual was due to spring onto the world scene before the close of the 19th century. In August 1896, two prospectors caught the flash of gold in a tributary of the Yukon River in far northern Canada. By 1898, the word had spread so widely that 41 ships were on regular runs between San Francisco and Skagway, the nearest port to the Dawson find in the Yukon. Tickets on those ships sold for $1,000 apiece, while one source[11] estimates that 100,000 men were to use them, or travel the arduous land route to the far north. Only 30,000 to 40,000 made the full trip, and only about 5,000 ever panned for the yellow metal. But the rush ended almost as quickly as it began, within three years, and after yielding some 2.5 million ounces. With it ended the most fabulous 52 years in the history of gold.

Gold's *monetary* history had been given a tremendous boost during that period as well. One by one, the major countries of Europe and North America switched from a silver money standard onto gold. By 1914, 59 nations were on the gold standard, and only China among the major countries remained on silver. The United States shifted in 1900 onto a measure of gold value for the dollar: 25⅘ grains of 90 percent fine gold became the standard unit of value. "All other forms of money issued or coined in the U.S. shall

---

[11] Pierre Breton, *The Golden Trail* (Toronto: Macmillan, Ltd., 1954).

be maintained at a parity of value with this standard," read a portion of the enabling legislation. The gold price was \$20.67 per ounce, the level of most of the previous two centuries.

The unity of belief in a gold standard was not to be long-lived, however. With the outbreak of World War I, most European countries suspended their gold standards. By 1919, Britain had also suspended its gold standard, although the United States remained on it until 1933. Britain and a handful of other major European nations made brief returns to a gold exchange standard in the late 20s, but at the prewar price of \$20.67 per ounce. This was despite a major increase in the general level of prices for commodities in the interim, and was a contributing factor in the eventual downfall of the gold standard in the Depression. In 1931, the pound sterling was devalued and gold bullion hoarding forbidden in Great Britain.

In March 1933, the Roosevelt administration took the United States off the gold standard by banning the hoarding of gold by citizens and denying the export of it. Later that year, Roosevelt and acting Treasury Secretary Henry Morgenthau, plus Jesse Jones of the Reconstruction Finance Corp., began a daily ritual of fixing the gold price over breakfast, gradually increasing the price in the mistaken belief that a higher gold price would help pull the economy out of the depression. The reality became clear by January of the next year with the result that Roosevelt decreed a one-move hike in the price by over \$14 per ounce to \$35. There it remained until the devaluations of 1971 and 1973, when the official dollar price for gold was raised to \$42.22 per ounce.

With this extensive and dramatic history, gold has been ingrained into the traditions and legends of a great portion of the world's population. However, it is from most recent times that memories flourish. Citizens of countries ravaged by the wars and inflations of the 20th century covet gold most in today's world. Americans are just now being added to the list.

Gold was a principal commodity hidden by Jews in their capital flight from Nazi Germany. Untold hundreds, perhaps thousands, were saved the annihilation of concentration camps through gold bribes to soldiers or border guards (but not the SS or Gestapo). The pattern was repeated throughout countries desolated by the Nazis in the war, and by families trying to escape being forced to the East by the Soviet army in West Germany and Austria, after the war. Many Greek families were saved by the hiding of gold coins, even in window and doorjambs of their homes, when the war destroyed the Greek economy and the drachma. They still had buying power for necessities. Those who could hide none were often wiped out.

The French represent another case, torn as they have been by two vicious wars and by the destruction of inflation as well. Not only has gold provided necessities in times of German occupation, but it has withstood the 14 devaluations of the franc since World War I. A Frenchman who has salted away a few 10- or 20-gram bars in the mattress from time to time over the past 60 years has smiled at his gold value increase from $20.67 to the 1974 peak of $195, while the paper francs in his wallet dropped to $1/_{250}$ of their 1914 value!

Not only Europeans have felt oppressive need to hoard gold. India has been the most consistent absorber of the metal in recent years, taking on the order of 12–13 metric tons in bar form alone annually since 1970. The prior year India soaked up 22 tons. Hoarding done through jewelry in that country is even more common, a function of price and the incredible availability of 18–22 carat gold chains, pendants, and rings amid the worst squalor of the impoverished and disease-ridden sections. The Indian buying of gold represents a family's insurance policy more against drought or monsoon destruction of food supplies than against war, inflation, or devaluations. It is also a common practice in that country to hide "black money" — profits not declared to tax authorities — through purchase of small bullion bars, which are smuggled in.

Another strong factor in the hoarding demand from the Far East has been Indonesia, where inflation since the mid-1960s has been the prime motivator. Indonesia has absorbed 106 metric tons of gold, net, since 1968, including one dishoarding year, 1972, where a loss of 15 tons was recorded at the time of a stabilizing currency. The hoarding process resumed in 1973 and was expected to continue.

Investment and speculative demand picked up sharply in 1973, according to the Consolidated Gold Fields report. For the first time in several years West Germans and Swiss were important buyers, and Italians increased their normally significant share. Japan's first year of legal gold ownership in 1973 took some 40 tons, about half going to inventory at the Bank of Japan.

In light of gold's physical attributes, its usefulness and acquisition difficulty, its radical history and financial or personal protective value in the past 60 years, all acting in combination with the new surge in worldwide inflation/recession fears, the recent fascination with the metal should cause only a modest wonder. Few concepts short of motherhood can combine as many beloved qualities, both emotional and physical, as does gold.

Notwithstanding the foregoing, Americans reacted to their new gold ownership potential with what appeared to be a big yawn. Certainly bullion purchases in the first three months of 1975 left a good deal to be desired, according to brokers. However, gold coins, both national and commemorative, received much interest, as did gold futures trading. Futures traded on the nation's leading exchange, the International Monetary Market of the Chicago Mercantile Exchange, totaled 85,529 gold contracts in the first quarter of 1975, while New York's Comex was second with 76,604 contracts. Together they accounted for over three fourths of the gold futures traded in the U.S. during that period, with an aggregate face value approaching $2.8 billion. That is hardly evidence of a disinterested public.

Where Americans did withdraw from the supposed gold rush of 1975, their actions were psychologically motivated. The record gold price certainly contributed sobering thoughts. The numerous financial press stores were principally cautious, and federal government warnings were downright formidable, with the heavy fact of the U.S. Treasury sale of 2 million ounces of gold in January 1975, plainly discouraging. In addition, the facts of gold bullion ownership, which were stressed in many of the articles of the time, are clearly bothersome. Costs of acquisition, physical storage, quality determination, and insurance are all depressing negatives. Despite this, the gold price held remarkably well until April 1975.

History may well record the non-gold rush of 1975 as largely caused by a deepening American conservatism and practicality over the difficulties of bullion ownership, rather than a lack of interest in the yellow metal. Coupled with the American lack of emotional involvement with gold, as it is felt by Europeans and many in the Far East, America's subdued interest in gold in early 1975 was most understandable.

An Inflation Hedge?

The strongest arguments in favor of gold ownership advanced by the financial gurus, center around its value as a hedge against inflation. The following comments by the Federal Reserve Bank of San Francisco provide the needed facts.[12]

> Whether or not gold proves to be a good inflation hedge for the private U.S. citizen obviously depends upon the amount of appreciation in the dollar value of his gold holdings between the time that he buys the gold and the time that he sells it (Chart 1). In this regard, our primary criterion for evaluating gold's performance as an inflation hedge is the degree to which the price of gold moves with the general price level (either up or down). The question of whether gold is a good investment depends upon factors other than its role as an inflation hedge, mainly the return available on alternate investments. . . .

---

[12] Federal Reserve Bank of San Francisco, *Special Issue: Gold,* Winter 1974–75.

CHART 1

U.S. Dollars Per Ounce

GOLD PRICE

Timing one's purchase obviously is very important. For example, someone purchasing gold in 1929 and legally entitled to hold it beyond 1933 would have seen each ounce of his gold investment increase by 69.5 percent, from $20.65 in 1929 to $35.00 on January 31, 1934, when the Roosevelt administration officially revalued gold. During the same interval the value of other U.S. goods declined by about 30 percent as measured by the wholesale price index. Hence, a gold purchase in 1929 would have been an unusually good investment because while most prices were falling, the gold price rose in succeeding years (Chart 2a).

On the other hand, if our hypothetical gold buyer had purchased gold in February 1934, after gold's official price had been raised, and if he held his gold until 1968, he would have gained only a 12-percent rise in price, compared with a 165-percent rise in wholesale prices (Chart 2b). Hence, during this 34-year period, gold would have been no hedge against inflation; indeed, our buyer would have lost more than one-half of the purchasing power of his gold.

Finally, if our buyer had purchased bullion in 1968, his gold investment would have been a good inflation hedge by the end of 1969, no hedge at all by year-end 1970 and 1971, and an excellent hedge by year-end 1972, 1973, and 1974

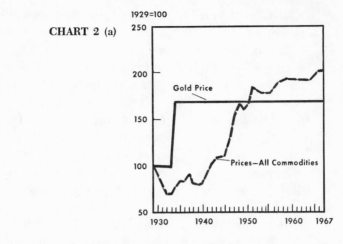

CHART 2 (a)

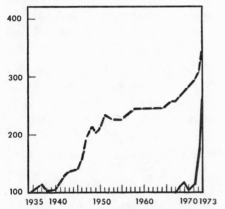

CHART 2 (b)

CHART 2 (c)

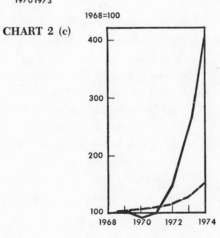

(Chart 2c). Nevertheless, there is no assurance that gold purchased now would continue to be a good inflation hedge. Gold purchased on December 30, 1974 at the London afternoon gold-fixing price of $195.25 per ounce, a record until that time, fell by $25.75 per ounce over the next week. *Ex post*, we see the necessity of timing one's gold purchases well if one desires to hold gold as a worthwhile inflation hedge.

As Chart 3 demonstrates, the variance in gold prices has increased as the price of gold has increased. Hence, the risk of buying high and selling low has increased through time; this risk, of course, is one of the costs of holding gold, of which more shortly.

In the most recent period, when gold prices have shown their most dramatic increases, prices of other internationally-traded goods have also risen very sharply. World export-price indices for all commodities—and primary commodities in particular—increased substantially between the first quarter of 1971 and the first quarter of 1974. During this three-year period, gold prices rose by nearly 290 percent, while export prices of all commodities rose by more than 50 percent, and those for primary commodities increased by more than 160 percent. Hence, the gold price has been moving in the same direction as the prices of all other internationally-traded goods.

Besides the 1968–74 experience, one other period in American history had no officially-fixed price of gold in terms of the U.S. dollar; namely, the Greenback Period from 1862 to 1879. The average monthly price of gold varied widely during this period, but by 1879, the United States was back on the gold standard at the pre–Civil War parity. The price level rose throughout the Civil War, then dropped 50 percent between 1865 and 1879, with the price of gold in greenbacks moving in parallel. A unit of gold in greenbacks that was worth a dollar before the war was worth $2.50 in 1865, before beginning to decline. Given this historical perspective, anyone wishing to make a good investment would have been well-advised to trade his greenbacks for gold at the

CHART 3

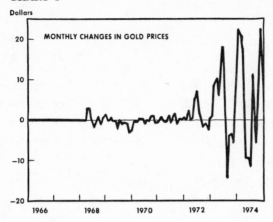

Dollars

MONTHLY CHANGES IN GOLD PRICES

beginning of the Civil War and then to trade back in 1864 when the gold price was at its height.

Different supply and demand factors operated during the 1862–79 period than during the more recent (1968–74) period. A century ago, the price of gold was essentially the dollar-pound exchange rate. With the United Kingdom on the gold standard, the Bank of England stood ready to settle transactions at the rate of one pound sterling per unit of gold. Hence, the gold price in terms of greenbacks was determined by the demand and supply for greenbacks vis-à-vis the pound sterling. Although gold was traded on the New York Stock Exchange, its price in terms of greenbacks reflected changes in the day-to-day value of greenbacks vis-à-vis British pounds in the foreign-exchange market. Today, no country operates on a gold standard; instead, all major currencies float against each other, and the gold price also floats freely in its own market. Nevertheless, one implication may be drawn from the experience of a century ago: if the price of gold is not fixed by government action to a given currency, then gold is a good investment only during inflation and is a very bad buy during deflation.

Where and What

London has clearly been the center of the modern golden age since the late 19th century. All of South Africa's gold was refined there in the early developmental years of that country's metal, and some still is. The city provided much of the capital for mining of South African gold from the outset. London was the premier market for the metal until 1968, when South Africa switched the bulk of its gold sales to Switzerland, although the London price is still the most widely quoted the world over.

The price of gold, which we know as being "fixed" twice a day in London, is set by agreement between the five firms that make up the London market: N. M. Rothschild & Sons (at whose offices the prices are fixed); Samuel Montagu & Co., owned by the Midland Bank Group; Sharps, Pixley, a subsidiary of Kleinwort, Benson, Lonsdale, Ltd., a merchant bank; Johnson, Matthey (Bankers), Ltd.; and Mocatta, Goldsmid, owned by Hambros Bank.

What is this illegal sounding gold price "fixing"?

First, it is the essence of legality and fair play; about as "British" an institution as exists. The pair of fixings represent a combination of auction and negotiated prices set in a gentlemanly way through the introduction of both buyers and sellers with the Bank of England near the open and close of business each day. The times of fixing are 10:30 A.M. and 3:00 P.M. The fixing price is agreed upon by the five bullion dealers, each representing their numerous clients: other banks, brokers, and fabricators. The fixings are the best publicized bench mark for gold prices on a given busi-

ness day, and are immediately relayed around the world
as soon as agreed upon. What the fixings *are not* is the
point of some confusion. They are neither the opening
prices for the day, nor the closing price for gold trading
in London. Business is done in the London gold market
both before and after the respective fixings. The fixings
do not represent the price at which the bulk of gold
trades are executed on any day. They are a price at
which some gold is traded (volume is never revealed),
and they do provide a point from which other dealings
may proceed. The actual method by which the price is
fixed gives the clearest picture of its worth to the
prospective gold buyer/seller.

Twice a day, four men representing the London gold
dealers walk up the steps of N. M. Rothschild & Sons
in St. Swithins Lane in London to join the manager
of that firm's gold bullion department in the fixing
room. The four sit, as their predecessors have since
September 1919, at separate desks around a large
room with a central table, at which sits the Rothschild
man. Each desk is equipped with a direct line telephone to the respective dealers' trading rooms and a
small Union Jack flag. Prior to the stroke of the appropriate hour all men confer with their trading rooms
to determine whether they have excess gold above that
which is matchable to orders within their firm, and
which they then wish to bring to market. Rothschild's
acts for the Bank of England and thus holds the
premier position in the market.

The Rothschild dealer, at the appointed time, selects
an opening price based upon what Rothschild has seen
of supply and demand for gold in relation to the previous fixing. This price is immediately sent to the other

four firms' trading rooms and to their clients. This is the true opening price, but may or may not become the fixing. It is stated a moment before the dealers' small flags are first flipped up, indicating that the dealer is talking with his trading room, and suspending the fixing process temporarily. Any dealer may flip his flag at any time during the proceedings.

Next, each dealer indicates whether he is a seller, a buyer, or has no interest at the opening price. Sellers state how many "good delivery" 400-ounce bars they are offering. Buyers indicate only their direction of interest, not quantity. When both buyers and sellers have revealed an interest, amounts of gold wanted by the buyers are then specified. If there is enough gold to meet the demand, the price is "fixed" at the opening level. If insufficient gold is for sale, the dealers may prorate the amount of bars for sale among the buyers and the price is "fixed." If the demand is too great, the price is moved up a notch and the process repeated until a balance is struck. The same method is followed on the downside if sellers outweigh buyers. The entire proceeding is secret with only the fixed price revealed.

This fixing system allows the Bank of England to bring its interest to the market at a fair point, but does not prevent the bank or any dealer from doing business with others before or after the fixing, and at prices away from the fixing level. Thus, the bench mark nature of the fixed price.

London dealers act strictly as agents for their clients, while the Swiss banks, who are in touch with the fixing via one of the four dealers (or all of them), act as principals, buying and selling for their own accounts and risk. As a result, during the business day in

Europe, Swiss banks make a firm "market" in 400-ounce gold bars, just as an American stock trader or specialist does for American Express or General Motors stock. For example, an October 1974 quote on a quiet day in Zurich's gold market, following a morning fixing in London of $155, was "154½ at 155½." Gold was being offered for sale at 155½ and bought at 154½ at that moment. This is the firm market during the day which operates completely separate from the fixing procedure. In fact, London dealers will offer quotes similar to Zurich's.

What then, one might wonder, is the main difference between the London and Zurich gold markets?

Aside from the fixing procedure, which doesn't exist in Switzerland, it is that nebulous commodity, secrecy. After March 1968, when South Africa wished greater secrecy in its gold sales to the free market, it moved its entire supply to the Zurich market to the obvious chagrin of London. After talks with the Bank of England in 1970, sales were split 80 percent–20 percent in favor of Zurich. The absence of more than 20 percent of the South African supply from the London market gives us one clear case of the price of secrecy, at least as far as South Africa was concerned: a near-century of traditional ties with London was overturned. Actually, London still physically receives more South African gold than Zurich, but much is for transshipment to ultimate buyers. Most arrives via the convenient Union Castle Line shipping routes into Southampton, still the least expensive method of transportation.

"The London gold market tends to be a bit more altruistic than do the Swiss," explained an official of a South African mining firm in London, "This is because they are agents only, not principals for their own account as in Zurich. But," he added, "three out of five dealers in London don't spend much time thinking about gold at all."

They certainly spend a lot of time talking about gold in Zurich, however. Naturally, competition with London is one of the key factors in conversation.

"What I want to make clear," offered one Zurich bank gold dealer, "is that we can buy and sell for our own inventory. We might have a few bars at a profit and can offer them cheaper than London. They're buying more from us than the Bank of England anyway."

"Why couldn't you have a loss on those bars instead?" I asked.

Looking rather wounded, he replied, "The way the gold price has gone?"

It can, of course, go down as easily as up, as Figure 1 shows. The point is that the London and Swiss gold markets differ in secrecy and method of doing business, not in quality or integrity of their dealers. Neither principals nor agents have a corner on the market.

Finding out what is *really* happening in the gold markets, who is buying, and who is doing the selling, is equally as difficult in London as in Zurich. It is simply not possible through direct inquiry. "In July 1974," a South African mining official revealed, "Italy's central bank was rumored to be a seller of gold. No dealer would verify this. But one could piece together bits of conversation and learn as much from what is not said, as what is. If, as it was rumored," he went on, "Italy was selling at the second fixing in London, the dealers who were not selling would know which dealers

FIGURE 1
Gold Prices, 1968–74

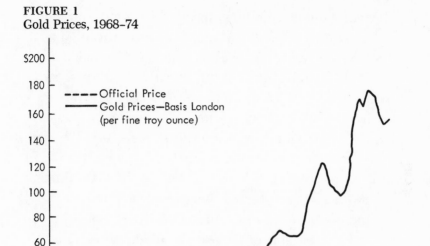

Dates on which the official price was set: January, 1879 – $20.67.
January, 1934 – $35.00.
November, 1971 – $38.00.
February, 1973 – $42.22.

Courtesy: Chicago Board of Trade.

were, and have a good feel for size. We had only to find out the size of the seller's offers, and knowing whom Italy usually goes through, we had a pretty good idea that the rumor was true."

What should you know about gold *physically* when considering its purchase in any of the numerous forms in which it is available?

In the case of bullion, the types of bars, their weight and fineness, the importance of refiner's marks and peculiar storage/authenticity problems are critical. Price variations by size are of nearly equal importance.

Americans find nothing short of a bewildering range of bar sizes available to them, and some variation as to fineness. In addition, wafers and other small nonbar forms are sold by jewelry and department stores. Swiss banks deal mainly in metric sizes, although this may change somewhat as American ownership asserts itself. These begin at the 5-gram size (0.177 ounce) and run to 1 kilogram (32.150 troy ounces, or 35.274 avoirdupois ounces). Gold is quoted in troy ounces; the two weights are given for comparison only.

Financial institutions and brokerage firms in the United States sell ounce sizes including $\frac{1}{2}$, 1, 5, 10, 16.075 ($\frac{1}{2}$ kilo), 25, 32.150 (1 kilo), 50, and 100. The 400-ounce standard bar is available both in Switzerland, as we have noted previously, and in the United States for anyone with $60,000 or more (at $150 per ounce gold price) who cares for them.

The *fine weight* of these bars is the weight of pure gold in each. The *fineness* is a ratio of parts of pure gold to total weight of the bar; i.e., 900/1,000. The most popular weights available from U.S. refiners are 999.5/1,000, a truly fine quality, although less than the best. "Four nines," or 999.9/1,000 fine, is featured by Swiss banks. A fineness down to 995/1,000 is also seen, but is obviously worth a bit less than the finer bars. This fineness ratio is stamped on each bar along with the refiner's hallmark—his name.

The best recognized of these hallmarks include Englehard, Handy & Harman, and Consolidated in the United States, and Argor or Johnson, Matthey in Europe. Unfortunately, there are some 59 recognized quality refiners around the world, and this presents a "good delivery" problem for buyers, since the names are hardly household words, and it must be remembered that gold is easily melted down, altered as to weight, and re-marked. The best test of reputation for integrity of the refiner is the acceptance by a financial institution of the mark. Banks will accept only well-respected hallmarks but will quickly raise the next question: How have you stored your gold since buying it? If it has not been held by another recognized institution throughout your ownership, your bank may require an assay of it. Starting at $30 a bar, an assay is an expensive and complicated chemical process, and one to avoid if possible. It must substitute authentication of gold fineness and lack of alteration for a previous record of acceptable storage. This peculiarity of gold bullion leads to a pair of rules which will be most helpful to you in considering gold purchase either in the United States or abroad.

1. Buy gold only from a recognized dealer or financial institution, *and* one which can arrange safe storage which will be acceptable to itself or another institution in later sale. Both conditions can be met by one institution, and, if possible, it makes the most sense to work with one institution. There is no point in moving gold bullion around if it can be avoided. In buying through a Swiss bank the temptation to have it shipped elsewhere will be reduced because of charges, and they will handle sale quite readily when you desire.

2. When buying bars on sight, ensure that you recognize, via a banker's list, the refiner's mark, and demand that the previous ownership record be established. This will require that the bar bear a serial number stamped by the refiner. Then, before buying, ask a major bank if they will accept the bar for later sale. Be guided by

their recommendation. Stamps and serial numbers can be forged.

The final difficulty in dealing with gold bullion is taxation. Most states in the United States now have sales or use taxes which must be paid when gold is delivered in those states. Foreign countries where gold is legal for sale often have value added taxes; i.e., West Germany, applicable to gold purchases. This is one area where at this time, Swiss banks have an advantage. They have no taxes applicable to your purchase of bullion, gold, or silver.

In summary, you may expect to pay the following charges for acquiring gold bullion, in addition to the normal 10–15 percent spread between the dealers' buying and selling prices:

1. *A Purchase Commission in the United States.* From 2 to 5 percent for 100-ounce bars and from 5–7 percent for smaller sizes. Commissions are not usually quoted in Switzerland, although small bars have a charge built into the net price.
2. *Sales or Use Tax.* From 4–7 percent of purchase price depending upon state where delivery is taken for storage. No such tax in Switzerland.
3. *Storage and Insurance.* Around $2 per month for a 100-ounce bar in the United States. One-eighth percent of value of holdings in a Swiss bank.
4. *Shipping Charge.* Ordinary mail plus insurance.
5. *Assay Charge.* Where bullion is purchased from a firm different than that through which it is sold, or stored by individual purchaser, from $30 per bar.

An example of bullion account charges is provided by Foreign Commerce Bank of Switzerland. For a minimum account of $5,000 invested in gold bullion, either in cash or on margin, there is a 1 percent purchase commission, storage of 0.15 percent of market value per annum, and a bookkeeping charge of $3.00 per account per quarter.

Thus, Swiss banks can be quite attractive for gold bullion purchases, based on the charges above, saving anywhere from 9–15 percent of purchase price in the United States on bars weighing 1 kilogram or more. Note: this purchase advantage is subject to rapid change.

Obviously, gold bullion has distinct cost and nuisance disadvantages. It also pays no dividend return and is subject to wide psychological price swings in the international market. This combination has caused many investors to turn to one of the other forms of gold ownership: coins, mining stocks, or futures, each of which have some advantage over bullion.

Gold coins have developed a large following for their handiness and portability. Storage is relatively easy in safe deposit boxes, depending upon quantity. The key points to watch for here are the premium price of the coin over its bullion value—called the coin's *agio* in Europe, and again the problem of fakes. A list of widely traded gold coins is given in Table 1.

The premium price of the coin over pure gold content can be determined by first calculating the current bullion market price times the fine weight of the coin given in the following tables of popular coins. Be certain you apply a troy ounce to gram conversion factor. Then obtain the current market quote for the coin. The difference between the two figures is the premium. If that premium is over 15–20 percent, there is sub-

TABLE 1
Gold Coins (weights in grams)

	Gross Weight	Fineness	Fine Weight
Switzerland			
Fr. 100			
Girl's Head	32.258	$900/_{1.000}$	29.032
Fr. 20			
"Vreneli" Girl's Head	6.451	$900/_{1.000}$	5.806
Fr. 10			
"Half-Vreneli" Girl's Head	3.225	$900/_{1.000}$	2.903
Austria			
4 Ducats			
Emperor Franz Josef	13.963	$986\ ^{1/9}/_{1.000}$	13.769
1 Ducat			
Emperor Franz Josef	3.490	$986\ ^{1/9}/_{1.000}$	3.442
100 Kronen			
Emperor Franz Josef	33.875	$900/_{1.000}$	30.487
20 Kronen			
Emperor Franz Josef	6.775	$900/_{1.000}$	6.097
10 Kronen			
Emperor Franz Josef	3.387	$900/_{1.000}$	3.048
8 Gulden			
Emperor Franz Josef	6.451	$900/_{1.000}$	5.806
4 Gulden			
Emperor Franz Josef	3.225	$900/_{1.000}$	2.903
Belgium			
Fr. 20			
Leopold II	6.451	$900/_{1.000}$	5.806
Denmark			
20 Kroner			
Christian X	8.960	$900/_{1.000}$	8.064
France			
F. 100			
Napoleon III	32.258	$900/_{1.000}$	29.032
F. 50			
Napoleon III	16.129	$900/_{1.000}$	14.516
F. 40			
Napoleon I	12.902	$900/_{1.000}$	11.612
F. 20			
"Coq," "Marianne"	6.451	$900/_{1.000}$	5.806
F. 10			
Napoleon III	3.225	$900/_{1.000}$	2.903
Germany			
20 Marks			
(various ruling princes)	7.964	$900/_{1.000}$	7.168
10 Marks			
Frederick III	3.982	$900/_{1.000}$	3.584

TABLE 1 (*continued*)

	Gross Weight	Fineness	Fine Weight
Great Britain			
£ 1 "Sovereign"			
George V	7.988	916 $^{2/3}$/$_{1.000}$	7.322
£ 1 "Elizabeth"			
Elizabeth II	7.988	916 $^{2/3}$/$_{1.000}$	7.322
50 p "Half Sovereign"			
George V	3.994	916 $^{2/3}$/$_{1.000}$	3.661
Hungary			
20 Kronen			
Emperor Franz Josef	6.775	^{900}/$_{1.000}$	6.097
10 Kronen			
Emperor Franz Josef	3.387	^{900}/$_{1.000}$	3.048
Italy			
L. 20 "Lator"			
Victor Emanuel II	6.451	^{900}/$_{1.000}$	5.806
Netherlands			
10 Guilders			
Queen Wilhelmina	6.720	^{900}/$_{1.000}$	6.048
Russia			
15 Rubles			
Czar Nicholas II	12.903	^{900}/$_{1.000}$	11.613
10 Rubles			
Czar Nicholas II	8.602	^{900}/$_{1.000}$	7.742
5 Rubles			
Czar Nicholas II	4.301	^{900}/$_{1.000}$	3.871
Turkey			
100 Piasters	7.216	916 $^{2/3}$/$_{1.000}$	6.614
South Africa			
Rand 2			
van Riebeeck, antelope°	7.988	916 $^{2/3}$/$_{1.000}$	7.322
Rand 1			
van Riebeeck, antelope°	3.994	916 $^{2/3}$/$_{1.000}$	3.661
Krüger Rand			
President Krüger, antelope†	33.931	916 $^{2/3}$/$_{1.000}$	31.103
Chile			
100 Pesos	20.339	^{900}/$_{1.000}$	18.305
Mexico			
50 Pesos			
"Centenario"	41.666	^{900}/$_{1.000}$	37.500
20 Pesos			
Aztec Calendar Stone	16.666	^{900}/$_{1.000}$	15.000
10 Pesos			
Hidalgo	8.333	^{900}/$_{1.000}$	7.500
5 Pesos			
Hidalgo	4.166	^{900}/$_{1.000}$	3.750

TABLE 1 (*concluded*)

	Gross Weight	Fineness	Fine Weight
2.5 Pesos			
Hidalgo	2.083	$900/_{1.000}$	1.875
2 Pesos	1.666	$900/_{1.000}$	1.500
Peru			
100 Soles	46.807	$900/_{1.000}$	42.126
50 Soles	23.403	$900/_{1.000}$	21.063
20 Soles	9.361	$900/_{1.000}$	8.425
United States			
$20 "Double Eagle"			
Liberty, Statue of Liberty	33.436	$900/_{1.000}$	30.092
by St. Gaudens			
$10 "Eagle"			
Liberty, Indian	16.718	$900/_{1.000}$	15.046
$5 "Half Eagle"			
Liberty, Indian	8.359	$900/_{1.000}$	7.523

° Minting of these coins began in 1962.

† Coinage began in 1967.

Source: Data from Union Bank of Switzerland.

stantial risk in the coin price, although, as with the U.S. $20 double eagle's 70–80 percent late 1974 premium, it can exist for years. The danger in the premium comes from three sources: new government minting of old dates, thereby increasing the supply of the "old" coins, government confiscation of coins at lower prices, and fakes.

It is true that coins are more difficult to fake than bullion is to alter. However, edge shaving on coins or manufacture with steel dies otherwise used for medallions is certainly possible. As Mr. Lloyd-Jacob of Consolidated Gold Fields puts it, "a simple mathematical exercise would tell one that with, say, a 25 percent or greater premium in a coin, a night shift run by a medallion maker would be a profitable enterprise." The most prolific manufacturers of fake coins, the Italians, imported two metric tons legally in 1973 for medallions, medals, and fakes. It is still *caveat emptor* for buyers of coins. In addition, market prices generally follow the wide swings in gold bullion and no dividend income is possible. Insurance may be purchased through special articles floaters in household policies.

The lack of dividend or interest return on both bullion and coins is best addressed through purchase of the stocks of gold mining companies, including U.S., Canadian, and South African. However, discussion of the merits of these issues is properly left to securities brokers or advisors, as they are traded, paid for, and stored like any other securities. As gold mining stocks are often discussed as hedges against an economic slump (see also Chapter 10), the chart in Figure 2 is pertinent here. Not noted, however, are the substantial price declines in the stocks after 1935. Homestake dropped from a 1936 adjusted high of 66 to 39¾ the following year, and a low of 22½ in 1942. (Although it crossed 60 every year through 1941.) Dome fell from a high of 61½ to 8 in 1942, and never topped 35 after 1937.

Gold futures, the trading of which began on four United States exchanges on December 31, 1974, have some peculiarities which merit attention.

First, these futures are simply commodity contracts to purchase a given amount of gold bullion at a specified date in the future. Specific contracts are traded with expiration dates in nearly every month of the year on one or another of the exchanges, but vary as to amount of the precious metal contracted for. All contracts are for gold fineness of at least .995 pure.

FIGURE 2
Gold Stocks in the Depression

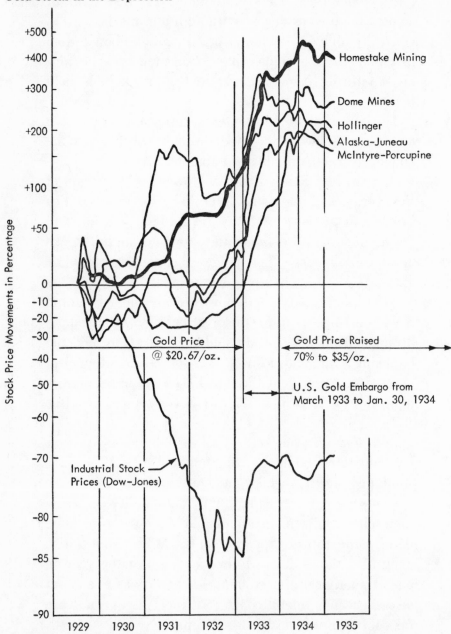

Courtesy: Franklin Capital Fund.

Contracts and Exchanges

International Monetary Market
of the Chicago Mercantile Exchange.......... 100 troy ounces
444 West Jackson Blvd.
Chicago, Ill. 60606

Chicago Board of Trade .... 3 kilograms of 32.15
LaSalle at Jackson   troy ounces each = 96.45
Chicago, Ill. 60604   troy ounces.

Commodity Exchange, Inc...................... 100 troy ounces
81 Broad St.
New York, N.Y. 10004

New York Mercantile Exchange............... 1 kilogram of 32.15 troy
6 Harrison St.   ounces.
New York, N.Y. 10013

Margins

The amount of cash which must be deposited for each gold contract will vary by the exchange and broker with whom you do business. A general rule of thumb: the exchange minimum margin will be about 10 percent of the contract value, with certain higher levels established by brokers, depending upon volatility of the commodity. Thus, a 100-ounce contract at $180 per ounce would be valued at $18,000, with an exchange margin of $1,800. The brokerage firm of Merrill Lynch, Pierce, Fenner & Smith, however, requires a $2,750 margin for this contract. If gold should become even more volatile than it was in early 1975, Merrill indicates that this house margin would be increased.

Quotations

Gold futures contracts are quoted each business day, based on actual sale prices, just as are stocks and bonds. The reprint from *The Wall Street Journal* in Figure 3 shows a typical range of prices over various contract expiration dates for the four major United States exchanges trading gold, plus the Winnipeg Commodity Exchange.

FIGURE 3

Gold Futures

Friday, February 21, 1975

	Open	High	Low	Close	Change	Season's High	Low
CHICAGO MERC. EXCH.—x100 TROY OUNCES							
Mar	186.50	187.90	184.70	185.70-186.—	.40to.10	195.00	165.00
June	191.00	192.00	188.90	189.'8-190.3	—.40to+.10	205.00	170.00
Sept	195.40	195.80	193.20	193.50	— .70	209.00	178.00
Dec	'202.20	202.20	197.80	199.-198.50	unch to—.50	215.00	182.00
Sales estimated at: 1,256 contracts.							
CHICAGO BOARD OF TRADE—x96.45 TROY OUNCES							
Mar	186.50	188.00	185.00	186.00	— .50	198.00	167.00
Apr	183.20	188.50	186.70	186.70	—1.50	188.70	174.50
May	189.70	191.00	187.50	188.50	— .90	198.00	171.00
July	193.00	193.50	191.00	191.50	—1.00	202.00	172.00
Sept	197.00	197.00	194.00	194.00	—1.50	202.00	177.50
Nov	199.50	199.50	197.00	197.00	—1.50	204.00	181.00
Jan76	202.00	202.30	200.00	200.00	—1.50	202.30	187.00
Mar	204.80	205.00	203.00	203.00	—1.50	205.00	189.00
May	208.00	208.00	206.00	206.00	—1.50	208.00	194.00
Sales estimated at: 315 contracts.							
WINNIPEG COMMOD. EXCH.—x400 TROY OUNCES							
Apr	187.70	188.00	185.70	185.70b	—2.00	210.80	142.00
July	191.80	192.00	189.80	189.80a	—2.00	208.00	151.70
Oct	196.00	196.30	194.10	194.00a	—2.00	213.50	164.60
Jan76	200.10	200.10	198.10	198.10b	—1.70	217.60	181.75
Apr	203.00	203.00	201.70	201.70a	— .70	203.00	191.40
Sales estimated at: 348 contracts.							
COMMODITY EXCH. (N.Y.)—x100 TROY OUNCES							
Feb	186.10	186.10	184.50	184.50	—1.60	191.50	165.00
Mar	186.70	186.70	184.60	184.70	—1.70	192.50	167.00
Apr	188.00	188.50	185.80	186.00	—1.70	195.40	168.00
June	191.00	191.50	188.80	189.00	—1.60	198.00	174.50
Aug	192.70	192.70	192.00	192.00	—1.50	200.00	177.00
Oct	197.00	197.00	195.00	195.00	—1.40	202.00	180.00
Dec	200.00	200.10	198.00	198.00	—1.30	205.00	183.50
Feb76	203.00	203.00	201.00	201.00	—1.20	208.00	188.70
Apr	205.80	205.80	203.80	204.00	—1.10	210.50	191.80
June	208.00	208.00	207.00	207.00	—1.00	208.00	194.50
Sales estimated at: 1,519 contracts.							
NEW YORK MERC. EXCH.—x32.15 TROY OUNCES							
Mar	186.40	187.40	184.80	186.00	— .20	197.00	168.00
Apr	187.60	187.60	186.60	186.60	— .60	188.40	175.40
May	189.20	190.40	187.60	188.80	— .20	198.00	174.00
July	192.00	192.80	191.20	191.20	— .80	200.00	175.00
Sept	195.80	195.80	194.00	194.00	— .40	203.00	178.00
Dec	199.00	199.00	198.00	198.80	— .60	206.60	184.00
Jan76	201.00	201.40	200.00	200.00	— .20	201.60	189.80
Mar	203.40	203.40	203.00	203.00	—1.80	204.80	190.00
July	209.40	209.40	209.40	209.40	+1.20	209.40	197.20
Sales estimated at: 347 contracts.							

a-Asked. b-Bid. x-Contract size.

Source: *The Wall Street Journal,* February 21, 1975.

Why Use Futures?

By far the most extensive users of any commodity futures are the manufacturers-producers of the commodity itself, and their customers-consumers. The markets were established for their principal use. They initiate trades on either the buy or sell side of the market in order to hedge the cost of their expected future business in the actual product.

A gold mining company might *sell* futures contracts at the going price for a given delivery date in order to protect itself against a real market price decline by that date. And conversely, a gold fabricator who regularly buys quantities of gold might *buy* future delivery contracts at a given price to protect itself against possible future price increases in the free market. Both the mining company and the fabricator can thereby "lock in" known prices for future deliveries and thus hedge their positions against market fluctuations.

In the first few months of trading gold futures in the United States in 1975, it became clear that the public participation in these markets was more significant than in the newly available bullion or "spot" markets. While comparable trading volume figures are not revealed for both futures and bullion, conversations with several brokerage firms engaged in both markets revealed they had no doubt that futures were receiving the bulk of the activity. While this could be reversed in the future, there are some basic advantages to futures trading compared with outright bullion purchase:

1. *Leverage:* For something between 10 percent and 15 percent of the contract value, a speculator can con-

trol a larger volume of gold than he might otherwise be able to afford. With this leverage on 15 percent margin, for example, a 15 percent gain in price of a long contract, from $160 per ounce to $184 per ounce, would *double* the money put up by the speculator. This contrasts with requirements that the full cash price of bullion be paid within two business days of purchase, or 50 percent margin be deposited for mining company stocks. In addition, a speculator's risk is theoretically limited to the amount of margin put up in the case of futures contracts, except in the case where additional margin is called for due to an adverse price move and the speculator does not wish to sell the contract and accept a loss. (See *trading price limits*, below.)

2. *Convenience* is the principal nontechnical advantage of gold futures, since only transactions in the contracts are involved. The problems of shipping, insurance, storage and assaying the physical gold, are eliminated. Even physical safekeeping of certificates is avoided as contracts are most often only bookkeeping entries on brokers books, with separate confirmations to customers.

3. *Commissions* for trading futures contracts are lower than those for either bullion or stocks, usually less than 1 percent of the contract value, compared to 5–7 percent for bullion and up to 20 percent buying/selling spread for gold coins. A typical 100-ounce future contract has a $45 round-trip commission on the Chicago Mercantile Exchange. Due to these low commissions, even persons wishing to take possession of the gold can purchase a contract and accept delivery at the close of the contract for considerably smaller cost than buying bullion outright.

4. *Pricing* of gold futures is based on actual transactions for a given day, such as those shown in Figure 3. This provides a firm indication of buy/sell prices and evidences a liquid market which may be more fluid than that for either coins or bullion. The latter are subject to dealer's repurchasing policies and the gap between buying and selling prices.

The clear and major disadvantage of gold futures compared to other forms of gold purchases is the risk of complete capital loss through an adverse price move of the contract, which is heightened by the relatively small margin. In the gold market where 50–70 percent price moves are not uncommon over a few months' time, 10–15 percent margin is not much protection, especially when the market is affected by as many obtuse international psychological forces as it is. Moreover, *trading price limits* are established for gold as well as for other commodities, and can prevent the contract holder from liquidating a position without greater loss than expected. These limits, recently $10 per ounce, set the maximum range which a contract price may move per day. If market forces dictate a greater price change, trading is halted and no contracts can be traded until a new price level is established. Three or four days of this can provide the ultimate in frustration.

As intriguing (and difficult) as gold futures may be, they are not readily available through your Swiss bank. No major Swiss bank traded them in early 1975, and given the banks' general sour taste from the UCB, Basle cocoa escapade, it is doubtful that they will any time soon. Smaller banks may, however. Check, if you are interested.

From the rusty gold brilliance of new Kruger Rands to the often startling moves in six month distant gold futures, gold is attracting the interest of more of the world's population than it ever has before. The range of opportunities to participate in its potential has likewise never been greater; almost as numerous as the proper cautions about its purchase and difficulties in its ownership. Swiss banks will lend their expertise to your acquisition of the yellow metal as they will most investments in the public domain. But, before you undertake gold purchases anywhere, be warned that the myths of gold infalibility are as numerous and widely expounded as the tales of William Tell. They have bases in fact, but their veracity is often problematical.

Chapter six

The Laundry List

THE SECOND FLOOR reception area in the Union Bank of Switzerland's Lugano branch is typical of rooms into which decision makers are ushered. It is a rather brightly lighted modern room, about 30 feet long with large, curtained windows and a purple (not magenta nor violet, but purple) carpet. Seven stuffed leather chairs and a semicircular sofa of similar material are grouped casually and face low, glass-topped tables. The large reception desk sits opposite one of two elevator doors at the end of the room near a long office corridor. It is presided over by an efficient-sounding guard in dark blue coat and tie with UBS emblems. His white shirt is starched: proficiency personified in Lugano. At the opposite end of the room is a door leading to a large conference room next to a second elevator door.

Similar reception rooms receive important decision makers and little decision makers at major Swiss banks. Most visitors to them have made one decision in common—to make use of a Swiss bank. In this re-

149

ception room they will meet their first bank officer, usually prior to being taken to a second, smaller visitor's room, separate from his private office, where banking business will be discussed. *Sitzimmers,* the latter are called in Zurich.

Out of the UBS, Lugano, conference room poured, at the moment of my arrival, two bank officers, a secretary, and a wealthy-looking, well-dressed businessman of obviously Italian lineage.

"A decision maker," I thought immediately. "And one of his decisions has been to use this bank. Why?"

His briefcase seemed ordinary enough. His clothes, though expensive, revealed little. He conversed with easy smiles in Italian. The bankers' persiflage was given with similar smiles. The businessman didn't look like a money runner or drug dealer or racketeer, I thought. "But then why should he?" I caught myself. "What do those people look like?" It seemed safe to conclude that very few higher echelon money runners, drug dealers, or racketeers would *look* the part. Common hoods wouldn't be common hoods with sufficient money. I decided he looked more like a Milan industrialist or attorney. It was that private room with the bankers that had added a degree of sinisterness.

I looked at the other inhabitants of the reception room. They'd each made a decision about this bank, or someone had made it for them, otherwise why would they be here?

One was a lower income Italian in undershirt with a rumpled jacket hanging over it, sporting new leather sandals, with his wife and two children. There were also three European businessmen, all in their 60s, and all quietly reading either newspapers or bank literature taken from a large rack in a corner. A fortyish Frenchman with coat and no tie was staring at the ceiling. Another man — an Italian in his 50s or so (how do you tell the age of middle-aged Italians?) — was wearing crushed velvet pants and jacket with a shirt open to his chest, the vogue. His younger female companion was chatting brightly. He paid little attention. There were no other signs of circumstance evident among any of the waiters.

A diverse lot. They all had needs for this bank. They may have all lived in Lugano or its environs. Or perhaps not. Their banking decisions may have arisen out of the bank's pure convenience, or come from pure fear for their money, or out of motives of asset diversification, or to simply hide funds. Whatever. There was no way of knowing. And yet, I somehow felt I should know. This was a *Swiss bank* in one of the liveliest money movement areas in the nation.

There were no Americans waiting for a Swiss banker at UBS, Lugano, during my brief dalliance in its reception area. That was not surprising. Most Americans use the bank branches more readily accessible in Geneva or Zurich. Still, the presence of several nationalities among the customers of the bank and the absence of Americans during that particular hour prompted some questions.

Could Swiss bank services be so uniquely European or established for use of non-Americans that they are too "foreign" or unusual for U.S. citizens' banking habits? Are their services better, or competitive, or noncompetitive, with those offered by U.S. banks?

Or, on the other hand, are there special factors which make Swiss banks especially attractive for Americans? The reception room offered no clue.

Research later revealed that while banking services world-wide do differ, it is mainly in terms, not form. Americans will be inclined to use Swiss banks most logically through their wide range of services offered. They truly make up a full laundry list. The Swiss bank service list, however, would rarely be of interest without some prompting by United States domestic problems. Most of these difficulties have been discussed in previous chapters, but one is worth additional note: The shrunken list of available, safe, money-placement opportunities.

Americans who have traveled abroad since 1971, some 6.5 million persons per year on the average, are especially aware of the collapse of the dollar itself. ("Only Americans who travel overseas know what has really happened to the dollar," opines Camille Perusset, Geneva manager of Foreign Commerce Bank.) The once "almighty dollar" has at times been flatly unacceptable in Europe. In many circumstances in Europe or Japan today it buys less than in the United States, a function of both inflation imbalance and exchange rate changes. At home it buys less than half of what it did 20 years ago. And it is no longer convertible into gold by anyone, including central banks.

The collapse of the U.S. stock market on the order of 40–60 percent during 1973–74, depending upon which index you follow, was widely covered in every newspaper, radio or TV news program, and mass circulation news magazine in the nation. It directly affected nearly all 30 million U.S. stock owners, plus uncounted other millions of indirect owners through their pension

or profit sharing plans. It followed the previous deci-
mation of equity values by just under three years. The
only decent, consistent money made in securities since
1968, in fact, has been in gold mining shares or option
writing on the Chicago Board Options Exchange.

With the U.S. economy, during the spring of 1975,
in the grip of its second recession in four years, amid
sophisticated concern that this time there could be a
depression on the horizon, it appears unlikely that there
could any longer exist a myth of consistent gains for
this, or any other national economy. With the well-
documented troubles of several real estate investment
trusts, real estate syndicates, cattle feeding plans, and
oil drilling programs, even the special pockets of tax
shelter investment advantages have caution flags flying.

And yet, it was only back in 1967–68 that many
believed that the millennium had arrived. (It seems like
the Paleolithic era, now.) Professor Colyer Crum's
Investments class at Harvard was then selecting an
average gain of 30 percent per annum as the likely
growth of one's money in the stock market, or so he
told the Institutional Investor Conference in 1972.

No, Americans of all ages and economic persuasions
have become sadder but wiser about their capital uses
in just the short span of six or seven years. Even the
conference at which Professor Crum spoke in 1972 was
titled, "Is Growth Dead?" During 1973–74 at least, it
was. Savings accounts and certificates, Treasury bills,
and money market funds have provided the available
range of liquid investment alternatives. Long term,
some have found that the advantages of direct real
estate ownership overshadowed trusts or limited part-
nerships. Others have had gains in gold of one form or
another. Coins and stamps, antiques and art have ac-

quired a large following. Possibly even more persons have profited from foreign currency holdings. The 1960s money placement vehicles in the United States have been supplanted by a varied, but basically traditional, list. It is, in fact, a highly conservative series.

It is in this group of alternatives that the Swiss deal most extensively.

The Currency Issue

I suspect that the more sophisticated persons in our midst would now be very inclined to agree with a statement made in 1972 by Albert Wojnilower, economist for the investment firm, First Boston Corporation.

"Additional capital outflows [from the United States]," he said, "are likely to develop over the years as even those Americans with no particular international business connections learn, like everyone else in the world, not to keep all their eggs in one basket, and gradually and modestly diversify their assets among different currencies."

More recently, stronger advice has been given. *Fortune* magazine recently suggested, "There is a good case for looking hard at the [investment] opportunities abroad. Small investors interested in high yields on short term bank deposits can do far better outside the U.S."[1]

Foreign currency gains against the dollar have been significant, too. The 72 percent increase in the price of

---

[1] A. F. Ehrbar, "It Can Pay to Send Money Abroad," *Fortune*, August 1974.

the Swiss franc against the dollar, or the 60 percent gain in the Deutsche mark in the four years through 1974, has attracted more attention than just that of the treasurers of our multinational corporations. Any further gains in these or other foreign currencies will likely be observed by a far larger number of persons than the number *au courant* with currency price changes at the times of the dollar's previous devaluations. What is more, the major negative aspect of the idea of currency diversification, those explosive foreign exchange losses sustained by major banks in 1974, have come from currency *trading* on margin or futures, not long-term holdings. There is a great difference, as anyone of the thousands of investors caught by stock market margin calls in recent years could explain. While speculators are being frightened in foreign exchange, long-range investors are fortifying themselves with such facts as the growth of the Swiss franc *even after* the second devaluation of the U.S. dollar in February 1973. Table 2 shows monthly

TABLE 2
Swiss Franc Record 1970–74 (francs per U.S. dollar)

	1970	1971	1972	1973	1974
January	4.30	4.29$\frac{1}{2}$	3.86$\frac{1}{2}$	3.63	3.28
February	4.29$\frac{1}{2}$	4.29	3.85	3.13	3.12$\frac{1}{2}$
March	4.31	4.28$\frac{1}{2}$	3.84	3.23$\frac{1}{2}$	2.99
April	4.29$\frac{1}{2}$	4.29	3.86	3.24$\frac{1}{2}$	2.93
May	4.31	4.08$\frac{1}{4}$	3.86	3.09$\frac{1}{2}$	2.98$\frac{1}{2}$
June	4.30$\frac{1}{2}$	4.09	3.73$\frac{1}{2}$	2.93	3.00$\frac{1}{2}$
July	4.29	4.08	3.77	2.84	2.97
August	4.28$\frac{1}{2}$	3.99	3.77$\frac{1}{2}$	3.03	2.95
September	4.31	3.95	3.80	3.01$\frac{1}{2}$	2.93
October	4.32	3.98$\frac{1}{4}$	3.79$\frac{1}{2}$	3.09	2.87
November	4.30$\frac{1}{2}$	3.94$\frac{1}{2}$	3.77$\frac{3}{4}$	3.20	2.71$\frac{1}{2}$
December	4.30$\frac{1}{2}$	3.94	3.76$\frac{1}{2}$	3.23	2.55

Source: Franz Pick, *Pick's Currency Yearbook* (New York: Pick Publishing Co., 1970–74).

changes in the franc per dollar exchange rate over five years.

Investment diversification in strong currencies on a long-range basis has made and will continue to make sense, as Wojnilower predicted. It is one of the prime points which Swiss bankers will stress as an advantage of their accounts.

This foreign currency matter brings into focus the first important property of Swiss bank accounts: multiple currency availability. This fact will require one of your first decisions when considering opening a Swiss account. In which currency should it be held?

Banking practice will not permit you to hold two or more currencies in a single account. If you wish to open a dollar account and later switch funds to francs, a new franc account is opened. Obviously, the banks don't care for this additional paper work if it can be avoided, and thus encourage a thoughtful decision before opening any denomination account. This is true no matter whether it is a current or savings type account. You can, of course, hold accounts in several currencies at once if your deposits are worthwhile in each.

Second, it has been my feeling that there is little point in opening a Swiss account to hold it in dollars, unless it is only a temporary expedient, and then the bank will frown upon it. Why send funds such a distance to hold money in your own currency? If they are shortly to be invested in a Eurocurrency fiduciary deposit or invested in a securities portfolio, the bank will usually hold funds "in suspense" until the investments are made, or will place them into an account denominated in the currency from which you wish to make your fiduciary deposits or draw investment proceeds. In either case this might be dollars, although this has not made sense when viewed against the recent record of Swiss francs, Deutsche marks, or guilders against the dollar. Since an investment portfolio may acquire securities of any currency denomination, it has been preferable to accept investment proceeds in one of these strong currencies and open the account in this denomination.

However, it should be pointed out that you may well have another reason for opening a dollar account at some point. If you have shown a gain in guilders or marks versus dollars, after holding the other currency for some period, you may wish to take the profit into dollars and await a future time when the exchange rate is a bit cheaper before buying the foreign currency again. This can be done; in fact, it makes sense to do so. But it should not be done with small amounts, unless you wish to incur the unhappiness of your Swiss banker. A sensible amount to carry in your account when planning to make currency switches is around $5,000, although smaller amounts will certainly be accepted in such exchanges.

The Current Account (*Kontokorrent* in German, *Compte Courant* in French) is the starting point for use of all services at a Swiss bank, as it is with banks worldwide. It may be opened for as little as $100, as we have noted elsewhere. There is even a report in the U.S. congressional testimony of Robert Morgenthau that one individual opened several Swiss accounts a few years ago in the amount of $50 each, and gave them as Christmas presents. However, Swiss bankers will discourage you from depositing such small amounts. The paper work inflation has been too great, and they don't need that sort of business. The private banks will definitely not accept miniscule amounts at all, although they will not state a general minimum as a rule. As we'll note later, minimums at private banks have to do with your desires for investment portfolio management, not the opening of an account.

If you wish to open an account for less than $1,000 at any of the Big Three banks, you should be prepared to accept some limitations on activities in the account. You may be advised, for instance, that the bank will not hold the amount in more than one currency. Since each currency requires a different account, the bank will not be inclined to spread a few hundred dollars around among several different currency accounts.

Account Paperwork

Account forms are simple at most Swiss Banks. They will follow the format of Figure 4 with little variation.

For around SFr. 1,000 account value, the major banks will issue you a checkbook without charge. It will be a dollar checkbook if the account is held in that currency, or any other currency you designate. A checkbook which has no currency indicated can also be obtained, allowing you to write checks in any money, wherever you happen to be. When this type check arrives at the bank, they will convert the appropriate amount from whatever currency the account holds and pay the check in the currency you have designated. (See the following Chapter.)

FIGURE 4
A Sample Account Form

Gentlemen:

I wish to open the following account(s) with your bank:

☐ Current (checking) account in   ☐ Swiss francs
                                   ☐ US dollars
                                   ☐ _____

☐ Time deposit for_____ months in ☐ Swiss francs
                                   ☐ US dollars
                                   ☐ _____

☐ Cash deposit account

☐ Savings account

☐ Investment Savings account

Full name: Mr./Mrs./Miss _____

Address: _____

Nationality:_____ Date of birth:_____

Country of domicile:_____

I wish to confer power of attorney on the following person(s):

1. Full name: Mr./Mrs./Miss _____

   Nationality: _____ Date of birth: _____

2. Full name: Mr./Mrs./Miss _____

   Nationality: _____ Date of birth:_____

All correspondence is to be   ☐ sent to the following address
                                   ☐ retained by the bank

Name: _____

Street:_____

City & postal code:_____

Country:_____

☐ I enclose check for_____

☐ I instructed (name of bank)_____

☐ to transfer the amount of_____ to you in my favour.

_____   _____
(place & date)   (signature)

Once the current account has been opened, you will receive a letter similar to the following in confirmation:

Dear Sir(s),

We are pleased to confirm herewith having opened in your name on our books a (name of currency) current account at the following conditions:

Interest: None bonified on credit balances (or stating interest payable on savings accounts)

Turnover
Commission: $1/_{20}$ of 1% per six months on the larger side of the ledger incl. balance. Items resulting from bullion, foreign exchange and stock exchange transactions effected through our intermediary being exempt.

The minimum charges are:
the equivalent of SFr. 5 — up to a turnover of SFr. 10,000. — the equivalent of SFr. 10 — for a turnover exceeding SFr. 10,000 — (incl. balance)

This account is subject to the general conditions printed overleaf. The number assigned to the above account is _____, which may, however, only be utilized in conjunction with the name of the account holder. Transfers in your favour must be payable to your name plus indication of the above punch-card number.

As acceptance of these terms, please sign and return the attached duplicate copy of this present letter.

Very truly yours,
YOUR SWISS BANK

Thereafter, usually at six-month intervals, you will receive a statement indicating the transactions in

FIGURE 5

(Bank name)						
(City in which account resides)						
Please examine this statement of your account and report any discrepancies to us within four weeks.				Kontokorrent per Compte courant au Current account as per (date)		
(Account name)		Konte Compte Account No: 123.456.07 A				
Wahrung Monnaie Currency	Franken					
Datum Date	Text Texte Particulars	Val	SOLL DEBIT	HABEN CREDIT	Saldo Solde Balance
25 09 75	TRSF	18		11 459.55	11 459.55

your account for the period covered. It will be similar to that shown in Figure 5. The numbers included are for example only.

In addition, the statement will have totals for numbers of entries and the number of days the account has been held during the period covered by the statement. Statements are generally sent airmail and always, as is the case with any communications from a Swiss bank, are sent in unmarked envelopes. The only indication of their origin will be the Swiss city postmark and "Helvetia" on the stamp or imprinted postage. If Swiss bank accounts are to be private the Swiss believe they should be private from the postman as well as anyone else.

Your current account carries no interest payment for nonresidents of Switzerland. If residing there you may obtain 0.5 percent interest on current account balances. Since Swiss residency is virtually impossible for foreigners to obtain, the details of how checking account interest is acquired are not salient here. However, Swiss residency for foreigners is an interesting point of contention within the country. The Swiss are so strongly opposed to allowing any additional foreigners into the country (there are about 1 million "guest workers" there now, over 15 percent of the population versus 1.5 percent alien population in the United States) that a national referendum to expel up to three-fourths of the foreign workers was voted upon in October 1974. It was rejected by two-thirds of the popular vote, but was the object of a great heated debate and uncertainty as to outcome prior to polling.

The Savings Idea

Naturally, Swiss banks have a series of savings accounts available, and they are not unlike those offered by American banks with one exception: most have notice of withdrawal requirements. This, in turn, varies with the term of the account. Interest rates were raised during 1974 and are now quite competitive with U.S. banks.

The basic savings account, sometimes called a deposit account, is available from the major banks at 3.5 percent interest per annum, and is the least competitive to U.S. banks. The interest is paid and compounded once a year, usually December 31. There is no daily compounding to raise the effective rate of return on your funds. This account permits withdrawals of up to SFr. 10,000 per month but requires 30 days' notice for withdrawals in excess of this level. Interest on this account (and all others at Swiss banks) is subject to the standard withholding tax of 30 percent of interest paid. It is deducted by the bank prior to crediting to your account. More on this below.

A second savings account is available at 5 percent interest and allows up to SFr. 5,000 withdrawal per month. Six months' notice is required for larger withdrawals. Interest is paid and compounded annually after the withholding deduction.

The third savings account is the investment savings account or special account. It now pays 6 percent interest per annum. A once-per-year withdrawal of SFr. 5,000 is allowed, but additional withdrawals require a full six months' notice. Again, withholding tax is deducted at time of annual interest payment.

Aside from the deposit account, interest rates paid to savers have become attractive vis-à-vis American rates, given the Swiss condition of withdrawal notice. This is the first time in several years that any equality has existed, and is likely a reflection of the 1973–74 slowdown in Swiss bank deposit growth from the torrid pace of the previous five years. The negative interest rate of 2 percent per quarter which was in effect from July 1972 until October 1973 on deposits above SFr. 100,000 and the lack of interest permitted on accounts above SFr. 50,000 until October 1974 undoubtedly contributed to this deposit-growth hiatus. (The new 10 percent interest penalty on large Swiss franc deposits will likely have a similar effect.) The individual user of Swiss banks has benefited by these regulations by the raising of savings rates, although the lack of compounding interest and the withholding tax reduce the effective comparison to U.S. bank rates. In any case, it should be remembered that the status of interest rates payable on accounts can change rapidly. Always check rates prior to making any deposit.

There are two other means of raising your take on savings deposits at a Swiss bank. One is the medium-term bond (*Kassenobligationen*), which is issued for varying maturities and at varying rates. The bonds are available in multiples of SFr. 1,000 at the following maturities and rates: three or four years at 6.75 percent per year; and five to six years at 7 percent; and seven to eight years maturity at 7.5 percent per annum. One important feature of these bonds is a negative one: they may not be sold prior to maturity. There is no secondary market or way of releasing funds until the bond matures. They can be pledged against a loan, however, if the urgent need for cash arises. These bonds are therefore somewhat less flexible than the certificate accounts available from U.S. banks, where the funds may be obtained at only a loss of interest, albeit a substantial one.

Another method of increasing interest return on funds deposited with a Swiss bank was a most popular idea during the 1973–74 period of high interest rates. This is the fiduciary deposit sent from your Swiss bank into the Eurocurrency market, usually in London. The fiduciary deposit is one which is not widely known outside Switzerland as it involves separating the risk (largely theoretical) from the name in which the funds are held. It works this way: a major Swiss bank is authorized in writing to place a given deposit (usually a minimum of $25,000 for a CD), with a large international bank outside Switzerland for a given period of time. The funds are placed in the name of your Swiss bank at the other bank but at your risk. Thus the fiduciary connection. The interest rates obtained are the high interbank rates which prevail in the international money market; during 1974, rates between 11 percent and 13 percent were obtainable, with maturities ranging between 30 and 360 days. An additional advantage to this form of large deposit is that it is not subject to the 30 percent Swiss withholding tax, even though it is placed through your Swiss bank, since the interest is earned outside Switzerland. Such fiduciary deposits are available in any currency except Swiss francs. A fee of between .25 and 1.0 percent per annum will be charged by the Swiss bank for placing the deposit varying with deposit size and maturity.

In line with the fiduciary concept is the private loan aspect of this relationship. The bank may act in its own name between a client wishing to borrow funds and another client wishing to loan them with the borrower determined by the lender. In this case the fiduciary relationship may transfer more risk to the lender than with the fiduciary bank deposit, but interest rates may be increased as a result.

The Swiss 30 percent withholding tax on interest payments is a bothersome factor for anyone considering a Swiss account. Depending upon your personal inclinations, this tax withheld is largely retrievable, however. As a result of the Double Taxation Treaty between the United States and Switzerland, you may claim a refund of this foreign tax on your U.S. tax return for the year in which it was paid in Switzerland. All but 5 percent of the 30 percent tax withheld is recoverable in this manner. For example, let us say that you have held a $10,000 equivalent deposit in a Swiss savings account at 5 percent interest for a year. The interest payable will be $500, of which 30 percent or $150 must be deducted for Swiss taxes. This reduces your effective yield to 3.5 percent unless you claim the tax expense on your U.S. return. If you do make the claim, your tax bill will be reduced by $125, leaving only 5 percent of the $500 or $25 as your net cost. In this way your effective interest return is raised to 4.75 percent per annum, less the time required to file your tax return and receive the benefit of the deduction.

Securities

Let there be no doubt about the interest of the Swiss banks in securities portfolio management. Despite the sour nature of the subject by year-end 1974, caused by the worldwide clawing of most investors by this generation's most virulent bear market, one has only to observe the window displays along Zurich's Bahnhofstrasse or bank branches throughout the country to see Swiss banks' interest in securities management. Quotations and latest prices of all issues trading that day on the Zurich Bourse plus 50 major New York Stock Exchange issues seem to be the minimum available by closed circuit television displays for passersby. The most elaborate reminder of Swiss banks' role in the international securities markets is at the head office of Swiss Credit Bank on the Paradeplatz in Zurich. Visible from any of a half-dozen large windows at the corner of the Bahnhofstrasse is an eight-paneled revolving stock price board stretching nearly to the ceiling. It contains four closed circuit TV displays rolling stock prices upward, a series of electric quotation panels with latest prices and net changes on a full range of Swiss and U.S. shares plus 16 clocks showing times for each major time zone in the world. It serves as a monument to the interest of Swiss banks in international investments.

Clearly, the Swiss banks are among the world's most international investment sources, following as they do some 15 stock markets from Tokyo and Hong Kong to London and New York. Their success in this pursuit, or lack of it, is not published by any of the banks. The only clues we have to results come from the mutual funds run by the larger banks. As Tables 3, 4, and 5 in Chapter 8 show, the performance records of most funds, other than those specializing in gold or real estate, is little better than their American counterparts. In defense of the Swiss money managers, it must be said that the recent bear market has left no stock exchange in the world untouched. Only timing differences in the bear's gash of stock values was revealed.

A somewhat more positive factor in the portfolio management arena in Switzerland surfaces in management fees the banks will charge to "run" your portfolio. Most Swiss banks do not charge a management fee per se. There is a significant word of caution necessary here, however. True to form with many fees and charges at Swiss banks, the small items and individual fees for various services can add to a greater total than the single set fee, usually 0.5 percent, charged by U.S. securities management organizations. The most common Swiss bank management conditions are revealed by Swiss Bank Corporation procedures.

The bank indicates it will not accept a managed account of less than SFr. 1,000,000., and that for this size portfolio they will charge SFr. 2,500. per year (2.5 per mil of value) for "full management." In addition, they will be paid for brokerage fees, since banks in Switzerland are brokers as well as advisers. On top of these charges will be a securities custodial fee which amounts to 1.25 per mil of value annually, per stock held. If the shares are held at a correspondent bank or subsidiary of the Swiss bank in New York, the charge is $6.50 per 100 shares held. In general however, the charges amount to less than for a managed account in the United States. Quite clearly, these charges can rapidly add up, thus the insistence upon the relatively high minimum portfolio size. By "full management," Swiss Bank Corporation means review of the account as needed and issuance of quarterly written reports on the progress of the account.

However, Swiss Bank Corporation will accept a portfolio of securities from you down to around SFr. 100,000. for management on a "nonfee" basis. Such nonfee accounts receive infrequent review, perhaps monthly, and will not include quarterly written reports. Any reports or actions required by the client on such accounts are charged according to the amount of work involved, whether it be for a written progress report or establishment of a Liechtenstein trust. These nonfee accounts are still subject to the custodial fee for securities safekeeping, as well as brokerage charges as incurred.

The other major banks as well as the private banks have varying minimum managed account sizes. Union Bank indicates it prefers SFr. 500,000 minimum for full management, while Swiss Credit Bank says it has no minimum per se, if the account is given on a full discretionary basis. Again, they will not charge a separate fee for management but will levy individual fees plus brokerage and safekeeping charges depending upon the communication needs of the client. Most private banks look to the level above SFr. 500,000 as minimal portfolio size.

The physical form in which your securities may be held can vary considerably depending upon the country of domicile of the company whose shares you have purchased. Swiss shares are *bearer* shares, and will be registered in the name of the bank through which you purchase them and then endorsed in blank. This form may also be used for any of the 70 U.S. stocks listed on the Zurich Bourse. Where American corporate shares are purchased, other than those listed in Zurich, they are registered in your name, but may be held physically at your Swiss bank's subsidiary in New York, or may be registered in that subsidiary's nominee name and held there at your discretion. All American registered shares, even if listed on the Zurich Bourse, are bought and sold through the U.S. market. When this is done by your Swiss bank you will pay extra for the privilege. The additional charge results from the required payment of U.S. brokerage commissions by the bank, plus their charge of normal Swiss brokerage on top. While this latter charge is not large, amounting to 1 percent of value on stocks trading under SFr. 150 per share and 0.625 percent on stocks above this price, plus SFr. 1.15 per mil of value in taxes, it simply adds to your costs of doing business. Unless you have a total portfolio managed by one of the Swiss banks at their discretion, it makes better sense to order purchase and sale of individual American stocks through your American broker, in order to save the Swiss brokerage fee.

A final fact about which you should be aware when considering portfolio management by a Swiss bank is that they manage an enormous number of investment programs. In order to be able to keep their fees as low as they are (subject to change, of course), they do not believe in adding managers for your convenience. As a result, each portfolio manager handles a large number of accounts. As many as 1,000 accounts may be run by a single person, although the bulk of these may be essentially inactive accounts. One private bank in Geneva manages "several thousand" accounts, but has only 15 persons actually doing the managing. Personal attention, unless you ask for it, is a rare commodity at most Swiss banks. Exceptions are at the very small banks, including some of the private banks. Foreign Commerce Bank's Geneva manager told me that this was one of the features of their service. "We have few enough accounts that we can get to know them all personally," he reported. He estimated about 50 accounts per manager.

This is not to suggest that you won't be treated warmly by a larger bank at which you have your securities portfolio, especially if it is of healthy size. You may expect a personal conversation with your manager during a trip to Switzerland, and he will be available for telephone consultation very readily, so long as the practice is not overused. If so, you will be charged for it.

The major Swiss banks and a few of the private banks have established stock brokerage affiliates in the United

States to facilitate their trades in the American market. This also makes the capture of brokerage commissions that much more lucrative for them where both Swiss and American rates are charged. For reference, Union Bank of Switzerland owns Swiss-American Corporation, New York, members of the NASD and the Pacific Stock Exchange; Swiss Bank Corporation owns Basle Securities Corporation, New York, members of NASD. Swiss Credit Bank owns a portion of SoGen, New York, with four other European banks and indirectly owns a 17 percent interest in the American firm of White, Weld, Inc., New York, who are members of the New York Stock Exchange. In addition, the bank holds a 40 percent interest in White, Weld Finance Corp. in Europe. Julius Bär & Co. owns Bär Securities of New York, members of the Midwest and PBW Exchanges.

Private Banks

While dealing with the subject of securities, we must note the important role that the private Swiss banks play in securities portfolio management. The most significant part of this role has often been considered that of the unlimited liability of the bank partners in standing behind their portfolio management.

"The Swiss private banks," explained one private banker, "have always had unlimited liability. This means the definition of such banks has required a partnership. And I believe this in turn has led clients to believe we might be more cautious with their funds."

The private banks were the forerunners of modern Swiss banking, establishing their operations even before the turn of the 19th century, as we have seen. This has led to their reputation of deep tradition, conservative methods, and for those now in operation, a belief that they are run by people of personal wealth and substance. Yet, proof of this reputation is difficult to come by.

The private banks are not required to publish annual balance sheets as are the public banks. They do business in small, externally austere buildings, marked only with obscure brass plaques stating their presence. They are not permitted to solicit client business in any direct way. They discourage portfolios being brought to them under the substantial size of $250,000, although, as one bank partner remarked, "for close friends, we might take $100,000 or even $50,000." Friendship and references are the principal means through which the private bankers obtain their new clients. They represent the ultimate in privacy in a nation where privacy is both a legal and habitual watchword.

Some private bankers believe this is all about to be torn asunder. The largest in their midst has incorporated. On January 1, 1975, Julius Bär & Co. of Zurich became a limited company, discarding the partnership mantle that it has worn since 1895. While Bär officials explain the move as purely pragmatic, involving such mundane considerations as their heir's succession, social security taxes, and modern banking methodology, other private bankers aren't so sure.

"It could start a trend which can only end in all of us being forced into limited company status," observed another private banker with a frown. "A great tradition may be lost."

Bär partner Hans Bär agrees that a trend toward

limited liability status will be forthcoming in the private banking group. "But it will be a matter of their seeing the significance of the tax legislation which went into effect this year [1974], and its increased personal and partnership liabilities for social security taxes."

Over and above the ostensible reasons which mark the emergence of Julius Bär & Co. as a public bank (although it will still be closely held by the Bär family), are the more obvious considerations of protection of personal assets in the current era of wide swings in securities values, other major bank losses in foreign exchange, and perhaps most likely, the future need for capital to continue growth. Whatever the full story, it is clear that the private banking scene in Switzerland will never be quite the same after the Bär reformation.

All this notwithstanding, what can private banks do for you?

They will provide all the special services which go with asset management: accounting, special reports, tax return information, and personal consultations — if you have the portfolio size and contacts to be properly introduced to them. They dote on personal service.

"A client can visit our highest level officers, and always meet with the same people," offers partner Pierre Keller of Geneva's Lombard Odier. "Typically this means a partner, his assistant and his secretary. We like to see our clients regularly, or at least correspond regularly with distant accounts."

I asked Mr. Keller what he would most like Americans to know about private banks in Switzerland. "We in the private banking group," he said, "attempt to be very professional, high quality managers of securities portfolios. We would hope to stand up to any leading professional managers in comparison. This and personal attention to client requirements are our most important assets."

Perhaps behind this is the importance of the client relationship itself. From the initial question, "Who gave you the name of our bank?" asked by private bankers of persons requesting their services, to their conservative reputation and professional services with close client attention, it is the formation of a *proper* relationship with affluent clients that the private bankers desire most.

"It is said," offered one private bank partner, "that a banker is often a confessor to his client. Over the years, there is built a tremendous mutual confidence between the two."

That is the sort of relationship private bankers would like you to believe in before sending your funds to them. When you do, be certain the funds are sizable as well.

Investment Funds

For those of us with something under the normal $100,000-"plus" required to obtain a managed securities portfolio at a Swiss bank, the major banks and a handful of the private ones have long provided their own mutual funds. The oldest date to the 1930s. As with stock brokerage functions, Swiss (and most other European) banks are permitted to sell, manage, and advise on their own mutual funds, where U.S. banks are not. Where the American banks went through the trauma of having their investment activities stripped from them by the Glass Steagal Act of 1933, with certain exceptions such as trust management, the European banks did not. Thus the promotion of their mutual funds, and revenue from stock brokerage.

The Swiss bank fund business is sizable, if still tiny compared with the giant U.S. fund industry. The 1973 year-end assets of all Swiss bank funds ran to $4.9 billion, with some $4.0 billion administered by the Big Three banks, (at the prevailing exchange rate of 3.23 francs per dollar) as compared with $46.5 billion assets of the U.S. fund industry on the same date. Of the Big Three Swiss bank fund assets on December 31, 1973, Swiss Credit and Bank Corp. held 22 percent each, with Union Bank the market leader at 56 percent of these assets.

Swiss bank funds are available for purchase with relatively small acquisition charges, the maximum of which are around a 4 percent spread between bid and offer. Swiss bank fund shares are issued somewhat differently than American mutual funds, in that they are often quoted on the Zurich Bourse in the open market, but have special share issues offered by the banks as well. These bank issues are a constant offering. They are, however, made on a net price basis where the Bourse prices require adding of commissions. A comparison of the pricing structure for a few of Union Bank's funds in mid-July 1974 will give you an idea of how this pricing structure operates.

Bond-Invest, their international bond fund, was available for SFr. 74 per share, from the bank, net. The same day's price on the Bourse was SFr. 72.50 plus commission and tax. Fonsa, the Swiss securities fund, was offered at SFr. 89.50 by the bank, net, and at

SFr. 88 plus commission on the Bourse. A far larger spread was seen in Safit, the South African fund on that day. It was offered at SFr. 370.50 by the bank, but available at SFr. 352 on the Bourse. Obviously, it can pay to do a little shopping when considering acquisition of a Swiss bank fund.

Most Swiss funds are available with no minimum size purchase requirements through your Swiss bank, providing you have a current account there. When purchased through the Bourse, a minimum 100-share purchase is usually required. Here your bank will act as agent for you just as with any stock purchase. Regular investment plan purchases can be arranged and dividends/capital gains can be automatically reinvested. Sale of fund shares can be made on the open market or directly to the fund management at the fund's managing bank.

Dividends paid by funds investing less than 80 percent of their funds outside Switzerland are subject to the 30 percent Swiss withholding tax. Those which are 80 percent or more invested outside the country are not subject to the tax.

Recent pertinent information and price records of the largest Swiss bank funds are contained in the tables in Chapter 8.

Stock Exchanges

The Zurich Bourse is the point of focus for the Swiss securities industry, although there are Bourses in Geneva and Basle as well. The Zurich Bourse dates to 1744 and features trading in some 70 American stocks,

192 Swiss and other foreign issues, and 1,540 separate
bonds. However, the market is very thin by U.S. standards. Large block trades are a rarity and even small
blocks are often difficult to execute. The market is
dwarfed by the size of the banks dealing in it. The
trust assets of Swiss banks exceed the Bourse's total
capitalization by nearly six times.

Trading volume figures issued by the Bourse are
given a Swiss franc value of SFr. 65.4 billion for 1973,
down from over SFr. 74 billion in 1972. The Bourse does
not issue share volume figures, making comparison
with the U.S. market difficult. However, taking a $40
per share average recent value for stocks traded on the
New York Exchange, a 15-million-share trading day
would represent about $600 million value. On this basis
about one and a half months' volume on the New York
Exchange would equal the *annual* volume on the Zurich
Bourse. Since average share prices are considerably
higher on the Zurich Bourse than in New York, this
figure is only a rough estimate.

Gold

In addition to the detailed discussion of gold in Chapter Five, it is pertinent to list here the key requirements for purchase of gold bullion and its safekeeping.

The Big Three Swiss banks have established the
world's largest volume gold market. As noted earlier,
Zurich gold pool dealers are principals in the market.
That is, they buy and sell for their own account and
risk, with long or short positions as they see fit. The
normal unit of sale is known as the "standard" bar of

400 troy ounces, at least 995 parts pure. When one obtains a Zurich quote on bullion, it is for this bar or larger quantities. Early 1975 prices put the tag per unit around $72,000. For smaller sizes, say down to the one kilogram bar, (32.15 troy ounces), you can expect to pay a premium of about 15 percent per ounce over the standard bar price. All the banks have gold counters where units as small as 10-gram bars may be purchased at daily changing prices. Premiums are built into these prices, so that as with anything we buy in small unit sizes, they will be more expensive than the standard unit.

With the entry of the American public into the gold market during 1975 for the first time in 41 years, it is likely that the premiums for smaller bars will increase. The pattern will largely follow that charged for the yellow metal by American banks or brokers. Zurich will not, according to one senior gold dealer there, be left behind in the premium market. However, Swiss banks do not usually charge a commission per se for gold purchases. Prices are on a net basis. What form commissions, if any, will eventually take can only be a matter of conjecture at this writing.

Swiss banks will store gold bullion for you with no precise minimum requirement as to size lot. Their charge is 0.125 percent of value of gold stored, per year. However, a good rule of thumb for requesting safekeeping of bullion is, if you could carry it, don't ask your bank to store it. Swiss bankers will suggest you rent a safe-deposit box for storage of anything less than a 400 ounce standard bar, but will probably store down to one kilo bars if you are not planning to go to Switzerland.

Another tip about gold purchases. In ordering gold from your Swiss bank, don't plan to buy odd amounts of gold. Place orders for kilo bars and not odd ounce sizes. Swiss gold does not come in 15-ounce or 50-ounce units—or any in-between except 32.15 troy ounces: 1 kilogram. Orders for gold should be placed in kilogram units, therefore, and the small tola bars ignored in long-distance gold purchase orders.

Americans in Zurich

American banks and multinational corporations have been as mindful—probably more so—of the advantages of operating from a base within the Swiss Confederacy as have the many individual Americans who have availed themselves of Swiss bank accounts. While, as we have seen, one can hold a Swiss account for a small amount of money, the larger the stash the greater the advantages. With literally millions at their disposal, the giant American banks have found both the listening post aspect of a Swiss unit and the deposit gains worthwhile.

American-owned Swiss banks must be incorporated under Swiss law and operate under full aegis of that law. Thus, as was discovered by Jerry Goodman at UCB, Basle, they are Swiss legal entities and are controlled by a board of directors the majority of whom must be Swiss citizens. The voting stock ownership may be foreign controlled. Most American-owned banks in Switzerland provide the full range of banking services, but with some variation from bank to bank. American banks will not accept numbered accounts,

however, as a general rule. Two exceptions are Foreign
Commerce Bank and Bank Indiana. But these are not
subsidiary operations of large American banks. They
are independent and privately financed. Neither Bank
of America, Chase Manhattan, nor First National City
Bank accept numbered accounts. As in every other
bank, however, the full weight of Swiss bank secrecy
applies to regular accounts. Their employees are subject to the same penalties for indiscretion about accounts as are employees of Swiss-owned banks.

The American domestic branches of the banks
listed at the end of this chapter will provide you with
any details of services available at their Swiss units.
However, it is sensible to remember that any communications or orders given through a branch of a U.S.
domestic bank, which also has a Swiss unit, are governed only by American banking privacy rules, not
Swiss.

Perqs

Swiss banks, especially the private members of the
group, are justifiably known for their years of service
to generations of the same families within the country.
Through these long years of banking relationships,
close ties have been built. As sizable fortunes have
been amassed and left to management of the same
bank over 50 or 75 years, the closeness of the ties and
offered perquisites have grown. New depositors should
hardly expect them, and will likely be offered only a
few, and then only with satisfactorily sized accounts.

Most banks in Switzerland will make their legal

departments available (always for a fee) for the drawing and notarizing of wills. They often have expert real
estate management services which may also be had
for a fee, assuming that you are legally entitled to own
Swiss real estate (only Swiss residents or Swiss-con-
trolled corporations with foreign owners). Tax return
preparation is a common service offered by the major
banks, as are travel reservations through their extensive travel departments.

The banks will gladly assist, again for a fee, in establishing a Swiss corporation for you, or in setting up
a trust, including those in Liechtenstein. They most
often will provide bank officials to be named to the
boards of trustees or directors of these entities, as well.
They may even "provide a cook for local residents,"
as one private banker observed with a smile in Geneva,
underscoring the range of services available. But along
with theater tickets and secluded dinners, that sort of
perquisite is best considered only a private accom-
modation for their best clients.

In all, Swiss banks have long been precisely what
many American financial institutions are now aspiring
to become, the great financial department stores of
their nation. Because of legal restrictions within the
United States, it is doubtful that many institutions here
could reach the range of services provided by the Swiss
banks. Stated publicly or not, most U.S. financial institutions must look upon Swiss banks in this sense
with some envy. With these services set behind the veil
of banking secrecy, few institutions anywhere in the
world can match the power and prestige in their own
countries that the Swiss banks enjoy in their tiny alpine
land.

American Banks in Zurich (including addresses, telephone numbers and principal officers)

American Express International Banking Corporation
Paul Rohner
Bahnhofstrasse 20, 8001 Zurich, Tel. 23 57 20

Bank of America, NT & SA
A. H. Kohler
Borsenstrasse 16, 8022 Zurich, Tel. 27 06 10

Bank Firestone, Ltd.
R. Bachmann
Bleicherweg 15, 8039 Zurich. Tel. 36 71 44

Bankers Trust, AG
J. Hahn
Dreikonigstrasse 6, 8022 Zurich, Tel. 36 67 37

Brown Brothers Harriman Services AG
E. Muller
Stockerstrasse 38, 8002 Zurich. Tel. 36 41 00

Chase Manhattan Bank (Suisse)
A. Welti
Genferstrasse 24, 8002 Zurich. Tel. 36 49 36

Chemical Bank
R. Gut
Gartenstrasse 32, 8039 Zurich. Tel. 36 04 40

Continental Illinois Bank
S. C. Rey
Bahnhofstrasse 18, 8022 Zurich. Tel 27 48 10

Dow Banking Corporation
E. P. Fassler
Bahnhofstrasse 24, 8022 Zurich. Tel. 27 44 50

First National City Bank
E. Giger
St. Peterstrasse 16, 8001 Zurich. Tel. 44 22 41

Foreign Commerce Bank
K. Munger
Ballariastrasse 82, 8038 Zurich. Tel. 45 66 88

Morgan Guaranty Trust Company
P. H. Schaad
Stockerstrasse 38, 8022 Zurich. Tel. 36 65 36

Twenty-Five Important Services of Major Swiss Banks

Board of Directors (or Trustees), Members for
Certificates of Deposit
Checking Accounts
Corporate Underwriting
Factoring of Receivables
Fiduciary Deposits
Foreign Exchange
Foreign Trade Financing
Incorporation
Investment Counseling
Investment (Mutual) Funds
Leasing, Capital Goods
Legal Advice and Tax Information
Letters of Credit
Loans: Personal, Consumer Goods
Mortgage Financing
Precious Metals Dealings
Safe Deposit Boxes
Savings Accounts
Savings Certificates
Securities Brokerage
Travel Services
Travelers Checks
Trust Arrangements
Wills

Chapter seven

Those Swiss Myths

SWITZERLAND'S fame as a nation of precision quickly strikes air travelers to Zurich or Geneva. How many international airports have a large lighted sign visible from all parts of their sizable waiting rooms, announcing "MEETING SPOT," and adorned with two red arrows pointing to a bright red, six-inch spot on the sign?

A telephone call from one of the large lighted booths at the same airport introduces the caller to the most efficient phone system on the continent. The phone box collects *centimes* for a call, registers the amount on a meter below the phone face and ticks off elapsed money, showing the caller exactly the amount left for the call. Running short? Just deposit another coin for more conversation.

From these lighter examples of precision to the famed chronometer accuracy of Swiss watches, which Omega advertises as the reason for its selection as the official watch of the U.S. moon voyages, to the clockwork timeliness of the National Railways, the Swiss mirror accuracy with the definition of a finely cut diamond. Ironically, in so doing, Switzerland has also become the myth capital of the free world.

Surprising? Probably, unless you've been there.

Certainly, the Swiss themselves strive to dispel the imprecision of myths and rumors, which are anathema to them, especially in the world of finance which has its own claims to accuracy and precision. They would prefer perfect precision. One basic reason for the dichotomy is, of course, the Swiss' equally famous bank secrecy, whose purpose is to hide private facts. The secrecy hides the precision which bankers normally exude on interest rates to four decimals and monthly payments to the day. Secrecy tends to cloud statistics. It complicates meanings of statements which are offered as clarification of unfamiliar motives. The function of secrecy is imprecision. How is one both secret and precise? No wonder the myths, right?

Unfortunately, it is not bank secrecy which has initiated most of the currently popular myths about Swiss banks. Only the numbered account still retains a myth shroud which can be blamed directly on bank secrecy, despite constant efforts to clarify it.

For example, the idea advanced in recent novels, such as Frederick Forsyth's *The Dogs of War,* that Swiss banks might be rather passé has nothing to do with bank secrecy. The suggestion simply ignores widely known facts. The curiosity over acceptable minimum account size in the tiny nation belies the readily available, published statements of most banks. The gold backing to the Swiss franc is no more secret than any statistic published by the National Bank, but is still taken to mean far more than any banker intends it should. The alleged austerity of the banks themselves is quickly dispelled by their promotional and cultural activities both within the country and overseas. The handiness of a multicurrency checkbook should be obvious to anyone who travels or does business internationally. This feature is promoted by the banks, and yet few people seem to know that this service is one of the most useful of those offered by Swiss banks. Like green thumb gardeners, the Swiss banks seem to grow a yard full of myths without ever trying, one of the peculiar phenomena of the confused financial milieu of the mid-70s. Since these myths blind would-be Swiss account holders, they deserve a bit of broom work on their mist shrouded foundations.

Who's Passé?

Little did the Swiss banking authorities imagine in October 1974, when they ended a drive to discourage desirability of the Swiss franc for the world's peoples, that they would be forced to return with two new discouraging steps within three months' time. The scenario unfolded simply enough. Shortly after visiting Zurich during the second week of October 1974, where I exchanged dollars at the rate of 2.89 francs (34.6 U.S. cents per franc) the Swiss National Bank removed their prohibition against interest payments for single new accounts (or increases in existing accounts) above SFr. 50,000. Within three weeks the exchange rate collapsed to under 2.60 francs per dollar (38.4 U.S. cents per franc). The franc was then at the pinnacle of a 65 percent gain in the franc per dollar rate in a period of three and a half years. The spiral had been over 10 percent from the time of my visit.

In deference to the heavily export-dependent Swiss industry, Swiss banking authorities were shortly forced to admit a (for them) bothersome fact: Swiss banks, nearly seven years after the height of their popularity, still featured the best monetary bargain in the immensely deteriorated international financial scheme: their own money. Their admission took the form of imposing a new "negative" interest rate (the previous 2 percent per quarter rate had been eliminated in July, 1973), of 3 percent per quarter on the average account balance exceeding SFr. 100,000, plus the absence of any interest on deposits of SFr. 50,000 to SFr. 99,999. They were instituting a *charge* to depositors of 12 percent per year when account balances averaged over SFr 100,000 ($38,400 at the prevailing exchange rate). In blunt terms, the Swiss banking authorities were saying once more, "if you like our banks and our money so much, you pay us to leave your money here."

Naturally, the move was not met with unbounded enthusiasm by the members of the working Swiss bank industry. It simply put a wet blanket on new business, despite the bankers' already protective inclinations for Swiss industry. They didn't want the franc to become a reserve currency for the world, a role which many outsiders believe only makes sense. "Look," Swiss bankers say, "what happened to the pound and dollar and those economies as a result of their reserve currency role."

There was, too, another side to the move. Hans Bär, senior partner of Julius Bär & Co., made the point: "The last time we took the same measures in 1972, the dollar was at 3.75 francs. By the time the measures were completely removed, the dollar was down to 3 francs." Hardly evidence of success.

But there were more problems to come. Prior to the end of 1974, Bär's concern was justified again. Following the 3 percent negative interest rate imposition, a brief rally moved the exchange rate to 2.80, whereupon it again collapsed to the 2.50 franc per dollar level. By late January 1975, the Swiss National Bank was compelled to move again, this time to a 10 percent per quarter negative interest rate on deposits over SFr. 100,000. The banks were charging 40 percent per year for the safekeeping of your money in amounts above roughly $40,000! The previous lack of interest on deposits over SFr. 50,000 still applied. How was it possible? Surely this was sufficient deterrent to prevent the inflow of buyers of francs, or so the Swiss banking authorities thought. Wrong again. By March 1, 1975, the rate had moved to 2.42 francs per dollar. The franc gain was approaching 20 percent in four months' time.

In fact, there was a reason — a loophole which prompted Bär's lack of enthusiasm back in November, 1974. It is most important to potential account holders. The series of penalty regulations issued beginning in 1972 and continuing through 1975, all contained a provision which stressed application to *single accounts* at the prescribed levels. Thus, a new depositor could obtain normal interest on deposits *under* SFr. 50,000 by opening any number of accounts below that level. What is more, nothing in the regulation prevents foreign banks from acquiring Swiss francs in any quantity outside Switzerland. It is these loopholes which, despite the difficulty in dealing with them due to Swiss determination to maintain a fully convertible franc, will likely be addressed by the banking authorities should a continued climb in the franc's price take place.

This exercise in popularity should erase any lingering doubts about the importance of Swiss banks in the recent recessionary climate, although it is judicious to note that Swiss banks and Swiss francs are not inseparable. Whatever the Swiss banks' disadvantages of costs, inconvenience, or relatively lower interest rates, they still have a corner on the most desirable currency in the world. Either directly or indirectly, it must be purchased from them. With only about $15 billion worth of Swiss francs in the money supply (M1) versus something over U.S. $285 billion floating about, the basic supply-demand forces are revealing themselves in a rising franc price. They have shown few signs of relenting.

The importance of this to those considering using Swiss banks is unmistakable. In the international money arena, where all relationships are purely relative and nothing is absolute, Swiss franc interest-bearing deposits under the SFr. 50,000 level appear the best the world has to offer. Barring additional penalties yet to be devised and/or announced by Swiss banking authorities, the small supply Swiss franc float cannot meet demand for the foreseeable future. The myth that Swiss banks have somehow become passé while featuring the world's most popular (or at worst, one of two most popular) currencies, has been laid to rest. It will take a startling turn of events for resurrection.

Two for the Seesaw

Of course, there are always events lurking in the wings of the Great Money Game stage that can alter basic trends in currency prices. Prices of currencies can be changed by a wide-ranging combination of forces. If we may view the price relationship between any two currencies as being a seesaw contest between the respective countries, the price of one country's currency in relation to the others may be moved up or down by an increase or reduction in pressure on either of the two currencies. The two most important, though by no means the only, pressures are the inflation/recession prospects in one country relative to the other, and the balance-of-payments prospects in one country relative to its business partner.

In simplified terms, if domestic inflationary pressures increase in one of two nations riding a currency price seesaw, and do so relative to its seesaw partner, the seesaw tends to drop on the inflationary pressured end, attendantly raising the price of the currency on the other end. In addition, the relative lowering of general interest rates, a recessing economy, or a worsening balance-of-payments expectation, has had a similar downward "seesaw" pressure for the country experiencing these difficulties, relative to another with better prospects.

With floating currency rates, the strength or weakness of a currency in relation to any other is a direct reflection of how the financial world perceives that country's *relative* economic position. This position is transmitted by official statistics and both published and private opinions offered by foreign exchange dealers, bankers, and corporate treasurers, who create a pervasive psychological mood which is akin to that surrounding that great confounder of public logic, the stock market. Over the longer term there is often a more predictable direction to single currency prices than individual stock prices. But currency prices swing day to day by the tenuous thread of psychology. Daily or even weekly currency price undulations can be just short of maniacal, as foreign exchange traders at a host of shocked banks could testify in 1974. As we have seen, the Swiss National Bank's imposition of the negative interest rate had both temporary and artificial effects on the dollar/franc price, superimposed on a longer term uptrend of the franc. The move was a complex psychological undertaking. The direction of exchange rate movement became a matter of near-term opinion. It turned out that the short term opinion was wrong.

Thus, currencies may be understood as akin to the public stock of a nation. Their price relationship to any other nation's stock is the seesaw we have noted.

The foregoing discussion has treated the currency seesaw as being bilateral, that is, involving only the exchange rate between two currencies. Of course, the relationship is more complicated than that. A general trend in a given currency's price affects its seesaw relationships with a number of different monies. For example, the dollar has been under general downward pressure vis-à-vis several currencies since 1971. The question becomes, which ones and why? The downdraft has been against those with relatively fewer national economic problems behind them than the United States, or by 1975, when the recession was becoming worldwide, against those currencies which represented countries with apparently less troublesome problems.

In this multi-lateral sense, the seesaw analogy becomes a group affair, with a given major currency weighing on one end of the board and a group of relatively better-off currencies on the other end. At the same time, the original major currency is riding a seesaw with another group of nations doing relatively poorly compared with it. The analogy becomes a bit tenuous here, but is valid. Whether one discusses bilateral or multilateral exchange rates, *both* favorable and unfavorable relative pressures can weigh on *either* end of the seesaw, giving us four directional variables to affect the exchange rate itself. These variables are psychologically activated by a group of special financial opinion makers over the short term, while longer term trends have shown a momentum which has been more universal.

Since the world has had only a brief modern experience with floating exchange rates (since 1971), and less than a decade of playing the Great Money Game, we have a limited amount of data upon which to build long term currency price patterns. Purely empirical evidence shows the Dutch guilder, German mark, and Swiss franc in long-term uptrends with only brief reversals. The U.S. dollar and the British pound, meanwhile, have revealed steadily declining channels with only short-term upticks. The lightest child on a seesaw doesn't gain weight overnight, no matter how many artificial blocks he places on his end of the seesaw, even though these too will affect the balance of the board. The strongest international monetary thinking has been that Switzerland's franc is one of the lightest kids on the international money block. It will end up relatively higher on the currency seesaw than most other players over the longer term, unless the Swiss banking authorities find a large concrete block to place on their end of the teeter-totter, or the heavy-weight United States or Britain lose some of their difficult economic poundage. Recessionary psychology, gold politics, oil money flows, and additional discouraging moves by Swiss banking authorities are the likely external pressures which will most affect the dollar/franc price seesaw in the near future.

Dealing in Size

With few exceptions, persons asking me about this book have been of the opinion that they would need a good deal of money to open Swiss bank accounts. "They must be for high rollers," was a typical observation. This is not necessarily so.

The only practical rule of thumb for account size at Swiss banks is that the more funds you have, the more services you will be able to make use of and the more valuable the banks will be. Like financial department stores, the shop becomes more significant in your total financial plans as the range of products of which you can avail yourself grows. This concept does not exclude the average person with a few dollars to invest or place on deposit. It simply means that he or she will be tapping only a small portion of what Swiss banks have to offer, and that this situation must be compared with the inconvenience of doing so.

But the major Swiss banks, including the Big Three and the Cantonal Banks, will accept small deposits. It just pains them to do so. A senior official of a Big Three bank explained:

> It is terrible that we can't help the small man as much as we'd like. They need help in protection against inflation as much, probably more, than big investors. But how could we handle 10,000 new accounts for a few hundred dollars each? Staff costs alone would kill us. And yet, we have always offered our services to the smaller account, so we must continue

Even more straightforward was the observation of another major banker. "We will take the small accounts because we feel we have to. But please don't encourage them. They cost us money."

The fact is that the major Swiss banks will accept accounts as small as $100 now, and even took $50 accounts a few years ago. The real question should be, for what reason do you want to put $100 in a Swiss bank? If it is only a token of total resources, don't bother a Swiss bank until you have sufficient funds handy to avail yourself of well more than a current account deposit. If it is the last $100 you have, don't send it to Switzerland—at recent inflation rates you'll need it here tomorrow for necessities. Even $1,000 is not considered important at Swiss banks, which are used to dealing in hundreds of thousands, as the Clifford Irving case revealed during my research on that subject.

Having obtained the details of the Irving hoax from a few bankers and several published reports, I wanted to verify them with the principal bank involved, Swiss Credit Bank. Dr. Hans Mast of that bank agreed to have his legal department look into the facts and verify what

I had written. A short time later, I received a series of
written comments on the facts, one of which caught my
immediate attention. Where I had described the
$50,000 which Mrs. Irving had deposited as "obviously
a sizeable account," the bank made the observation,
"actually accounts of that size are rather frequent even
for private persons." Obviously a big fish in the Swiss
bank pond must have more weight to it, or so they
would have us believe.

Somewhere between the $50,000 involved in the
Irving case and the $100 mentioned above is the
sensibly sized minimum account you should consider,
which does leave some leeway. Foreign Commerce
Bank has a $15,000 minimum now that they are flush
with funds as a result of several recommendations by
the financial gurus. Private banks aren't interested in
what size account you open so long as you wish their
securities portfolio management services, and those
minimums start at about $250,000 unless you are a
very good friend of one of their peers.

It remains true that unless you have sufficient resources to make interest paid on savings or CD accounts worthwhile, you must be content with your pure
percentage gain on available assets. Making 17 percent,
for example, on $1,000, or $170, isn't much in pure
dollars. But 17 percent is a *very* good percentage return
on any asset, in one year or less.

With $1,000 or $2,000, 5 percent interest return is
hardly worth the bother of sending the funds to Switzerland, unless you want to speculate on the franc/dollar
rate for better return.

This should be your basic account size criteria:
Open a Swiss account only with an amount which, at

current interest rates, will satisfy you in dollar yield as a worthwhile return. Otherwise, be satisfied with solid percentage gain potential. If $500 is the minimum worthwhile annual dollar yield for you, you'll need to deposit around $10,000, depending upon the type of account and the interest it pays. Going several thousand miles by mail, cable, or phone to obtain less dollars in interest return will add unnecessary bother, underutilize your Swiss account, and therefore suggests you may not have sufficient reason for opening one. But, for SFr. 1,000 you'll get a multicurrency checkbook . . . and know the truth about the small account myth, at least.

Play Money

Your first visit to a major Swiss city will likely bring you face to face with one of the numerous electronic timepieces posted as sentinels outside jewelers' shops or banks. Most of these marvels tick off not only hours, minutes, and seconds, but tenths of a second as well. If your reaction to these Olympics-style timing devices is similar to mine, you'll wonder why passersby on a busy street need such precision. Sharp eyes can only recognize three or four tenths per second and then become glassy after five seconds.

Practicality isn't the point, of course. Those electronic hair splitters are positioned to demonstrate the watch sellers' *capability;* he has a toy which cuts time into pieces virtually too small to see. Think of what else he might be capable.

The exposition of the fast electronic timepieces is

similar in a real sense to the Swiss bank's multicurrency checkbooks. They both impress with their capability. Their usefulness is up to you. The banks want you to be aware that they deal in *any* currency; the jewelers, that precision is their hallmark.

For most people, the multicurrency checkbook, where you write on the blank check whatever currency you wish to use to pay a bill or invoice, will be far more useful than a rare timing clock or watch. In fact, an American resident of Switzerland throughout the 60s, who was intimately involved with Investors Overseas Services of Geneva, believes Swiss banks' multi-currency checkbook is the *only* true advantage of Swiss accounts over other banks. Wherever you rank it, the any-money checkbook is a bright idea for anyone who travels or does business abroad, or who might in the future. And, it can be just as useful in the United States. A dollar check, no matter on which bank it is written, will probably be acceptable with proper identification. Only the collection time is different.

The multicurrency check function is simple. By writing a check in any currency you select, and without regard to the currency you hold in your Swiss account, you have at your disposal a truly international currency, and one which will be accepted anywhere a check is accepted. Paying a hotel bill in London? Write "£" on your Swiss multicurrency checkbook, pay the hotel directly in their currency, and avoid the usually barn-wide spread that hotels use in currency exchange. Your Swiss bank will exchange funds from your account, no matter what currency the account is held in, when the check arrives for payment. Your account remains in its original denomination. And since the check will be paid by your Swiss bank as written in any currency, it is as simple to write as your U.S. bank's check.

This multi-currency checkbook is eminently useful in business as well. You receive credit for payment at the time the check is accepted by your foreign supplier or seller of services, since it is denominated in his own currency and will in turn be accepted directly by his bank. There should be no waiting for collection on his part.

The principal disadvantage—in fact, the only one I can think of, aside from letting the payee know that you have a Swiss account—is that the exchange rate between account funds and the foreign currency check is not determined until the check reaches your Swiss bank. This could be as long as one or two weeks from the date of presentation for a bill in any city outside Switzerland. If the exchange rate between the denomination of the bill and the denomination of your account in Switzerland moves against you during the check clearing period, you will lose something as a cost of convenience. On the other hand, if one had kept a Swiss account in Swiss francs over the past three years, the rate changes against most currencies would have had the effect of providing a discount on your bill or invoice, a pleasant dividend.

Thus, the Swiss have offered a device in the multi-currency checkbook which both advertises their capabilities in international currency handling, and dispels the myth that Swiss francs aren't useful to anyone but those persons going to Switzerland. While there is certainly no guarantee that the dollar/franc rate will continue to benefit holders of francs in the future, it should be useful to know that if you wish to hold francs as protection in a Swiss account, the same action provides you with convenience in check writing and might gain an exchange rate dividend besides.

There's Gold in Those Francs

Probably the most pervasive myth about Swiss banks, again involving their currency, has to do with the gold backing to the money. The point is made in most treatises, market letters, advisory services, and books about international finance, that the Swiss franc is backed 100 percent by gold. If one takes the narrowly defined money supply (M1), this is true in terms of *coverage* of the volume of money at free market gold prices. The rough coverage in November 1974, according to Union Bank of Switzerland, was SFr. 48 billion worth of gold at the Swiss National Bank versus about SFr. 43 billion in M1 money supply.

That is 110 percent coverage and more. What is overlooked in this simple statement is that the percentage cover figure is virtually meaningless to the average person holding Swiss francs. Contrary to this very popular myth, Swiss francs cannot be exchanged for gold any more than the U.S. dollar can be by the average person, or even the top players of the Great Money Game. While the currency is *covered* by gold sufficient to buy out every franc in existence (again in M1), there is no legal way of doing so. The franc is not redeemable in gold at the Swiss National Bank. True, one can buy gold bullion or coins with francs (or any other currency) at any bank or exchange house in

Switzerland. But this is not the same as redeemability. One can buy any form of gold in the United States with dollars too, but the dollar is not convertible into gold by anyone, including other governments, through any government agency. And if this is the case, what good is the 110 percent gold cover of the Swiss franc, any more than the 17 percent gold cover of the dollar (at free market prices)? True, it *sounds* better, but if there is no way to take advantage of that cover, of what value is it? The term "backing" is too strong and not based on legal fact.

In fact, however, there is a value to the term "backing," but not the one that is popularly believed. It is the value of the gold as a potential support to the currency in international trade as a reserve behind the balance of payments of any given country. In this regard a far more important statement about the gold "backing" of a country is the backing to the balance of payments or trade account deficit/surplus. But that sounds complicated, so the "cover" to the currency is quoted instead.

Gold backing to a balance of payments deficit simply provides the country with one means of settling that deficit without printing new money or borrowing internationally. While settling such deficits by gold payment has been something most nations are loath to do, the availability of gold to do so provides one more measure of strength of a nation's finances.

This balance of trade/payments consideration touches upon still another myth about Switzerland, which is that the nation's trade account is very solid. It is not. Switzerland has run a chronic balance of trade deficit. In 1974, imports to Switzerland were

about SFr. 40 billion versus SFr. 32 billion in exports:
an SFr. 8 billion trade deficit. Against this figure, the
SFr. 48 billion in gold reserves is meaningful. It means
that the country could finance six years of similar trade
deficits out of its gold stock alone. In this sense, the
gold backs the currency because theoretically the franc
would not have to be devalued to bring this account
into balance. However, we are overlooking the fact that
nearly all of that trade deficit is also covered by the so-
called invisibles of the payments account: direct
dividends from Swiss firms abroad, banking, tourism,
and insurance. Thus, there was virtually no balance-of-
payments deficit expected for 1974.

With this additional bolstering to the franc, Switzerland's gold resides in unused splendor in the National
Bank vaults, "backing" a currency which cannot be
exchanged into it, and "covering" a nearly nonexistent
balance-of-payments deficit. It is plainly a powerful
reserve, and one which is not likely to change negatively in the foreseeable future. Its existence and
expected immutability provide significant psychological reasons for international interest in the Swiss
franc.

One piece of evidence of the psychological factor at
work where gold reserves are large, was provided by a
Wall Street Journal report on currency strength versus
gold reserves.[1] It quoted results of a study made in late
1974 by a Boston-based statistical services firm com-
paring the gold coverage of a nation's money supply
with the price change of its currency against the dollar.

---

[1]Charles J. Elia, "Heard On The Street," *The Wall Street Journal*,
April 7, 1975.

While the relationship was not stated as causal, it is, nevertheless, interesting. Valuing the gold portion of reserves at $168.50 per ounce over the period 1970–74, the Swiss franc had gold equal to 76 percent of its money supply; the franc gained 51 percent against the dollar. The Netherlands' gold was 64 percent of money supply; the guilder gain was 36 percent. Austria: 60 percent gold, 41 percent currency gain. West Germany: 38 percent gold, 41 percent currency gain. The Boston firm's conclusion: "The strong currencies aren't necessarily that way just because of the gold, but because they [their respective governments] tend to think along broad monetary policy lines which assign weight to gold reserves, among other things."

In sum, the gold backing to a currency carries either psychological or disciplinary weight in the Great Money Game, but not redeemability.

The Numbers Game

The list of reasons against attempting to open a spy- or Mafia-famed numbered account at a Swiss bank is formidable, and its advantages truly few (see also Chapter 8). And yet, this one type of account has gained more fame for Swiss banks than any other, and continues to be of greatest interest of any available. It is the stubbornest holdout among myths related to bank secrecy, and reports of its demise as a provocateur of rumor are, as Mark Twain observed under parallel personal circumstances, exaggerated.

The first misconception about the numbered account is its exact meaning. All accounts at Swiss banks, as with any modern bank anywhere in the world, are numbered; that is, they have numbers assigned to them. But in Switzerland, a "numbered account" properly refers only to those accounts which have the connection between the number and name of its owner separated and kept secret except to a very few employees of the bank branch where the account is opened. This is accomplished by holding all account records in number only when they are handled by regular employees of the bank. The bank's vault or minimum-access locked files contain the names corresponding to the numbers. Still, some persons must have access to the connecting papers. The customer's man who opens the account will obviously know the tie. So will some back-office person and secretary responsible for correspondence between the bank and the numbered account holder, unless it is always given in person. And the bank manager will have access to the name-number association record if he so desires. Compared with regular accounts, where any employee having to deal with the account, from the investment department on securities trades, to bullion or foreign exchange clerks and interest recording staff, can see the name on any account, the limitation to a few persons handling numbered account records is sharp. But it is not a fail-proof concept. Given the legal stifling of comment about any Swiss account, numbered or not, this limited access only offers a degree of improved protection against inadvertent remarks or accepted bribes.

The active myths about the numbered account are still multiple, if gradually declining. The purest of these myths is that they are the only accounts afforded the full protection of the secrecy laws. Of course, we have already stated that all Swiss accounts have precisely the same safeguards, numbered or not. Correspondingly, violations of criminal statutes in Switzerland will pry open both numbered and regular accounts with equal ease. The press made a good deal of fuss about the alleged numbered account into which Edith Irving deposited the McGraw-Hill funds, claiming that it was a "super-secret" account. There is no such thing. Moreover, Swiss Credit Bank later announced that the account was a regular account, not a numbered account at all. And the bank insists that it would have handled the matter of information about either a numbered or regular account in the Irving case in precisely the same manner.

The idea that numbered accounts are widely used in intelligence gathering activities to wash informational money payoffs and other nefarious activities was probably true at one time. Intelligence services have used numbered accounts in the past, but such use has almost certainly lessened. Spies dislike nothing more than publicity, which they have certainly received in Switzerland. With the availability of several other bank secrecy havens in the world, few self respecting spies any longer need the difficulty of opening numbered accounts in the land of the yodel. What is more, regular accounts held by paper (but legally established) corporations serve the purpose just as well. Thus, much of that intelligence gathering money which has not left Switzerland is probably buried under corporate facades in regular accounts.

The same conditions apply to Mafia/underworld money. The plausibility of past reportage of the Mafia/underworld use of numbered accounts has made the concept virtually irrefutable. But equally irrefutable is the high degree of probability that most such funds have journeyed away from the light of publicity, however shrouded by secrecy it might have remained for a time. On too many occasions the time period has been only temporary; and a temporary cover isn't worth the risk. What is more, any such illegal underworld funds almost certainly had to be placed in Switzerland without the complicity of any major Swiss bank, as I suggested in Chapter 2. Now with all the fame gained by such potential uses of Swiss banks, the bankers have become both more aware and diligent in ferreting out the simple masks used to cover these funds. Why undertake the difficult in Switzerland when the simple will suffice elsewhere—say Lebanon, Mexico, or Hong Kong? Both the spy and Mafia uses of Swiss banks are likely, at best, overblown in their extent. At their least, they are pure myth. The truth probably lies somewhere toward the minimal end of the scale, with just one certainty in the entire matter: no one can know the full reality, not even the Swiss bankers. We have only probabilities.

"Banks which must depend upon customer confidence for their business, cannot act fraudulently for long," offers Swiss Credit Bank's Dr. Mast. "The interest of honesty in dealing with customers is primary. A bad account, a shady customer, simply cost too much. Look at the cost of the Irvings case [reportedly upward of $100,000 in direct expenses for the banks involved]."

In addition to these myths, pure or diluted, there is the naïve belief in some quarters that one can open a numbered or regular account with equal ease. Not so.

Partly due to the infamy which now surrounds numbered accounts, partly for legal reasons, Swiss bankers
become suspicious when being asked by Americans to
open these accounts.

"We are very reluctant for Americans," one major
bank customer's man explained to me, "because
Americans are required to declare existence of their
foreign accounts to the IRS. Therefore, we must
wonder why they want the most protected of secret
accounts?" There may be reasons, he implied, but the
modest request to open one will still be met with
suspicion. This skepticism progresses to questions of
those wishing a numbered account. They will always
be asked in person; numbered accounts cannot be
opened by mail in the practice of most banks. The
apparently innocuous inquiry as to whether one will
accept correspondence at home or business is another
key for the Swiss banker. A negative reply for either
address, or even a demurral, will raise further doubts
about the legitimacy of the account. Why would one
not want to receive unmarked Swiss letters at his most
useful address?

"We will definitely refuse the account if we are
concerned about its reality," offered a banker, "and
we will either refuse it outright, or set a very substantial
minimum on it. One we are quite certain cannot be
met." These numbered account minimums are usually
left vague until other questions have been answered.
As a result, one may hear amounts ranging from as low
as $25,000 to that stated publicly by a "Big Three"
bank at $100,000. The Swiss know that those prospec-
tive numbered account users who truly want the ac-

count will ante up. Only competition from smaller banks keeps the minimum size within reason. Some would say even that "reason" is a substantial deterrent to a numbered account. They're catching on.

Since numbered accounts are opened in person only, the prospect will be asked to produce a passport identification and register the account in that name alone unless accompanied by others joining the account, also in person and with passports in hand. Most banks will not accept numbered accounts from corporations any longer, a function of dislike of the anonymity they afford, nor will they accept any "dummy" or anonymous names. I have yet to find a bank making an exception to the anonymous name prohibition, although I have been told that some small banks will.

Over and above these inquiries and roadblocks is the matter of references. With numbered accounts they are *de rigueur* at most banks unless you are already known to them. The reference matter requires a bit of verbal juggling on the part of the Swiss bankers, and in some cases references may be checked only for existence, not for direct inquiry about a prospective account holder. But of one thing you may be certain: Your Swiss banker cannot tell your reference his real reason for inquiry. To say that the inquiry is being made for the purpose of your opening a Swiss bank account would be an admission that you were seeking one, and later if an account was opened, prima facie evidence that one could exist. This is a potential violation of the bank secrecy laws, something fervently avoided. Instead, the inquiry to your reference may come as an alleged information request from a prospective business associate or a Swiss exporting firm wishing to extend you credit, but not for the purpose of opening a bank account.

If the foregoing hurdles haven't deterred all prospective numbered account holders, a final inconvenience can be added. Persons traveling outside the United States are required to declare whether they are carrying $5,000 or more in cash on any one trip. There is nothing illegal about carrying the funds, but they must be declared. Since numbered account deposit minimums are substantially above this level, several trips would have to be made to avoid the traveler's admission and identification on capital export. This transfer can be accomplished more readily by bank draft directly to the Swiss bank after formalities have been attended to on a personal visit, but the Bank Secrecy Act requires domestic bank notification to the Treasury of all transactions involving $10,000 or more. Thus, the multiple payment inconvenience is still left, if privacy is to be maximized. Even then, a record of all payments over $100 is kept on file at your bank, a product of the same act. That desire for privacy through a numbered account in Switzerland has taken on the aspect of being surrounded by a barbed wire fence. Funny, that seems to be what Congress had in mind.

What are the advantages of the numbered account? For nonresidents of Switzerland they are miniscule. As we have seen, the obvious one, increased secrecy protection, is both a sometimes matter and a relative one at that. Increased secrecy does not come from increased legal protection, but only prevention of multiple-person access to bank records. This access can only be circumvented by specific information

ferreting about a specific account, or bribes of connected employees. Formal legal proceedings undertaken from the United States, even under the new
Mutual Assistance Treaty (see Chapter 8), require equal
concurrence of a Swiss court for either regular or numbered accounts. Thus, the question is one of whether
it is likely that anyone, including those attached to a
U.S. government agency, would go to bribery efforts
over your account. If so, the numbered account might
be useful. If not, why bother?

There can be some advantage in holding a numbered
account for inheritance purposes, but, again, this same
advantage applies to the regular account. Since there
is no inheritance tax applied in Switzerland, someone
wishing to draw on joint account funds held under individual signature rights could do so upon the death
of one party without probate of the funds. But this
would require the omission of such funds in U.S. reports required for estate purposes, a clear violation
of U.S. tax laws.

Since these deterrents would seem to turn away all
but the most ardent criminals or those persons with
some other compelling reason to snare a numbered
account, we can reveal that which most curiosity seek-
ers will never see elsewhere. This is what a numbered
account looks like:

430 879 XQ3

That's it, at least at one large bank. Two sets of
three numbers followed by a combination of three
letters or numbers. But this number varies from bank
to bank. It can be five numbers followed by two letters,

as well. Or any other combination. Even this is imprecise in the land of great precision.

The Great Ice Box

A final myth about Swiss banks is perhaps the simplest to dispel. For lack of a more precise sobriquet, "frigid gnome" will do. More a function of the alpine remoteness of Switzerland than anything to do with bank secrecy is the long-standing popular belief that Swiss banks and bankers are cold, austere, and given to scurrying to hidden mountain vaults with the world's money. This image can only be entertained by persons unenlightened by a visit to the country. Once inside, the myth disappears like snow in a spring meadow. All but the private banks are very publicly oriented, and the private concerns are legally prevented from so being by a provision of the Federal Banking Act which prohibits them from soliciting public business. Their small brass name plaques on older austere-looking buildings are more than revelations that gnomes live there. They are the private bankers conservative reaction to the law.

The major banks, and even many smaller public institutions, are solicitous of public business to the full measure of the law. Enormous window displays of fine graphic treatment of historical periods, modern art, housing construction, or the Swiss tool and die industry, are constant features of the large banks along the Bahnhofstrasse in Zurich or the Rue de la Confederation in Geneva. Three-foot high gold coin replicas adorned the windows of one bank in Zurich in 1974.

Real gold coins from a dozen countries embellish the street display of another. Paper money from every conceivable nation is placed on view. Television presentations of constantly changing stock prices from around the world are ubiquitous in every major city bank window. This is all done with taste, mind you, but one still has the impression that the only bank-offered commodity that has not yet been flaunted are the bankers themselves. So far, they only make speeches, preside at public gatherings, and serve in the army.

The major banks are prolific publishers. Union Bank's red-bordered pamphlets cover every conceivable subject from gold to foreign exchange, from founding a business in Switzerland to their annual report. Swiss Credit Bank and Swiss Bank Corporation publish nearly as many informational pieces, along with monthly bulletins featuring extensive graphics. Swiss Bank Corporation published a 500-page 8 × 10 inch, gold monogramed, hard-covered history of the bank to celebrate its 100th anniversary in 1972 and undertook a series of public events that year that may outdo the U.S. Bicentennial celebrations. The same bank's Centenary Foundation donated over SFr. 1 million in the first 20 months of its operation to charitable causes in the country. The bank's Foundation for Promotion of Housing Construction began construction on 637 flats in five Swiss cities, and acquired land or projected an additional 730 more in two years' operation to the beginning of 1974. A competition organized by the bank to test Swiss knowledge of money matters and banking services drew 87,000 entries from around the country in 1973.

In 1972 and 1973, Union Bank organized a series of

After Work Concerts in six cities as part of an ongoing cultural program. They were attended by nearly 27,000 people in the second year alone. The bank also participated in six domestic and five foreign fairs during the same year.

All of this is only the tip of the iceberg of Swiss bank promotional activities. Regular speeches by senior bank officials are made around the globe, with the Economic Clubs of Detroit and New York being two favorite U.S. forums for their pronouncements. Banker participation in private monetary conferences are frequent, if not as common as direct speeches. Radio, television, and press interviews are granted regularly, if with a somewhat wary countenance. Visitors and prospective customers are greeted with an openness which can be disarming to the uninitiated "frigid gnome" believer. Dinners and cocktails flow easily, even in staid Zurich, for those with important business to transact or where even a brief rapport has been established.

The inclination of Swiss bankers to be open and friendly has its limits, of course. It is fair to say that they fall far short of the image projected by the cold, austere banker myth which still lingers almost inexplicably in the nonfinancial world. Swiss bank competitors know better.

A favorite Swiss saying goes, "Don't sell the rabbits' fur before he's been shot." Where Swiss myths are concerned, we can add, "and be sure it's a rabbit, not a banker, before you shoot."

Chapter eight

The Pros and Cons

EVERYTHING we do with our money must have its list of advantages and disadvantages. That's as basic as apple pie. And it is certainly true about Swiss banks.[1]

But there is a problem. The reasons listed in favor of Swiss bank accounts by most potential depositors aren't "normal." That is, they don't fit the usual pattern for choosing one's bank. Normally we consider quite simple reasons for selecting one bank over another, and the banks promote them in vying for our cash. Inevitably they are: convenience, costs, personal relationship, or services. However, Swiss banks are inconvenient for everyone but the Swiss, and most offer little in a personal relationship potential as a result. Plus, they are more expensive to use than U.S. banks. That leaves only services in the usual list, and, as we have seen, these they have in abundance. You just have to overlook the inconvenience, impersonality, and costs

---

[1] Author's note: This list must necessarily touch upon facts and comment made, in some cases, in other parts of the book. A certain amount of redundancy is regrettably unavoidable.

to obtain them, and in so doing, ignore three out of four advantages which most banks think are important. Unless Swiss bank services can overcome their other disadvantages, clearly there must be new advantages that Swiss banks have over their competitors. There are, but those new advantages add complications. First, let us look at the "normal" aspects of a banking relationship.

Convenience, Costs, and Personality

Most major banks are so determined that a branch on every corner is the formula for success that they are virtually falling over one another seeking space. Among the more vehement in the branching vocation has been Barclay's Bank of Britain. Through its International Division (renamed from DCO: Dominion, Commonwealth and Overseas) Barclay's has acquired more than 5,000 branches in nearly 50 different countries. More than 45 percent of these are outside the United Kingdom. Other British banks are nearly as aggressive. National Westminster has about two thirds the foreign branches of Barclay's, and Lloyd's Bank in 1974 acquired the near 50 branch system of California's First Western Bank in a major competitive move against Barclay's in the Golden State. The two most expansive U.S. banks, Bank of America and First National Citibank of New York, have 104 and 252 foreign branches, respectively. While this represents a considerable falling off from Barclay's pace, it also reflects a sharp difference in the size of domestic markets and the practice that a bank doesn't go afield to obtain what it can get at home.

And the Swiss? Internally, they are the greatest of branch bankers. Their convenience is spread through 473 banks with over 4,500 branches in an area only the size of Maine. However, the Swiss branch banks combined have only ten true branches outside Switzerland. In the United States, they have opened only five branches. Swiss Bank Corporation has branches in New York, Chicago, and San Francisco. Swiss Credit Bank will accept deposits through New York and Los Angeles. But Union Bank of Switzerland, with nineteen "representative" offices worldwide, has only three in the United States, and none accept deposits. They are in New York, Chicago, and San Francisco. What is more, the banks in Switzerland have jointly agreed to limit their domestic expansion until 1977. Hardly aggressive banking at all.

This suggests the Swiss know something about their drawing power. Given their deposit growth in the past few years (except 1973, when the Big Three showed a small deposit decline due to the negative interest rate and curtailment of expansion), they clearly haven't needed to open convenient branches to get foreign deposits. Convenience simply has not been nearly as important to Swiss banks' foreign operations as to major American or British banks.

Swiss banks certainly cannot have the personal relationship factor working for them with Americans. It is rather difficult to hold a "personal" relationship across an ocean, even though a correspondence can be developed. They emphatically do not advertise themselves as "friendly", either, and in offering depositors a four-language statement only twice a year, can hardly be considered warm communicators. Swiss banks also do not have a list of free services or give away items as are often touted by banks in the United States to tempt your money into their vaults. Indeed, the personal touches offered by Swiss bankers are few, and usually, when given, follow the arrival of your deposit, rather than preceed it.

We have already noted the costs of doing business with Swiss banks in general terms in Chapter 6. Additional details are below under the heading "Some Negatives." Suffice to say here that Swiss bank fees add up rapidly to more than those charged by most American banks.

The Drummer Factor

Illegalities aside, who in his right mind would send a decent amount of money 3,000–6,000 miles away, if it weren't for some concern or outright fear for its safety or its potential at home? At the same time, the sender's neighbors haven't budged a dime. Who would brave language barriers and increased banking costs in Switzerland if there wasn't a fear for privacy or profits at home? Others seem to think the Citizens' Bank of Sheboygan is terribly private/profitable. Taking advantage of a monetary crisis or the alpine rise and fall of a floating currency to invest through a Swiss bank may evoke a gambler's instinct in one person and leave another cold. The remoteness of the Swiss money depositories from the United States may chill the security thoughts of someone who has never been more than a few blocks away from his hard-earned green, but be of precisely no concern to someone who makes a living by telex or international telephone circuits.

The winds over Watergate and the recurring financial storms of recent years have definitely blown a good deal of money across the Atlantic, much of it to Switzerland. And yet, by winter 1974–75 no harm had come to 99.9 percent of American bank accounts as a result of these storms.

In all, this suggests a "different drummer" factor is at work on Americans considering Swiss banks. Either that, or almost everyone with a Swiss account is doing something illegal. Since we can't know that aspect of bank business, although we have discussed several known cases of it, let's consider what might be causing a "drummer" action. It looks suspiciously like an education process, and not by the Swiss. They rarely publish anything in the United States but an annual balance sheet in the *Wall Street Journal*.

A more likely source of the drumbeats has occurred through sharply heightened public familiarity with the scope of the world's economic ills. The popular media, both sophisticated and mundane, have made "inflation," "monetary crisis," and "devaluation" household words within the past seven years. And yet the media have rarely suggested solutions, if any indeed exist. They have done little but explain the complexities to a still puzzled public. It seems logical to assume that a curious and directly affected public has turned increasingly to a new source of understanding and solution: those "new Jeremiahs" and other prophets of the gloom noted in Chapter 2. They are among the few who appear to "understand" the situation, and most important, they offer solutions — admittedly bleak, but solutions. And they are being read. Harry Browne's book, *You Can Profit from a Monetary Crisis*, sold more than 250,000 copies in hard-cover during 1973–74. He along with Harry Schultz and James Dines, both of whom say they have "thousands" of subscribers to their investment letters (Dines employs a staff of 30), have been the leaders in explaining the monetary muddle. Their solutions to your problems with the world's monetary mess all include gold and Swiss banks. It is distinctly possible that they are being listened to, along with businessmen, economists, and educators who are familiar with Swiss banks.

In identifying this additional factor for the popularity of Swiss banks in recent years, we are led to an observation which will be useful perspective for our pro/con balance: the popularity (and therefore the plus-column balance) of Swiss banks is now being increased in their favor by the political and economic troubles of the world and our personal fears about those troubles. Switzerland has the image of mountain retreat tranquillity, both real and fabled, compared to the world around it. As we recognize this image, bolster it with many rumors and a handful of facts during troubled times, we are readily inclined to make pluses out of Swiss bank minuses or super-pluses out of modest advantages.

Through numerous conversations with Swiss bank users and potential users, it has become clear that their first view of Swiss bank advantages and disadvantages comes from their ability to protect money against threats perceived, plus profit motives, personal financial condition, and illegal temptations. With these subjective factors in mind, coupled with the push being given by economic drummers, we can now examine the true pros and cons of Swiss banks.

A pattern will develop from the following discussion which, if you fit it, will reveal you to be far more likely to profit from a Swiss account than those who don't.

Privacy

The Great Theme upon which the strongest Swiss pluses are built is privacy. It plays counterpoint, background, and main melody at varying times. And it typifies the subjectivity of certain arguments. Privacy for whom? Privacy compared to what? Privacy for what reasons? These are valid questions which we must presume entail some boundaries, and perhaps suggest the greater need for awareness on the part of many persons who find it uncomfortable to think internationally about money.

Certainly, there is privacy in the United States. It does appear to have been well eroded from past levels with gulleys made by credit card computer systems, data banks, and the recently court-approved Bank Secrecy Act.

In 1971, Professor Arthur R. Miller of the University of Michigan Law School told the Senate Subcommittee on Constitutional Rights that the average American was the subject of between 10 and 20 dossiers in government and private files. By 1974, the Subcommittee's investigation of this phenomenon was still continuing, spurred by what many observers are now suggesting is too easily forced accessibility to confidential information. In no way has this been made more clear than through the dramatic revelations of the Watergate scandals, of course. Daniel Ellsberg's psychiatrist, many of those connected with the "plumbers" activities, and the juries' convicting top White House aides would suggest those observers have valid concerns. Charges of CIA domestic spying, White-House directed IRS audits, and FBI files on leading Congressmen have added to our fears.

As previously explained, the U.S. Bank Secrecy Act of 1970 now authorizes your bank to reveal to government authorities any check you have written in an amount over $100. Banks must also immediately report to the IRS the transfer of $10,000 or more from any account, and you must declare any amount of $5,000 or more taken overseas. The act's ostensible purpose is to trace illegal, principally underworld, money flows where crimes are suspected. Many people concerned with civil liberties believe it could be used far more extensively against average citizens than simply on a Mafia or tax-dodging money hunt.

All this notwithstanding, privacy still exists in the United States in relative strength to many foreign countries. We are constantly reminded of this through the suspension of liberties and investigation of citizens through the unending stream of South American coups. The Chilean military overthrow of the Allende regime in 1973 was a notable recent example; reports of CIA involvement only strengthened the point. The Portugese counter-coup in early 1975, with its suddenly Communist-leaning government, should remind us how quickly even modest freedoms can be dispatched. Nevertheless, we have been forced in the United States to add some doubts to our feelings of secure monetary privacy. These doubts have spurred a degree of urgency in discovering the kinds of privacy offered elsewhere.

There is privacy in Mexico, for instance, at least

where bank accounts are concerned, since they have numbered accounts as does Switzerland. This, clearly, was a fact not overlooked by those involved with money "washing" in 1972, prior to certain deposits being transferred to the Republican National Committee and CREEP. The same type of secret numbered accounts are available in Lebanon, Hong Kong, and Singapore. But none have the solid criminal penalties for violators of secrecy that Switzerland does. Few have the 100-year tradition behind bank secrecy that Switzerland does, either. And none have the 700-year history of privacy found in the alpine country. As we have seen, that history has been the basis for the Swiss granting political asylum from persecution in other countries, as well as monetary privacy, for many years. Alexander Solzhenitsyn is only the most recent of a long line of political escapees to Switzerland, which also includes Napoleon III and Lenin. That tradition of providing protection from political denials of privacy is also part of the firm ground upon which Swiss banking secrecy is founded. It has been continued and strengthened through the 20th century.

Probably the most demonstrable evidence of Swiss determination to maintain monetary privacy occurred in the early 1930s, when Switzerland reacted to Hitler's fanatical despotism in Germany. The Nazi regime in 1933 had become infuriated over the flight of capital from Germany, a flight which was frequently stopping just over the border in Switzerland. Literally thousands of Germans had sent funds out of their country in anticipation of Hitler's suppression of civil liberties. Thus, a law was promulgated in Germany ordering all citizens to declare their foreign holdings. Failure to comply carried the death penalty. Most Germans who had exported capital felt they had no choice but to put their trust in the Swiss not to reveal information on their personal finances, and a great many Germans did not report their accounts across the border. And a great many Gestapo agents were sent into Switzerland as a result. The latter's methods and techniques are still described by the Swiss as "diabolical and clever."[2] They included not only bribes but efforts to deposit funds under suspected account names at various Swiss banks. If the funds were accepted by a bank, this was considered proof that the person named held an account at the bank. If that fact hadn't been reported, the death penalty was invoked. One famous inducement case involved a young lady employee of a Swiss bank who had made a few offhand comments about depositors to her boyfriend, undoubtedly, as it turned out, with some prompting. He, of course, was later exposed as a Gestapo agent.[3]

As these methods of ferreting information became known to the Swiss government, it reacted to further protect the banking secrecy tradition. In 1934, the Swiss National Council ratified a law which put banking secrecy under official protection of the penal codes. The law, which was revised in March 1971, reads in part:

> 1. Whoever divulges a secret entrusted to him in his capacity as officer, employee, authorized agent, liquidator or commissioner of a bank, as a representative of the Bank-

---

[2] Swiss Bank Corporation, Swiss Credit Bank, and Union Bank of Switzerland, booklet, *The Truth About Swiss Banking* (undated).
[3] Ibid.

number of potential candidates. Remember, the person you want is almost certainly now employed and not answering help wanted ads.

4. Ask tough questions in the interview.

Your candidate may have 20 years of yesterdays. You cannot review them adequately in a 30-minute interview.

The interview should be longer than that and should cover the candidate's goals, his track record, his outstanding qualities, and why your firm interests him.

5. Check secondary references.

Talk to the references he gives you, but be sure to talk also to all previous bosses as well as co-workers. Do not ask for their views in writing. You will get more candid opinions in person or over the phone.

6. Push for a positive choice.

You should wind up choosing between two or three outstanding candidates. If there is only one, keep looking.

"The tunnel may seem long," says recruiter Broyles, "but at the end of it will be a winner."

One Reason for Opening a Swiss Bank Account

Opening a Swiss bank account is a good hedge against inflation, one expert says.

"Inflation has become a way of life for our federal government," says James Kelder, author of "How to Open a Swiss Bank Account" (Thomas Y. Crowell Co, New York, $9.95).

"That means the dollar has become a soft currency. It will continue to lose value compared to a hard currency like the Swiss franc."

Here is Mr. Kelder's case for putting your savings in hard (meaning shrink-resistant) money such as Switzerland's.

In late 1970, the dollar was worth 4.31 Swiss francs. So a $1,000 deposit in a Swiss bank would have given you a balance of 4,310 Swiss francs.

Since then, the dollar has diminished in value.

On Sept. 1, 1976, the dollar was worth only 2.47 Swiss francs. So the 4,310 francs in the Swiss bank was worth $1,744.93.

In addition, the account would have earned at least 3.5 percent interest, compounded annually. That would have added another 438.1 francs, or $177.36.

The total: $1,922.29.

The same $1,000 deposited in an American bank would still be worth $1,000 plus interest.

Swiss bankers welcome small accounts as well as large ones.

"Many of Switzerland's most respected banks will open an account for $100 or less," Mr. Kelder says.

Of course, there are drawbacks, such as these:

• Swiss banks pay interest on only the first 50,000 francs in a non-Swiss account.

• Nonresidents are allowed only one interest-earning account.

• The Swiss government collects a 30 percent withholding tax on all interest income. Americans, however, can get five sixths of the tax refunded.

And then, there is no Federal Deposit Insurance Corp. insurance of Swiss accounts.

Stock Prices During Election Years

Stock prices tend to peak late in the year when Americans elect a President.

William X. Scheinman, of Arthur Wiesenberger & Co., Inc., makes that observation in a series of stock market studies called "Timings."

He says there has been a further tendency in the past 100 years for the market to reach important peaks during all years ending in 6.

Stock prices during all election years of this century, he adds, have persistently tended to rally from a June low to an August high.

Where does the market go from there?

"If the incumbent party loses the presidency, then the August high, which incidentally is usually lower than the January opening, tends to be the high point for the remainder of the year."

However, if the incumbent party holds on to the White House, Mr. Scheinman says, the outcome is different. Then the August high is not only typically higher than the January opening, but it is also followed by a higher year-end high.

There is no clue to what happens if Wall Street decides to break a century-old tradition.

THIS STAMP GETS YOUR LETTER WHERE IT'S GOING.

THIS STAMP GETS YOUR LETTER WHERE IT'S GOING, AND EVEN HELPS GET IT THERE FASTER BECAUSE IT'S DATED, CANCELLED, POSTMARKED BY THE POSTAGE METER THAT PRINTS IT. ESPECIALLY IMPORTANT WITH POSTAL COSTS RISING, YOU ALWAYS HAVE THE RIGHT DENOMINATION. THE POSTAGE METER MAKES AN AUTOMATIC BOOKKEEPING RECORD, AND YOU CAN NEVER LOSE OR TEAR A METER STAMP.

≻∺ Pitney Bowes

Because business travels
at the speed of paper.

PITNEY BOWES, 1365 PACIFIC STREET, STAMFORD, CONN. 06904. 190 OFFICES THROUGHOUT THE U.S. AND CANADA. POSTAGE METERS, MAILING SYSTEMS, COPIERS, COUNTERS AND IMPRINTERS, ADDRESSER/PRINTERS, LABELING AND MARKING SYSTEMS.

ing Commission, officer or employee of a recognized auditing company, or who has become aware of such a secret in this capacity, and whoever tries to induce others to violate professional secrecy, shall be punished by a prison term not to exceed six months or by a fine not exceeding 50,000 Swiss francs.

2. If the act has been committed by negligence, the penalty shall be a fine not exceeding 30,000 Swiss francs.

3. The violation of professional secrecy remains punishable even after termination of the official or employment relationship or the exercise of the profession.

This law and the practice of numbering accounts protected a great number of Germans, despite the Gestapo efforts which continued for many years. It remains the key for any individual's belief that his money matters will remain private while they are being dealt with in Switzerland. It is a virtually unique concept in the world, and with the backing of history, has made Switzerland both famous and wealthy, and made several million persons more confident about their financial resources. Quite clearly, this privacy has attracted many persons of doubtful intentions who have made the system work for illegal gains, as we noted in Chapter 2. This has led to some highly celebrated court cases, all of which serve to focus the world's attention on Swiss banking secrecy. Some of this attention has been highly critical. However, as an editorial in *Barron's* (January 20, 1969) put the matter: "Just because almost all other countries have given up what for centuries had been a globally upheld financial freedom, the Swiss are not believed to have the slightest inclination to follow suit. . . . Why should the Swiss banking system give up the very discretion for which it is world-renowned and respected?"

It would seem that this is the context in which potential depositors should view Swiss bank privacy. Governments have great abilities to deny privacy. It is up to individuals to take personal steps to protect it.

However, as was also pointed out in Chapter 2, Swiss bank secrecy is hardly absolute. When one wanders into the quasi-legal world of tax avoidance or potential fraud, privacy can disappear as quickly as the spring alpine snow.

As the Big Three Swiss banks stated the matter in their booklet, *The Truth about Swiss Banking:* "Contrary to popular belief, there are limitations on banking secrecy in Switzerland. Banks are obliged to furnish pertinent information when the higher interest of the public or the state are involved, particularly in cases defined as crimes by Swiss law. The purpose of banking secrecy is to protect the innocent, not to shield the guilty, and history has demonstrated its usefulness."

If that sounds a bit smug, you should ask the Irvings.

One important aspect of Swiss bank privacy, the difference between numbered and regular accounts, has already been discussed in Chapter 6. Suffice to say here that there is no legal difference and only small practical differences between the two. The availability of numbered accounts cannot be considered a plus for Swiss banks in any legal sense.

Judicial Assistance

Since taxation is one of the more onerous burdens faced by citizens everywhere, its avoidance (not a crime in Switzerland) is often the moral peg onto which a citizen hangs his devices to gain Swiss privacy. The recently concluded U.S.–Swiss Mutual Assistance Treaty brings this point into focus. The treaty is the culmination of several years of negotiations between the Swiss and American authorities over the issue of illegally gotten money flows from the United States to Switzerland—principally underworld money. The treaty was prompted by pressure from criminal law enforcement officials, securities law regulators at the SEC, monetary authorities at the U.S. Treasury, and the Internal Revenue Service. They all wanted the cooperation of the Swiss in tracing alleged criminals through name- or event-associated data. The Swiss staunchly refused to cooperate in investigation of alleged crimes on the basis of tax avoidance because they don't see it as a crime.

The matter of tax fraud versus tax avoidance requires some clarification as there is a fine line between the two. Basically, fraud is involved where a statement is made or documentation given about alleged non-existence of certain income. Tax avoidance is the simple omission of reporting the income without any supporting statement or data. This technicality is one upon which Swiss and American authorities agree, but act upon in different ways. The distinction is not usually important in the United States except in fixing the degree of penalty; both avoidance and fraud are crimes. With the administered tax system in Switzerland, only fraud is a crime.

This distinction is recognized in the Mutual Assistance Treaty and was a fundamental point of argument during the Swiss National Assembly's ratification process. (See Chapter 9 for a leading Swiss banker's comments on this point).

As the Treaty stands, the Swiss will not cooperate in fishing expeditions into their banks, nor on tax avoidance matters in the United States. The Swiss federal government would cooperate where fraud against a Swiss institution is suspected, or where documentation denying tax avoidance exists along with reasonable evidence of the avoidance. The Swiss are also prepared to assist with special measures against organized crime.

The following general summary of the Treaty is pertinent.

A LAYMAN'S SUMMARY OF THE
UNITED STATES–SWITZERLAND
JUDICIAL ASSISTANCE TREATY*

The United States and Switzerland signed the Treaty on Mutual Assistance in Criminal Matters in Berne on May 25, 1973. [It had been ratified by the Upper House of the Swiss National Assembly and was awaiting ratification by the Lower House prior to U.S. Senate discussion, on January 1, 1975]

The Treaty contains 41 articles grouped in nine chapters and a Schedule listing 35 categories of offenses to which the Treaty is applicable. It is supplemented by six exchanges of letters interpreting language used in certain provisions of the Treaty.

The Treaty represents the first major agreement for the United States with any country in the area of mutual assistance in criminal matters. For Switzerland, it represents the first agreement of this type with a country having an Anglo-Saxon system of law. A number of the provisions of the Treaty are based on provisions in the European Convention on

---

* Courtesy of the United States Embassy, Berne, Switzerland.

Mutual Assistance in Criminal Matters to which Switzerland is a party.

Portions of the Treaty establish an obligation to furnish assistance in connection with investigations or court proceedings on selected offenses. Compulsory measures are generally required in connection with criminal offenses in both countries and are listed in the Schedule to the Treaty. The document does not create any new crimes in either nation. It is limited to providing each country additional evidence and information for use in prosecuting crimes established by its domestic law. This includes assistance in locating witnesses, obtaining of statements and testimony of witnesses, production and authentication of business records, and service of judicial or administrative documents.

Organized crime cases are covered by special sections of the Treaty and provide for extra assistance where such cases are involved. The document recognizes the widespread dangers of such crimes to society and that the international scope of operations justifies needs for special legal assistance.

Tax crimes are excluded from the Treaty and are governed exclusively by the Convention of May 24, 1951, on Avoidance of Double Taxation, between the United States and Switzerland. Tax matters where organized crime is concerned are delineated in the Treaty itself.

Certain provisions of the Treaty deal with the Swiss concept of banking secrecy and provide for highly selective and limited occasions under which this secrecy can be overcome, especially in connection with serious crimes in the United States.

Finally, it is expected that most requests for assistance under the Treaty will be undertaken at the requests of the two countries' Departments of Justice.

Full copies of the Treaty may be obtained from the United States Department of State, the Department of Justice and the Department of the Treasury.

Another factor relating to privacy is that prompted by concerns over a pending or threatened dissolution of marriage. Lawyers say that such actions may be one of the major instigations of Swiss account openings. Here, Swiss authorities have little interest in providing exceptions to their fabled privacy. A husband may stash away funds in a Swiss account and even swear to its nonexistence in an American court (running risk of perjury, of course), and have little chance of being discovered. Even if the American court requested assistance of a Swiss court in determining bank balances, experts say it is doubtful if the Swiss court would find sufficient exception to banking secrecy to check all Swiss banks for the existence of family assets. Sequestering funds from relatives, including a wife, is not a crime in Switzerland.

Interestingly enough, however, a wife may not be given the same protection in legal matrimonial proceedings under Swiss courts. Husbands can sometimes obtain permission to inspect a wife's account under Swiss law, an extension of the highly male-dominated society of the Swiss which only recently gave women full suffrage. Women's liberation is hardly considered an "in" concept in Switzerland.

In sum, Switzerland does indeed provide privacy that is almost unique in the world. Why you might wish to make use of that privacy, for positive or negative reasons, out of legal or illegal motives, is a personal consideration which must color that uniqueness for you.

Stability

A second major factor weighing on the plus side of Swiss accounts is stability. Stability of the government, stability of the economy, stability of the currency. Change and uncertainty is the single major factor in giving people sleepless nights about their money. Whether it is money in the stock market, money in a strike-torn, economically wracked economy, or money caught in the throes of a political coup or other upheaval, the fact of pending or threatened change in dramatic form is one of the most significant stimuli to our collective money-protective natures. The relative absence of these changes in Switzerland for the past 125 years has led invariably to its positive image as a safe haven for money. Here, history weighs so heavily that there can be little argument that political and economic stability of the country is a major plus for anyone considering a Swiss bank account. A brief return to that history can be helpful here.

As previously explained, the neutrality of Switzerland has been guaranteed by the major European powers since 1815, a factor which has not been changed by the colossal political and economic upheavals surrounding the tiny country since then. The Swiss, of course, would be the last to wish a change in neutrality status, and the European powers have largely found Switzerland to be a useful island in their stormy history. The federal government has flowered since 1848, not seriously threatened in its decentralized democratic form to this day. No other important country in the world has been excluded as a combatant in a war or untouched by revolution for as long. The Swiss are determined to keep it so.

As a result, when Americans on rare occasions are beset by concerns about a political change or a social upheaval in their country, as many have been over the past decade, they turn naturally to the political stability of Switzerland. It matches that of the United States, and, without a civil war in 125 years, even tops it.

Switzerland and America did undergo revolutionary changes within a decade of each other just before the turn of the 19th century. In Switzerland, as we have noted, this was also the period of the establishment of the major private banks giving them a lengthy record of stable growth after the upheaval. Of those formed at that time, the largest are now Lombard, Odier, Pictet, and Julius Bär (the newcomer of nearly a century later). They are estimated to account for approximately $5 billion in portfolio assets among them. The Big Three public banks date back nearly as far, with the oversubscribed sale of Swiss Credit Bank to the public in 1856 up to the 1912 merger birth of Union Bank. These giants are now believed to control assets and portfolios worth close to $100 billion, making them distinct rivals to New York and London banks in the Goliath world of high finance. In age alone, however, it is Barclay's of London which is the Methuselah: over 350 years have passed since its birth. Interestingly enough, despite the century-old beginnings of most important Swiss banks, it wasn't until 1907 that the nation formed a central bank. This was largely a function of the decentralized federal concept of government; there simply had been little need for one. Now, the country is the home of the best known *central* bankers' central bank, the place where so many of the late 1960s' monetary crises were thrashed out, the Bank for International Settlements in Basle.

While the Swiss banks were founded as an outgrowth of manufacturing or as a refuge for political escapees' funds, they emerged shortly as the most deft and experienced dealers in money and its investment for their clients. Three and four generations of families have held their accounts at the same bank and have been rewarded with not only success in investments, but numerous favors. The banking establishment and its clients have grown apace in service to country and local civic causes. Their ties are often inseparable.

By the time of World War I, Swiss banks had established themselves as important purveyors of funds to the country's own cantons and several foreign nations as well. We have noted this as a function of traditional Swiss interest in capital export. In the aftermath of the war, the banks became major lenders to war-ravaged countries and furthered their reputation as bankers who kept their pledges and were willing to take measurable risks in doing so. Through Zurich, Swiss bankers provided assistance to Germany in repayment of war reparations and floated loans to the French National Railways, the government of Italy (yes, under Mussolini), and several South American nations.

But it was not until the Depression when the Swiss banks withstood the Nazi inroads on their privacy and also kept their doors open at the time everyone else was closing theirs, that they set their reputation in granite. In 1931, Germany froze foreign assets and declared a moratorium on foreign payments. By 1933, there was a General Transfer Moratorium throughout Europe which also involved foreign assets in the United States. The U.S. banks' holiday occurred in March 1933. This was the infamous time when, "the American experiment in self-government was facing what was, excepting the Civil War, its greatest test. Even more perhaps hung on the capacity to surmount crisis than in 1881. In 1933, the fate of the United States was involved with the fate of free men everywhere. And through the world the free way of life was already in retreat."[4]

The Swiss banks did not retreat. Throughout the Depression they remained open and paid all deposits demanded. The penalty was financially heavy. Swiss bank assets declined by more than 50 percent between 1930 and 1936. Three large banks failed, Union Bank was reorganized, and government assistance was required for several others. But all deposits were paid. And the Swiss banks' stature in the financial world and in the public mind increased immeasurably.

The Swiss political stability is militarily backed up, not only with troops, but with a national mentality that accepts the military as an important fact of life, probably dating from mercenary days. Every man who is physically capable of doing so serves in the army reserves between the ages of 20 to 50. This includes annual drills of two to three weeks, plus an active duty period in the early years. Hardly a home in Switzerland is without a gun, and reservists carrying a weapon and pack during the summer are seen all over the country, including main city streets and rail stations, on the way to annual drills. The exercises of the 650,000-man militia and the willingness with which the men accept the concept has been the backbone of Swiss neutrality. They deeply believe that the best way to

---

[4] Arthur Schlesinger, *The Crisis of the Old Order* (Cambridge, Mass.: Houghton Mifflin Co., 1957).

stay out of war is to prevent one. Their army and reserves are their ounce of prevention.

As might be expected, clothed in such trappings of political and economic stability as we've noted, the Swiss currency has been just short of unique in its own record. It is the only major trading currency of the world not to suffer a devaluation since the Depression, and that devaluation, in 1936, was the only one of this century. Contrasted with the 14 suffered by the French franc, the 7 of the Italian lira, or even the 5 of the British pound, and 3 of the U.S. dollar, the record is unusual. Since the fear of devaluation is one of the prime movers of funds out of any given country, Switzerland has become the natural refuge for monetary protection. This is despite the facts that in such a small country the does not belong to the International Monetary Fund, should it need assistance, and it has been forced to take important steps to stop the inflow of funds in order to avoid hyperinflation from currency surges. Steps such as the negative interest rate imposition on foreign holdings of Swiss francs, first in 1972 and again in 1974 – 75, and the limitation on foreign purchase of Swiss securities in 1972 (rescinded in 1974), and even the initial float of the franc in February 1973, were considered necessary to protect the franc for the Swiss.

Still, along with the rest of the industrial world, inflation in Switzerland has been dramatic. From December 1971 to December 1973, the consumer price index jumped 19 percent. By 1974, the country was in two-digit inflation. Prices in Switzerland for foreigners who have suffered currency devaluations along with the Swiss inflation, are now a real deterrent to visiting the country. Such is the price of success in lack of devaluations for the Swiss, who, while finding tourist trade down, are not yet notably complaining about it (at least no more than their normal level of lament at lost business, which is hardly a stony silence).

Taken together, the total record of stability in Switzerland is an important advantage in holding a Swiss bank account. And yet, political stability there is meaningless unless you fear for it in your own country. A banking record which not only includes overcoming the vicissitudes of history, but a willingness to band together to solve the problems of the future as they arrive, is of little use to you unless you believe this might not continue to be the case at home. A currency more stable than the dollar is not a great advantage to the average bank account holder in the United States, unless he or she is looking for an opportunity to profit from dollar declines in the floating money market.

In sum, something must precede the "plus" mark for the value of Swiss stability; either fear, the profit motive, or some illegality. By itself, Swiss stability is no great advantage unless there is fear for instability at home. But when you want the warmth of stability the Swiss have it in historical abundance.

Services

Having dealt with two of the broader advantages to holding a Swiss bank account in balance with three obvious disadvantages, we can now turn to the more practical and potentially profitable pluses on the ledger. Here we find, first, something of a reverse play on the convenience issue. While depositing funds in a

Swiss account is clearly less than convenient for Americans unless you happen to be going there, it is equally true that once your money is there a Swiss bank can do more for you than any American bank. (Other foreign banks can do almost as much, however.) Just how much your Swiss banker can do, or will do, is a function of how much money you place under his care. The $2,000 savings-type deposit won't gain anything but less interest compared with an American bank, plus a minor play on the future value of the Swiss franc if the deposit is held in that currency. While, as we have previously pointed out, the major banks will accept deposits as low as $100, the general demeanor of the officers admitting to this fact was such that they clearly hoped you wouldn't take advantage of their low offer. When you move into the $5,000 to $10,000 range, or can place blocks of $10,000 into your account at will, the Swiss bankers become both more useful and friendlier. Thus, any plus to be given to minimum account size is a relative one. I wouldn't rate the small minimum a plus at all, but rather would rate the number of services you can obtain with a larger deposit individually as pluses.

The Swiss banks' simplest convenience is in trading currencies, if that is your forte. Swiss bankers won't automatically do this for you, even with contingent instructions, nor will they recommend it unless you have a high five-figure account. But they will accept your orders to buy and sell foreign currencies, and once your banking relationship is solidly established they will discuss lending you between five and ten times the amount of cash you commit to a currency trade in order to leverage your purchases. Since Swiss banks are day-to-day traders in foreign currencies they can make you one too, once the proper relationship is established.

A word of caution here: With the great publicity given to the German banks' foreign exchange losses and subsequent collapses in 1974, plus the losses sustained by a handful of Swiss banks in this area, including the Union Bank customer who lost nearly $50 million alone, bankers everywhere are very cautious about foreign exchange trading. Swiss bankers' new conservatism in currency trading is therefore based on sound experience, and their cautionary comments are compelling. My suggestion to prospective currency traders is to use at least 30 percent margin on all trades, a level which is now widely agreed upon by the banks, unless you have a large reserve fund to add to your account.

Lombard, Odier & Co. gained something in its public reputation when it advised clients in August 1970 that the Swiss franc could be revalued upward. Patient clients who switched into that currency and waited until May 1971 when the franc was revalued nearly 14 percent against the dollar reaped profitable advice, especially if purchases were leveraged.

I have heard Swiss bankers tell clients in May and June 1973 that the dollar was too cheap against the Swiss franc, and that they were selling Swiss francs and buying dollars. The franc was then selling in a range between $0.32 and $0.34. By July, the franc topped at nearly $0.37 but the rise between May and the peak was over 15 percent, quite sufficient to wipe out the cash balance in a 10 percent leveraged account. By January 1974, however, the franc had dropped back to nearly $0.30 providing a handsome profit for shrewd timing the previous summer. But with the January 1975 price above $0.40, that was hardly a good long-term hold, either. A good many traders have been caught in this alpine rise and fall of the Swiss franc. Such are the vagaries of the currency markets: risky and sophisticated, but a prime source of potential profit through the convenience (in this case) of a Swiss account. Consider currency trading a plus at a Swiss bank only if you are a well-to-do speculator.

Closely allied to this ease of currency trading through the Swiss banks is their investment management function and reputation for being capable advisers in securities throughout the world. With some notable exceptions mentioned in Chapter 2, this is a fair claim. The Swiss are reported to now manage some $100 billion in investment portfolios. Some of this is invested in gold and real estate. But in general, they have maintained a solid record in securities, according to most reports. Here too, the Swiss can do for you what American banks cannot. They can buy or sell securities on your direct order. They act as brokers, as do most European banks, and will also handle your portfolio of securities on deposit with them under virtually any objectives you desire, but without the complications of an American trust account. This is often done under power of attorney at their discretion. However, there is a variance here. Most banks prefer discretionary accounts for clients not residing in Switzerland, this in order to facilitate action when time is essential. But with the recent condition of the securities markets, some banks now insist on your concurrence before taking any action. They're covering their flanks. As discussed in Chapter 6, the discretionary power is also a function of the fee charged for portfolio management. This is, therefore, an important point to check with the bank of your choice, based on the above guidelines.

The Swiss banks consider their international outlook to be a major selling point in banking service. They point with pride to their geographically diversified analytical departments in securities, real estate, and loans. The three major banks and a handful of the private variety have established in-house mutual funds, many of which specialize in securities of one foreign country or an international region.

This is as it should be. In a country of only 6.5 million people residing in an area the size of Maine, containing few natural exportable resources, the Swiss must be international entrepreneurs. So must the British and Japanese with both more people and less land. But where these two nations became traders and manufacturers, as did many Swiss, there was a stronger inclination to choose business in its purest form: money, in Switzerland. Thus, much emphasis on *international* finance. Whether this is a real across-the-board advantage to Americans is less than certain. Where Swiss bankers are major traders and market makers in precious metals, where they participate in international loan syndicates through one country or a dozen, where they are proud, ethical bankers across many borders, they have few peers. When they focus on foreign securities through one or two analysts looking into all the stocks in Japan, Hong Kong, and Australia, or have two or three analysts divining the whole U.S. stock market, some holes must appear in the theory. Still, performance has been no worse than their banking counterparts in the United States in most instances. That is hardly laudatory by 1975, but at least they don't suffer in the comparison.

One rule to remember about Swiss bank investment departments is, Do your required reading. This includes, foremost, their public funds' investment results. With at least 15 stock markets to choose from, plus all of that privacy to discover the true state of affairs, if they can't perform, their willingness to manage your money or trumpet international expertise is little more than meretricious. Be prepared for less than American SEC-required data, however. If they wanted you to have that much information they'd register with the SEC and sell their funds here. They don't want to.

To aid in your decision about assigning a plus to the banks' investment results, Tables 3, 4, and 5 showing the Big Three banks' funds will provide you with a yardstick.

While we are discussing securities management, don't forget the matter of brokerage commissions as explained in Chapter Six. They are cheaper in Switzerland than in the United States unless your Swiss bank is transacting in the American markets for you. Then, Swiss brokerage will be added to the American charge, running your fee to a level which should be unacceptable.

Even more sophisticated in the securities area is the currency switch prior to investment in a foreign security. With the 1974 removal of the U.S. Interest Equalization Tax (I.E.T.), Americans will find it profitable from time to time to buy foreign securities directly in the country of domicile. Prior to the tax removal an

TABLE 3
Union Bank of Switzerland Mutual Funds

Fund	Year Founded	Total Assets at Financial Year-End (in SFr. millions)	Price per Share at Financial-Year-End (in SFr.)					1974 Cash Dividend per Share (in SFr.)
			1970	1971	1972	1973	1974	
AMCA (U.S. and Canadian stocks)	1939	299. Dec. 31	210.44	219.46	240.41	173.66	96.80	1.10
BOND-INVEST (international bonds)	1970	2,409. Dec. 31	108.50	114.94	122.80	109.04	90.04	5.30
CANAC (Canadian stocks)	1955	80. March 31	225.61	245.16	251.66	242.19	230.74	4.60
CONVERT-INVEST (international convertible bonds)	1973	89. March 31	—	—	—	—	86.75	5.00
DENAC (retail trade, food processing industries' stocks)	1963	14. March 31	109.63	115.56	132.76	133.36	101.28	2.10
ESPAC (Spanish stocks)	1962	26. Oct. 31	268.59	278.47	374.47	430.27	385.07	10.00
EURIT (European stocks)	1959	64. Oct. 31	214.81	202.34	254.63	248.18	157.40	4.50
FONSA (Swiss stocks)	1950	330. June 30	174.84	199.21	221.28	235.49	189.83	5.20
FRANCIT (French stocks)	1960	19. Dec. 31	125.27	114.36	136.41	122.74	74.96	3.00
GERMAC (German stocks)	1963	28. Dec. 31	139.75	156.93	170.15	144.28	128.03	3.60
GLOBINVEST (international stocks)	1969	231. June 30	84.65	101.31	113.21	100.29	81.62	1.70
HELVETINVEST (Swiss fixed-income securities)	1972	99. Oct. 31	—	—	109.50	111.11	103.92	5.70
ITAC (Italian stocks)	1959	7. June 30	302.44	249.38	279.57	288.46	222.36	3.50
PACIFIC-INVEST (Pacific area securities)	1970	67. June 30	96.00	105.19	121.22	110.74	84.64	2.50
ROMETAC-INVEST (raw material and energy stocks)	1972	56. Oct.	—	—	—	477.50	362.64	12.50
SAFIT (South African stocks)	1949	237. March 31	609.79	696.93	698.25	834.88	1540.63	15.00
SIMA (Swiss real estate)	1951	1214. Sept. 30	293.77	327.86	357.77	394.11	413.49	7.40

Source: Union Bank of Switzerland.

TABLE 4
Swiss Bank Corporation Mutual Funds

Fund	Year Founded	Total Assets at Financial Year-End (in SFr. millions)		Price per Share at Financial Year-End (in SFr.)					1974 Cash Dividend Per Share (in SFr.)
				1970	1971	1972	1973	1974	
INTERSWISS (real estate)	1954	366.0	Dec. 30	890.00	1,044.00	1,248.00	1,214.00	1,060.00	48.00
INTERVALOR	1970	116.0	April 30	91.04	105.64	110.16	104.79	50.50	2.70
INTERCONTINENTAL TRUST (international securities)	1939	60.5	Aug. 31	332.00	341.00	384.00	309.00	192.00	11.00
SWISSIMMOBIL (Swiss real estate)	1961	292.0	Dec. 31	930.00	1,095.00	1,125.00	1,170.00	930.00	43.00
SWISSIMMOBIL NEW SERIES (Swiss real estate)	1950	228.0	Dec. 31	1,640.00	1,920.00	2,400.00	2,130.00	1,765.00	85.00
SWISSIMMOBIL SERIES D (Swiss real estate)	1938	89.0	Dec. 31	2,675.00	3,125.00	4,100.00	3,950.00	3,000.00	71.00
CANADAIMMOBIL (Canadian real estate)	1954	46.0	June 30	660.00	860.00	1,055.00	840.00	720.00	42.00

Source: Swiss Bank Corporation.

TABLE 5
Swiss Credit Bank Mutual Funds

Fund	Year Founded	Total Assets at Financial Year End (in SFr. millions)		Price per Share at Financial Year-End (in SFr.)					1974 Cash Dividend per Share (in SFr.)
				1970	1971	1972	1973	1974	
FONDS-BONDS (international bonds)	1970	1,238.9	Oct. 31	–	105.50	109.25	95.75	74.00	6.20
FONDS-INTERNATIONAL (international shares)	1970	207.9	Oct. 31	–	95.25	115.25	96.00	62.25	2.70
CANASEC (Canadian securities)	1952	73.7	May 31	728.00	881.00	999.00	816.00	707.00	21.00
USSEC (United States securities)	1951	83.0	Aug. 31	971.00	1,091.00	1,166.00	861.00	501.00	27.00
EUROPA-VALOR (European securities)	1959	57.1	April 30	155.50	162.25	171.75	171.75	135.00	5.00

Source: Swiss Credit Bank.

11.25 percent tax penalty was assessed in doing this, leaving mainly ADRs (American Depository Receipts) as most investors' choice in the foreign arena. Now, buying Heineckens in Holland, Sony in Japan, or Vaalreefs in South Africa may be more attractive than buying a dollar denominated ADR, convincingly so if the dollar is to acquire any future sinking spells. This type of transaction is one which your Swiss bank can easily handle for you, making a currency purchase (where permitted by the given country's currency convertibility), and then a securities trade virtually simultaneously. In fact, this idea had become so popular with investors outside the U.S. government jurisdiction that the Swiss banking authorities banned foreign purchases of Swiss franc denominated securities in 1972, to prevent a flood of foreign currencies from driving Swiss security prices and bank coffers to the ceiling. But the Swiss banker will now accommodate your wishes to buy other countries' securities in their native money, including Switzerland's. The approval to purchase Swiss securities came as a trade-off in cancelation of the United States I.E.T. Please note, however, that due to the soaring price of the Swiss franc in early 1975, there was talk of reviving the ban on nonresident purchases of Swiss securities. It could become a regulation any day.

Since about 1972, commodities have become an investment favorite of many Americans who have fathomed the peculiarities and risks of this specialized medium. Since about 1970, commodities have held far less than a favored position at Swiss banks. Many have rules prohibiting purchase of commodities through their investment departments. As one Swiss banker remarked at Dr. Harry Schultz' International Monetary Seminar in Montreal during October 1973, "Commodities aren't a popular investment at Swiss banks now. Maybe in 25 years." He was referring to the unlikelihood of the frowns being erased from Swiss Bankers Association members in the wake of the commodity scandal at UCB, Basle. By mutual agreement most bankers now find trading in commodities too risky. Gold and silver in some cases, but cocoa, wheat, and corn are out. This is not to say that you cannot arrange a commodities account after establishing a relationship with a Swiss bank. It is to say that you had better not plan to initiate your account with that as a main purpose.

Gold

One significant, but illegal, profit-making motive for the use of Swiss banks by Americans was removed with the 1975 legalization of gold ownership. Americans' inclination to take advantage of this new freedom was obviously diminished by the surge in gold's free market price to over $190 an ounce, but it seems likely that many will still make use of the opportunity. It is also likely that in the past many Americans made use of Swiss banks to buy and hold gold despite American law. Obviously, no figures are available. Some Swiss banks have refused to sell gold to Americans, at least by letter or cabled instructions. Very few were so nobly inclined if you walked into a bank branch in Switzerland and paid to walk out with the gold. A near-classic statement was made on the gold matter just a few years ago: ". . . the big Swiss banks have already drawn the attention of American citizens to the fact that the purchase of gold is against American law; some banks even went to the length of declining such orders."[5]

Now, and much to the likely relief of Swiss bankers, gold purchases by Americans are allowed, even though from the standpoint of legality such acquisition as a plus for a Swiss account is reduced. Swiss secrecy is no longer needed to shield the purchases. The plus is not eliminated, however. It is quite probable that you will be able to buy gold cheaper through a Swiss bank than in the United States. Chapter 5 has spelled out the details.

However you are disposed towards gold, the advantages of using a Swiss account for its purchase are decreased if you were planning a little illegal buying, and increased in practical terms, including cost savings, with the gold legalization for Americans.

Some Negatives

While the favorable side of the ledger for Swiss bank accounts is laden with personal considerations and therefore tends to be less definitive than one might wish, the negative side tends to be clear-cut. The arguments against a Swiss account are relatively simple and more tangible than the pluses. Because of this they are more visible and easily understood. It was probably this simplicity which prompted the talk show host

---

[5] Max Ikle, *Switzerland, An International Banking and Finance Center,* (Stroudsberg, Pa.: Dowden, Hutchinson & Ross, Inc., 1972).

mentioned in Chapter Four to conclude that there were few real advantages in holding a Swiss account. Yet, we must remember that since about the mid-60s the opposite has been true for the holders of several billion dollars who have transferred those funds to Switzerland. The somewhat nebulous positives have outweighed the clearer negatives for those folks. No doubt illegalities, especially where gold and taxes were concerned, have been a factor, although probably less than the popular image of Swiss banks would lead us to believe. In addition, pure profit motives through currency hedging, securities trades, or gaining adequate interest on funds while awaiting profit opportunities, have been prevalent.

A sizable bundle of money has gone to Switzerland. So sizable, that a Swiss banker was prompted to tell me in March 1974, "We are in a delicate position now. We don't want every Peter and Mary in America sending a few thousand dollars to us. But we have always accepted any size account when it was given to us. Now we are getting too many. But how can we discourage them?" That sort of thinking doesn't surface from Americans concluding that the minuses outweigh the pluses in Swiss accounts. Nevertheless, the minuses can be formidable.

We have already pointed out the most obvious negative to a Swiss account: its inconvenience and remoteness. One ramification of this is communications. While a jet flight from anywhere in the United States can get you to Switzerland in less than a day's flying time, your money and your epistles take a good deal longer. An airmail letter requires five to seven days from the U.S. West Coast to arrive in Zurich, three to five days from the East (assuming no special postal delays), and requires $0.26 postage per half ounce weight. A check sent airmail will take between two and three weeks to clear your U.S. account after your Swiss bank receives it, and can take longer. Up to six weeks isn't unusual. The process is a bit faster when a check is written on the Swiss account for deposit here, but not much.

Cable charges run in the $3 to $6 range depending upon the type sent, while telephone charges to Zurich are $6.75 for a three-minute station call from anywhere in the United States, and $12 person to person. Time works against a caller from the United States, as well. When it is a convenient 10 A.M. for your Swiss banker, it is 2 A.M. in San Francisco and 5 A.M. in New York. At 10 A.M. in Chicago it is 4 P.M. in Switzerland, allowing only a one to two hour time window to reach your banker and conduct business, office to office. All calls from the United States should be placed in our morning to reach a Swiss banker at his office, and on the West Coast they must be placed before 9 A.M. So much for the convenience of personal communication.

Other costs of doing business with Swiss bankers are bothersome too. While those banks usually levy no monthly service charge on checking accounts, contrary to most banks' practice here, that holds true only until you do something in the account . . . such as transact business. Then you are charged a modest fee for almost everything. There is a charge to collect a check from a foreign bank, a charge for conversion to a different currency (i.e., from dollars to Swiss francs), and several types of "handling charges." The holders of accounts at the ill-fated UCB, Basle, for example, while unable to do anything with their accounts for over a year, were charged a handling fee when the accounts were freed. The Swiss are paid for everything in one form or another.

Check writing per se costs you nothing at most Swiss banks. However, since the Swiss don't often use checks (their local transactions are usually in cash), they name these accounts "current accounts" and often require a minimum balance to issue checks. At major banks this is SFr. 1,000 for the "free" checking privilege. Granted, many U.S. banks levy similar charges for their international efforts; we rarely see them in an average domestic account. With frequent activity in your Swiss account they can add up quickly. It is wise to ask a Swiss bank for a list of such charges when requesting information about opening an account.

There is no such thing as deposit insurance on Swiss bank accounts, again contrary to U.S. practice, where individual accounts are insured up to $40,000 by the Federal Deposit Insurance Corporation. (Never mind that the FDIC only has cash on hand for such insurance to the extent of less than 1 percent of accounts insured.) The Swiss don't go through the formality of even that. In fact, it would be quite against their nature. One must presume the integrity and honesty of every bank. To do less would suggest some doubt about their tradition of stability, frugality, and even open their privacy to question. More than any insurance law the Swiss bankers rarely allow any deposit to go unprotected as to its integrity. No Swiss bank has failed, including those that closed during the Depression, and left its accounts less than fully paid unless there was criminal fraud involved. And such instances have been rare and at small banks. At UCB, Basle, depositors were paid off to the penny, and with interest where appropriate. This was done by parent Western Bancorporation of Los Angeles, undoubtedly with more than gentle prodding by the Swiss banking authorities. The fact that depositors were without the use of their funds for a year does not alter the fact that they were paid in full in Swiss bankers' minds. Besides, it was an American-run bank, they say, with just a hint of, "what else could you expect?"

Swiss bankers operate, as does all of Swiss industry, on an informal collective guidance system. It is most doubtful in the mind of anyone familiar with their policies and ethics that they would permit a major bank to close its doors without paying off each and every account. (See also the section on bank failures in Chapter 2.) The Swiss might well charge a service or handling fee for the protection in the unlikely event of a collapse, but there would not likely by any demurs to the payment in full. Where a bank is run by a foreign entity, even though it must be Swiss controlled, there could be some conceivable leniency in delay of payment. Nothing is certain in this world. But few things are more likely than a Swiss banker's belief in protection of reputation, integrity, and ethics. Thus, the lack of deposit insurance should not really be considered a negative for Swiss accounts. I list it here because it is an unfamiliar and therefore possibly negatively weighted factor for many Americans. It should also be a reminder that a small Swiss bank should be used only after a *very thorough* investigation.

Other clear negatives for most inquiries into Swiss

accounts have been discussed in detail in Chapter 6. They include the relatively low interest rates on savings-type accounts, the withdrawal notice required, and the Swiss withholding tax on interest paid.

A final annoyance about Swiss bank accounts is a problem shared with many American banks and other institutions, especially where extensive use of computers is made. This is the ubiquitous account error. It is compounded by receiving bank advisories and confirmations in three or four languages, or where the English language terms used aren't American phraseology. The problem stems from the familiar computer snafu often caused by the quality of the work force handling computer paper work.

Union Bank pointed out in its 1973 annual report, "The Union Bank of Switzerland will introduce integrated computer processing of all business transactions in the coming years within the framework of its comprehensive automation project." That announcement could strike some fear in the hearts of at least a few of those familiar with Swiss bank operations. The UBS project began with much fanfare, and similar efforts were started at the other major banks at about the same time. It ended in September 1974 as the manufacturer of the computer, Control Data, and the bank announced a termination of the project. It simply wouldn't work. Back to the drawing boards and use of smaller computers.

Regarding the previous difficulties encountered by the banks due to the swelling of transactions and accounts in recent years, Ray Vicker quotes Union Bank in his book, *Those Swiss Money Men*[6], as previously

---

[6] Ray Vicker, *Those Swiss Money Men* (New York: Charles Scribner's Sons, 1973).

reporting, "The fact that the speed and accuracy of the services provided by the Swiss banks have suffered, and that mistakes and delays occur more frequently is regrettable, but understandable." That bank had made the comment regarding its 77 percent increase in cash payment transactions and 71 percent increase in staff between 1966 and 1970. Vicker has another explanation. "There are a million foreign workers in the country doing most of the dirty and menial work. So, many of the less-educated Swiss who, under normal circumstances, might be swinging picks and shovels, are now working in Swiss banks. . . . Those proletariat may be handling your account."

You should understand this problem as a real, if correctable, minus on your Swiss bank scorecard.

Looking back over our plus-minus scorecard, the straightforwardness of the minuses tends to swing the balance against the subjective pluses. Very personal considerations which are out of place in this discussion, such as travel or residence plans, retirement or children's schooling, may readily carry the day because they reintroduce the deposit convenience factor. Then too, political and economic events of the next few years might compound our money-protective fears, some of which are already weighing Swiss bank privacy and national stability far ahead of their low interest rates and branch office remoteness. It is in the profit-making potential of Swiss banks that many Americans are finding the straw which swings the balance one way or the other. The greater your available funds, the greater your sophistication in investments, the more significant your fears about American political and economic problems, the more Swiss banks will become attractive for a portion of your funds. This is the concatenation between your personal circumstances and a Swiss bank.

Perhaps the Swiss bank ledger is summed up by an aphorism from the late Michael Arlen, given us by former newspaper publisher, columnist and raconteur, Lucius Beebe:

"I require very little of life," Arlen said, "I want only the best of everything, and there's so little of that."

In the final analysis, a Swiss bank account might add a finishing touch to that of which there is so little — if the paper work/computer doesn't get you first.

Chapter nine

Swiss Bankers Talk

SWISS BANKERS are not as closemouthed and reserved in public comments as is often thought to be the case. Leading Swiss bankers are regularly quoted in the European press, important American papers, wire services, and journals. The large banks publish regular newsletters or bulletins expounding their officials' views just as do large U.S. banks. Union Bank's foreign exchange department even publishes a biweekly paper of informal comments replete with cartoons.

Swiss bankers have, however, become most cautious and guarded with the press in general, a function of what they believe are excessive misunderstandings and misquotations on significant matters over the past several years. Banking secrecy, the U.S.—Swiss Mutual Assistance Treaty, and a few true disadvantages of Swiss banks for Americans are delicate points for most bankers. A discussion of these subjects and a few others with two leading Swiss bankers should be, therefore, of more than routine interest. Their candid comments were given to me privately and separately from one another and should be viewed in this context. Placement of their answers one after the other on the following pages is for reading convenience, and does not imply they were together discussing the questions asked.

The two men are important Swiss bankers in every sense of the word, and they represent two distinct points of view within their industry. One set of comments comes from a "Big Three" public banker; the other, at the time of the interview, a senior partner of Switzerland's largest private bank. Felix W. Schulthess is chairman of Swiss Credit Bank, the third largest of Switzerland's banks. Hans Bär is now Managing Director of Julius Bär and Company of Zurich, a firm which on January 1, 1975, became a limited company, a rarity among private banks. Their answers are edited only to avoid repetition of the same points.

Q: What are the major points of importance about Swiss banking secrecy?

MR. SCHULTHESS: Bank secrecy is a traditional part of Swiss law. It follows logically from the basic Swiss constitutional principle that every individual has a right to a private sphere protected from state interference—a right which bank secrecy helps to secure and preserve. There is also an important humanitarian aspect to be considered. For centuries Switzerland has offered political asylum to foreigners, providing a refuge not only for persecuted persons from many countries but also for their property. In the 30s the totalitarian regimes carried out intensive espionage in Switzerland in search of funds belonging to their nationals, and it was this that induced Switzerland in 1934 to include a special regulation in the Banking Law, whereby banking secrecy, which had previously rested in common law, was more clearly defined, while its violation was made a criminal offense subject to penalties. The secret services operated by totalitarian regimes since 1945 would also have had a much easier time had it not been for this provision. One can therefore say without exaggeration that the determination with which Swiss bank secrecy has been, and is being, observed has safeguarded the life and property of thousands of people.

However, it must be made clear that bank secrecy in no way hampers the fight against or prosecution of crime. It does not conflict at all with society's overriding interest in order and security; in fact, while bank secrecy in Switzerland is highly developed it is by no means absolute. Wherever higher public interests necessitate disclosure, the banks are under a legal obligation to give information. In particular, the banks cannot appeal to bank secrecy in criminal proceedings; in these cases they are bound to give evidence.

The banks' obligation to furnish information in criminal cases also applies to third countries to which Switzerland lends legal assistance. As is proper in a Western democracy, this obligation is precisely defined in law. Accordingly, neither the accusations of private detectives and investigators, nor newspaper stories or allegations on the part of lawyers or others, are sufficient to compel the banks to give information; for this purpose the decision of a competent judicial body is required. In addition, the crime in question must also be a punishable offense in Switzerland. Thirdly, also in accordance with generally recognized principles of international law, the requested support must not run counter to basic Swiss constitutional concepts. These limitations exclude, for example, political offenses, for which Switzerland as a country of asylum never grants legal assistance. They also exclude foreign exchange offenses since Switzerland imposes no transfer restrictions; for similar reasons they exclude tax offenses, provided these do not violate some article of Swiss criminal law such as fraud, and are prosecuted by foreign tax authorities on that basis.

Thus the purpose of bank secrecy is to protect private property and individual privacy, which are among the cornerstones of a free society; it has developed from the needs of the Swiss people; moreover it is in no way designed to aid shady or criminal dealings. Admittedly, Swiss bank secrecy may occasionally be used as a cloak for dubious practices, but the Swiss people and the responsible Swiss banks firmly disassociate themselves from these.

In fact, no country is in a position to offer advantages of a liberal order without accepting the possibility of its violation. This cannot, however, be used as a reason to suppress liberty. Incidentally, Switzerland has one of the lowest crime rates in the world, further evidence that bank secrecy does not provide a breeding ground for crime.

Q: Swiss banks have been accused of exporting their banking secrecy to other countries instead of keeping it in Switzerland. What do you think of this?

MR. BÄR: If you mean by exporting, getting someone to do something he wouldn't do elsewhere, I don't think we should, and I don't think reputable institutions do export banking secrecy. I don't want to see bankers going out and selling secrecy by saying "Come and open an account with me and avoid paying taxes." But if I sit here and only accept business sent to us, I am not exporting.

Q: But your reputation may export what you don't export actively. . . .

MR. BÄR: If I abide by my laws which include secrecy, how can I stop you from abiding by my laws, too? If you hear about my secrecy and want to come here and abide by our laws and make use of that secrecy, why should I stop you? If that makes you forget your laws that is your problem and your government's.

There is another aspect of the banking secret in Switzerland which we are forgetting. It is definitely being encroached upon by "salami" tactics. This is the gradual cutting away of small pieces of the secrecy through court cases, international pressure, even the assistance treaty with your country.

Frankly, the bank secret is not the product of the Swiss banking system on which I would like to build the future of my firm. I think it will change slowly by international attrition. But there won't be any new law suddenly tomorrow morning.

Q: Is the popularity of banking secrecy overrated then?

MR. BÄR: The drama is overrated. It is the journalists' fault. All these stories about anonymous accounts and bankers keeping money after someone dies simply aren't true. But they are reported and the clarification by the bank involved is only made later—and then not reported as well as the first story.

Besides this, there is a great difference between our beliefs about law in your country and mine. We all believe in our own laws — but don't always agree with each other's. We think Americans are constantly over-interpreting their laws. How can I know all of the American laws and be sure I don't violate them here? What do I really care about American or Canadian or Japanese law when I sit here in Switzerland? I will be honest, legal and ethical about banking secrecy in Switzerland, but I can't know all of what you consider honest, legal and ethical on this point in the United States.

Q: When should Americans use Swiss banks, and what are some of the disadvantages in doing so?

MR. SCHULTHESS: For U.S. firms and individuals, the decision whether or not to have dealings with a Swiss bank naturally depends primarily on whether they have business interests in Switzerland or at least in Europe. Thus import and export operations with Switzerland constitute the basis for a flourishing commercial credit business, which is conducted partly by the branch offices that the Swiss big banks, including Swiss Credit Bank, maintain in the United States.

A further basis for these transactions is provided by the financial operations of major U.S. corporations, which often manage their foreign interests, or handle their international finances, through a Swiss subsidiary. Moreover, substantial worldwide portfolio investments are channelled through Switzerland, prompting big U.S. investors, both institutional and private, to maintain business contacts with the Swiss banks. Furthermore, Switzerland is a tourist country, lying in the heart of Europe, with a sound and freely convertible currency; where U.S. residents who visit Europe regularly find it convenient to deposit some funds. Switzerland possesses a well-developed communications network, and an efficient banking system, giving customers all over the world easy access to their funds in Switzerland.

A further advantage, and one which is probably exclusive to Switzerland, is that the Swiss banks regularly serve their customers in all five major languages of the Western world, i.e., English, German, French, Italian and Spanish. For foreigners, it is therefore often more convenient to deal with a Swiss bank than with banks in other foreign countries. This gives a certain competitive edge to the Swiss institutions, which in international financial operations often act not only as financial intermediaries but also as translators.

Of course, it is difficult for a Swiss banker to see any disadvantages in holding Swiss bank accounts. As I have already explained, the basis of such an account must be a natural business relationship. Partly as a result of the totally unjustified fuss in the press about Switzerland's function as an international financial center, an idea has unfortunately gained currency in some quarters which may be summed up in the formula: "Money alone does not bring happiness, it has to be money in Switzerland." Such irrational motives, which often make a Swiss bank account a sort of status symbol, do not constitute a sound basis for business dealings with a Swiss bank; sooner or later they inevitably lead to disappointment. For one thing, it must be realized that interest rates in Switzerland are far lower than elsewhere. At present Swiss banks are only allowed to pay interest on very limited amounts of foreign funds, and on larger new deposits from abroad we are even compelled to levy a commission. Moreover, for people not in frequent contact with Switzerland or Europe, access to funds in Switzerland is relatively inconvenient.

MR. BÄR: First of all, we would have to be talking about an investor of means. I have no sympathy with this $10,000 bit. The potential holder must be of substance. The minimum on our advisory accounts is SFr. 500,000 — but there are no other minimums. If you come with SFr. 100,000 and try to tell us to buy ten different bonds, we will suggest you buy our bond fund instead.

Then, it must be a matter of diversification. Now that we know the dollar is not the only currency in the world — nor are U.S. securities the only securities, one must diversify assets. One can realize that Swiss bankers have the best worldwide experience by just looking at where we invest and in what things. In the Far East, in the Middle East, in Canada, in the U.S., stocks, bonds, Eurodeposits, gold. All kinds of investments all over — for many years.

I can also foresee the possibility of great inconvertibility of currencies. The worst possible collapse of the monetary system will be a return to bilateralism. It seems to be coming, and people will even more need our international view.

Look at the loan this fall [1974] from Germany to Italy: a loan in return for trade. This was the danger of the 1920s and now it is intimately involved with the whole question of the petrodollar.

Frankly, I think the petrodollar recycling cannot work. The situation is solvable only in one of two ways: a complete reduction in oil price to virtually old levels, or what we must call "political intervention" in the Mid-east. Right now, the staff work by central bankers is not being done. We are woefully behind in our creation of contingency plans.

Q: The U.S.—Swiss Mutual Assistance Treaty could have an important effect on American attitudes towards Swiss banks. What are your opinions about this treaty? Does it really just make legal what already exists?

MR. SCHULTHESS: The new Swiss-American mutual aid treaty, proves Switzerland's interest in promoting the rule of law on the international level. Seen from Switzerland, the main reason for the difficulties that arose in legal assistance between the two countries was that the United States, as a result of its internal legal system, was often not in a position to prosecute criminals or organized crime on the basis of its criminal laws, but resorted to prosecutions under the tax laws. As already mentioned, Switzerland could not grant legal assistance under the normal regulations of international law. This situation was unsatisfactory for Switzerland, too, because in the opinion of the Swiss authorities and bankers, bank secrecy, which provides no protection for national criminals, should not be used as a cover for international crime.

In view of this situation, a formula had to be found which would reconcile the basic legal positions in the U.S.A. and Switzerland in such a way that bank secrecy could be lifted when necessary in the fight against internationally organized crime, such as drug smuggling, even if U.S. authorities are not in a position to base their prosecutions on criminal law, as it would be in Switzerland, but rather on tax laws.

An acceptable formula is contained in the new treaty. It brings, however, no fundamental change to the concept or scope of banking secrecy, but removes a number of formal obstacles which in the past have impeded legal assistance in exceptional cases. Experience with the treaty will show whether difficulties in the fight against crime are really due so much to bank secrecy, as is maintained by U.S. authorities, or whether—and this seems much more likely—the problems lie in the basic concepts of U.S. criminal law, which make the proceedings in criminal cases much more difficult and complicated than in Europe.

MR. BÄR: The Mafia bill? We in the banking system believe it is a good thing. It finally serves to clear the air. There will no longer be any excuses to be damned if we do and damned if we don't. We have supported this all along.

But does it simply codify what has existed? No. It will provide a legal channel for Swiss banks to respond to proper questions from the American government. There will be some flak in our National Assembly—some points will be argued—but the treaty will be ratified in Switzerland.

Q: Perhaps it would be appropriate now to ask you what points you would like Americans to understand most about your banking industry—points which you feel they now misunderstand?

MR. SCHULTHESS: Above all, a word of warning is called for. Switzerland has an abundance of banks and not all of them are of the same quality. Furthermore there is no arrangement comparable to the U.S. deposit insurance. It is therefore advisable to exercise care in the choice of a Swiss bank. In my view one should select only those Swiss banks which can look back on a tradition of successful business activity and which have a worldwide reputation. This, if I may say so, does apply to my bank, Credit Suisse [Swiss Credit Bank], which was founded in 1856. But there are also many other institutions which come up to the required standard, such as the other two big banks and a number of highly reputed local and private banks. Finally, I would underline what I said just now: Do not regard an account with a Swiss bank as a status symbol, but judge it as you would judge an account with any other bank: by the benefits it can bring you.

MR. BÄR: First of all, the Swiss banking industry would be eager to improve its image in regard to its involvement in certain tax and recent foreign exchange matters by spreading the word that the fault in most cases, where one exists on the part of a Swiss bank, has been overplayed in the press. Swiss banks are basically very honest and there are very few exceptions to this. We would like our side of the stories told more effectively.

Secondly, we want to make it known that there are very few places one can go to obtain truly international expertise in one center, with as great a wealth of knowledge as to the Swiss banks. The proof is in the demand for our services from all over the world. . . .

Q: But hasn't your deposit growth slowed this past year?

MR. BÄR: For the Swiss banks as a whole, the explosion in deposits has stopped. But one must be careful about reading too much into any reported declines due to the phase-out of fiduciary deposits from balance sheets since 1972. But the basic demand for variety in our services grows still.

Finally, people must know that we are still a small country and a small industry. Our largest bank (Union Bank of Switzerland) is only the 50th largest in the world. We cannot do everything for everyone, even though we can do a great many things.

Technicalities

Answers to the following questions were provided by various bankers.

Q: May a Swiss account be opened in more than one name, and what are the inheritance ramifications of this?

A: Yes, a Swiss bank account can be opened by a husband and wife or any other persons who are legally associated. However, as with any bank account in Switzerland or abroad, including the numbered accounts, signature rights are important. If there are individual signature rights on the account, either or any of the account owners may withdraw funds at any time upon presentation of the single signature. This may be advantageous in the event that either party dies, in which case funds may be utilized or the account acted upon by the surviving party without any bank interference or Swiss government restrictions. In this regard it may be important to note that there are no inheritance taxes for nonresidents in Switzerland.

Q: Are commissions to purchase securities through Swiss banks higher or lower than buying directly in their country of origin?

A: Securities transaction commissions can be either higher or lower, depending upon the circumstances. They are higher by about half if the security is not issued by a Swiss company nor listed on a Swiss exchange. They are lower by about the same amount if the security is of Swiss origin or dually listed in its country of issue and on a Swiss exchange and purchased on the Swiss exchange.

Q: If a gain is made on securities bought through a Swiss bank is there a tax on that gain in Switzerland?

A: The only tax payable on returns obtained from securities in Switzerland is the 30 percent withholding tax on dividends or interest paid by the company issuing the security. There is no capital gain tax in Switzerland. However, the U.S. capital gain tax is applicable for U.S. citizens even though the securities are bought and sold in Switzerland.

Q: What are the advantages of a certificate of deposit compared with a regular deposit account in Switzerland?

A: Principally negotiability. A CD may be sold through a bank to a third party carrying its original rate of interest, where a normal deposit account is not a negotiable instrument. (This is also true in the United States.) In addition, CDs may be obtained through a Swiss bank via fiduciary deposits in the Eurocurrency market, sometimes for smaller amounts than the normal minimums of $25,000, thus yielding both high interest and negotiability. For example, January 1, 1975 bid rates for three-month Euromarket deposits were 10.125 percent for dollars, 9.625 percent for Swiss francs, 8.625 percent for Deutsche marks.

Q: Are Swiss banks required to hold large liquid deposits as reserves against total deposits as a means of protecting account holders?

A: Yes, not only as a means of protecting depositors but to aid in halting the inflow of capital by making it less attractive for the banks to use. Cash liquidity requirements are approximately 15 percent of total deposits. This has two components: the First Liquidity, which must be held by either the bank concerned or deposited with the National Bank and which must be available on one day's notice; it amounts to half of the cash requirement. The Second Liquidity, the other half of the requirement, can be deposited with any bank but must be available on 30 days' notice. In addition, 57 percent of all new current account deposits, since 1972, have to be placed as reserves with the National Bank, although they can be counted against the liquidity requirements as well.

Chapter ten

A Recession Shield

WHO SAID that Swiss banks can't be of much help to Americans caught in the throes of the worst recession since 1948–49 (or perhaps the Depression)? Given the caveat that no bank in the world can be of help to the person without money or a job, there are areas where Swiss banks may have advantages over other banks in difficult economic times. Barring sudden policy changes preventing foreigners from utilizing the banks fully, there are three major points of salvation that the Swiss banks offer. They also offer no guarantees.

Since banks during the period 1931–36, as well as in 1974, tended to become prominent casualties of economic slumps, the Swiss device of separating customer's holdings of gold or silver bullion from other bank assets and liabilities in the event of bank failure, could theoretically be of major importance to buyers of such commodities. Swiss banks, as we have already seen, were not immune to the rash of bank failures during the depression. From the year 1935 until 1942, some 35 banks were closed in one way or another, but only 7 through bankruptcy proceedings. Others were wound up through grace periods to meet liabilities, deferred payments, or agreements between creditors. Several were taken over by the two major Swiss banks with sizable asset blocks, Swiss Credit Bank and Swiss Bank Corporation. Union Bank was reorganized with a smaller capitalization during the period.

In bank closings, assets are frozen until a responsible party can sort out the claims against the bank or arrange a merger with another, solvent bank. No claims can be paid until all creditors are satisfied with the method of payment if the proceedings move past the voluntary reorganization or moratorium stage. This takes time. The Herstatt Bank of Cologne, Germany, which failed in June 1974, was still working on a creditor's plan in December, and could go many more months before a final plan is accepted — assuming there will be no new litigation which could further stall the referee's efforts.

However, under Swiss law, bullion and even coins, can be segregated by Swiss banks for their customers in "custodial accounts," which are similar to the fiduciary accounts utilized by the banks for time deposits with other major international banks on behalf of their customers. These custodial accounts, either in gold, silver, or fiduciary deposits are not considered part of the banks' direct obligations or assets. They are not counted in the balance sheet, nor are they a legal part of the bank's financial structure when held on a cash or fully paid basis.[1] They are not considered part

---

[1] Economic Research Council establishment, Vaduz, Liechtenstein, and the Union Bank of Switzerland.

of the bank resources against which creditors can make claims in the event of bankruptcy proceedings.

In short, the Swiss banks can park one's solid gold Cadillac in a garage other than their own, one which they consider fully safe in terms of protection against damage. If something should happen to their own parking lot, the other parking area should be untouched.

New regulations permitting banks to handle gold for Americans in the United States also permit those banks which act purely as agents for such purchases to exclude such purchases from their accounts. This leaves storage up to the buyer or the broker through whom the metal was purchased. The buyer must worry about the solvency of the broker or other storage firm. In Switzerland, storage is usually with major banks or warehousing firms whose solvency is either guaranteed by a group of banks, or whose only business is storage of precious metals and is fully insured.

It is still wise to remember that such serious economic dislocations as the depression have a habit of creating brand new problems entirely unlike those of the previous crash. The ultimate storage of one's precious metal pile should be a point of inquiry when wishing to take advantage of the custodial account provision of Swiss bank regulations. The simple segregation of such accounts at Swiss banks in the event of bank failure should provide both the owner of gold/ silver and fiduciary deposits a measure of protection worth considering in the recent economic plight.

An additional fact to note in regard to bank failures in Switzerland is that, while the major banks and leading private banks have most often taken care of each other in severe economic times, a potential negative about Swiss banks is the lack of government insurance of deposits such as is available in the United States. The fact that deposit insurance does not exist in Switzerland is a direct function of the people's lack of concern about it, according to one attorney in Geneva. That may be reassuring. But at those banks which have failed in Switzerland, principally smaller ones, depositors have stood in line for long periods to obtain their funds. In the case of the Arab Commercial Bank it was the better part of a decade. As with many other concerns during times of great economic stress, this deposit insurance issue provides a cue for utilizing only the largest of the public or private banks, if pure safety is a major worry. The late 1974 strength of the Swiss franc has suggested that this may not be too appropriate a cause for lost sleep, but the logic of bank size is a compelling consideration. Among the smaller banks, Foreign Commerce Bank calls attention to its precious metal custodial account segregation as an intended protective device for depositors.

A second significant area of Swiss bank assistance in difficult economic times is revealed in their history of freedom from foreign exchange controls. Not in the 225-year history of Swiss banks has there ever been a control placed on the export of capital from the country. This suggests the high degree of probability that any funds deposited in the country will be readily removable under any conceivable economic conditions. This, coupled with the multi-currency checkbook which permits issuance of checks denominated in any currency without regard to the currency held in the issuer's Swiss account, could provide an important means of financial mobility.

Foreign exchange controls are virtually unknown to Americans as well as the Swiss, save for the reporting requirement now in effect for transfer of $5,000 or more out of the country, and the former interest equalization tax which was a specialized form of exchange control. But the potential for imposition of direct low limits on the amount of funds which could be exported from the United States, a true exchange control, certainly exists under the inflationary pressures of the 1970s. While such controls would be the height of folly in a recessionary period, the economic situation is sufficiently fluid under recent weak dollar conditions vis-á-vis most major currencies that need for imposition of such controls could be argued. The financial gurus have been predicting the event for some time. Dr. Harry Schultz, in his ten-year look-ahead given at the 1973 International Monetary Seminar in Montreal, forecast a completely nonconvertible dollar, good for use in the United States, but neither transferable nor acceptable abroad. His reasoning: sufficient deterioration of investment prospects in the United States to make foreign potential far more attractive, followed by a snowballing outflow of American capital, justifying exchange controls.

The speed with which monetary controls can be instituted is virtually instantaneous. The dollar's nonconvertibility into gold was announced and made effective immediately by Presidential order in 1933 for citizens, and in 1971 for other governments. A similar move limiting paper dollar's convertibility into other currencies need take no longer.

Britain has lived with such exchange controls since 1947. There, citizens are limited to £25 cash on departure from the country, must obtain Treasury permission to hold foreign bank accounts and, as explained in Chapter Four, must buy foreign currencies for investment purposes from a special pool.

One measure of the value of holding foreign currencies outside a tight exchange control country such as Britain is the premium prevailing for investment pool currencies over the normal exchange rate. Ranging between 10 and 25 percent for most of the decade through 1974, the dollar premium hit 54 percent during the fall of 1974. Foreign-held proceeds of previous overseas investments would obviate the need for a British citizen to buy pool dollars for external investments, clearly at a substantial saving.

Whether exchange controls will be imposed in the United States and the form they might take is patently a matter of conjecture. But even with the substantial U.S. corporate and bank dollar holdings overseas, controls could be imposed swiftly. While the removal of the interest equalization tax in early 1974 and the Trade Bill of January 1975 indicate governmental thinking in the opposite direction, our "slumpflation" world could bring forth at least modest exchange controls at the literal drop of a balance of payments deficit. Americans with holdings of foreign currencies abroad could be the first beneficiaries of such onerous conditions. Switzerland's historic lack of such controls and international business outlook provides an ideal protection against this undetermined potential. Swiss banks provide a safe, as opposed to sorry, consideration.

The third shield that Swiss banks can provide against the untold troubles of a recessionary climate is in the very nature of their business structure. As financial department stores, Swiss banks are in a position to locate the most promising investment recovery prospects in the world. No need for an individual to uncover an emerging stock market rebound in Japan, the proper time to sell gold, or the deflationary prospects for the South African rand — a Swiss bank can do it for all customers. Considering the currency futures market? Interested in business risk insurance? Want advice about a three-month retreat in Switzerland? Ask your Swiss banker. That which he can't provide directly, his business associations will.

Intrigued by Swiss real estate as a hedge against inflation and recession combined? The major Swiss banks each have real estate mutual funds which permit foreign ownership where foreigners are normally prevented from buying Swiss real estate directly. The depth of Swiss bank services plus their well advertised international expertise makes them ideal vehicles for discovery of recessionary protective or recovery prospects. (See Chapter 6 for a listing of available services.)

While Swiss banks neither claim to be, nor have a record which supports anything close to infallibility, they are positioned to provide clients with "one world" investment vehicles. If they can't unearth leading prospects for money-making or money-saving around the world as the recession changes character to depression or recovery, it is unlikely any other single financial advisory source could either. But prejudices prevail. The East Grinstead Bank and Trust Company may be all you'll ever want for financial advice. Certainly, if you'd care to locate the best local financial advice in every country with protective/recovery prospects and deposit sufficient funds to entice each attractive unit, you won't need a Swiss bank.

But even then you might still need the Swiss franc!

Index

A

Account error, 250
Account size, 193–96, 235
Advantages of Swiss banks, 213–45, 257–58
"Affair Barilla," 93
Agenti di combi, 94
American banks in Zurich, 179–80, 182–83
American Century Mortgage Investors, 83
American Depository Receipts (ADRs), 243
American illegalities, 69–81
American mass media coverage, 26–27
American South African Ltd. stock, 24
Ampo Trading, 83–84
Ancien régime, testing of, 48
Arab Commercial Bank of Geneva, 28, 267
Arlen, Michael, 252
Arzi Bank of Zurich, 76
Assets of five largest Swiss banks, 6
Australia gold rush, 108, 116

B

Bail, orders for, 9–10
Balance of payments deficit, gold backing to, 200–201
Balance of payments prospects, 190
Bank
of America, 7, 180
of England, 82, 116, 129–30
of France, 116
Bank closings, 265–67
Bank Germann in Basle, 29
Bank holiday (U.S.), 231
Bank Indiana, 180
Bank for International Settlements in Basle, 230
Bank Leu, 52
Bank note situation, 54
Bank secrecy laws; *see* Secrecy
Banking
budding of, 51–55
evolution of principles of, 65
Banque Genevois d'Epargne et de Credit, 27
Bär, Hans, 172, 187–88, 254, 256–61
Bär, Julius, 230
Bär, Julius, & Company of Zurich, 52, 171–73, 187, 254
Bär Securities of New York, 171
Barclay's Bank of Britain, branches of, 214
Barclay's of London, 230
Barilla, Peter, 89–93
Barilla, Robert, 89–93
Barnato brothers, 117
Barron's, 26, 223

273

Basle Bankverein merger, 53
Basle Securities Corporation, New
    York, 171
Bentsen, Senator, 72–73
Big Three public banks, 175, 177,
    194, 206, 215, 224, 230, 254
Billion Dollar Killing, The, 10
Biodynamics, 83
Bond-Invest, 175
Bonjour, E., 45 n, 64 n
Branch banking, 214–15
Breton, Pierre, 118 n
Bribery of Swiss bank officials, 85–
    87
British bribery attempts, 85–87
British exchange control regula-
    tions, 82
    violations of, 82–84
Brokerage commissions, 239, 261–
    62
Browne, Harry, 20–24, 217
Burgundy War of 1476, 43
Business Week, 26

C

California gold rush, 108, 115–16
California's First Western Bank,
    branches of, 214
Calvin, John, 44
Capital, growth in, 54
Capitalists, rising class of, 50
Carihuela Investments, 83–84
Catholic cantons, alliance of, 55–56
Catholic counter-Reformation, 44
Cattle feeding plans, 153
Central government, formation of,
    56–57
Certificate of deposits, 262
Charter of Swiss bank, purchase
    of, 38
Chase Manhattan Bank, 75, 180
Checkbooks issued, 158
Chesler, Lou, 74
Chicago Board Options Exchange,
    153
Chilean military overthrow of Al-
    lende regime, 220
CIA's domestic spying, 220
CIA's use of Swiss accounts, 14

Civil War, 126, 232
Clarke, Stephen V.O., 103 n
Closed circuit television of stock
    prices, 166
Coggeshall and Hicks, 76
Coins, 54, 154; *see also* Gold coins
Collapse of banks, 27–30
Commodities trading, 243–44
Commodity contracts scandal, 8–9
Computer processing, 250
Comstock Lode gold rush, 116
Concerts, sponsoring of, 212
Confederation of Swiss cantons,
    42–44
    neutrality of, 45
Congressional hearings on secret
    accounts, 26
Congressional investigations, 2
Consolidated Gold Fields, 103, 109,
    140
Convenience, 214–16, 234–35
Coppola, Michael, 74
Corruption, 48
Costs, 216, 247
Cottage industries, 47–48
Cowles, Gardner, 74
Credit Mobilier, 52–53
Crete gold, 112
Croesus, 103, 112
Crum, Colyer, 153
Currency dealings, tax evasion on,
    80
Currency and Foreign Transactions
    Reporting Act, 72–73, 79
Currency issues, 154–58
Currency price changes, 190–93
Currency seesaw, 190–93
Currency trading, 235–36
Current accounts, 247
    confirmation, 160
    interest payments, 161–62
    paperwork for, 158–62
    starting point, 157
    statements of, 160–61
Custodial accounts, 265

D

Deak-Perera organization in New
    York, 23

de Gaulle, Charles, 105
Deposit accounts; *see* Savings accounts
Deposit insurance, 248–49, 267
Depression, 21–22, 119, 231–32, 266
  gold stocks in, 142
Deutsche mark, 155
Devaluation
  dollar, 7, 233
  pound sterling, 6, 68, 119, 233
  Swiss currency, 233
Dines, James, 24, 218
Dines Letter, The, 24–25
Diodorus Siculus, 111
Disadvantages of Swiss banks, 213–14, 245–52
Disclosure of information, prohibition of, 10, 12; *see also* Secrecy
Disraeli, Benjamin, 104
Disunity, 43–45
Dollar
  collapse of, 152
  devaluations, 7, 233
Dollar/franc price, 191, 193
Dollar/franc rate, 195, 198
Double invoice system, 99–100
Double Taxation Treaty, 165–66
Dow Chemical, 15
Dreyfus Sohne & Co., 52
Drug traffic funds, transfers of, 77–78
Drummer factor, 216–19
Dummy corporation, establishment of, 81

E

Eckstein, Hermann, 117
Economic difficulties, 49
Economic power, development as, 40–41
Egyptian gold, 111–12
Ehrbar, A. F., 154 n
Elia, Charles J., 201 n
Engelhard, Handy & Harman, 134
English machine-spun cotton, introduction of, 49
Erdman, Paul, 8–10
Escher, Alfred, 52

Eurocurrency market, 164
European illegalities, 82–87
European radio/TV coverage, 26–27
Everlasting Alliance, Treaty of, 42–43, 51
Export of blood, 45–47
Export trades, 47
Exports of spinning jenny spinning machines, 50

F

Falsification of documents and accounts, 8, 10, 13
Federal birth, 55–58
Federal constitution, 56
Federal Council, 56
  defensive steps against Germany, 61
Federal Reserve Bank of San Francisco, 123–27
Federal Reserve Board, abuses of stock purchase margin rules of, 76–77
Federal state
  existence of, 40
  significance of formation of, 64–67
Fells, Peter D., 102 n
Ferdinand of Spain (King), 105, 115
Ferrier, Lullin & Co., 52
Fiduciaria device, 90–92
Fiduciary deposit, 164–65
Financial department stores, 181, 270
Firestone Tire, 15
First Boston Corporation, 154
First National City Bank, 180
Floating foreign currency rates; *see* Great Money Game
Foley, Charles, 21 n, 23
Fonsa, 175
Forbes, 26
Foreign banks, 52
Foreign Commerce Bank of Zurich and Geneva, 23, 152, 170, 180, 195, 267
Foreign corporations, creation of, 97

Foreign currency holdings, 154
Foreign exchange
  business, extent of, 6
  controls, 268–69
  trading, 235–36
Foreign Investors Tax Act of 1966,
  97
Foreign trusts, establishment of, 97
Forsyth, Frederick, 185
Fortune magazine, 154
Fraud charges, 13
French blockade of English goods,
  50
French occupation, 48–50
French Revolution, 45–46, 48
Frigid gnome myth, 210–12

G

General Development Corporation,
  74
General Foods, 83
General strike, 58
General Transfer Moratorium
  (Europe), 231
Geon Industries, 83
Germann, Walter, 29–30
Gestapo agents, 59, 222
Gillette, 83
Glass Steagal Act of 1933, 175
Goebbel's propaganda measures,
  60–61
Gold, 154
  ancient history of, 111–15
  bar size variations, 134
  controversial nature of, 104–5
  fine weight of bars, 134
  fixing of price of, 128–31
  historical rush for, 103
  hoarding process in various
    countries, 120–21
  inflation hedge, 123–27
  interest in, 102
  legalization of ownership in
    America, 102, 104, 244–45
  London market versus Zurich
    market, 131–32
  market price runs, 102
  physical properties of, 106–7,
    133–34

Gold—*Cont.*
  premium for bars of, 178
  price fluctuations, 119, 133
  purchases of, 18–19
  refiner's hallmarks on bars of,
    134–35
  scarcity of, 107–9
  secrecy in market, 131–32
  standard bar of, 177–78
  trust in, 101–48
Gold backing, 4
  to balance of payments deficit,
    200–201
  to dollar notes, withdrawal of, 18
  to franc, 199–202
Gold bullion
  charges for purchasing, 136–37
  disadvantages, 137
  hoarding prohibition, 119
  key requirements for purchase
    and safekeeping of, 177–79
  odd amounts, purchases of, 179
  prices, 101
  properties of, 133–34
  purchases, 4
  rules for purchasing, 135–36
  safekeeping of, 178
Gold clauses in legal contracts, 102
Gold coins, 102
  advantages of, 137
  fakes, 140–41
  premium price of, 137, 140
  weights of, 138–40
Gold futures, 141
  advantages to trading in, 145–47
  commissions, 146
  contracts and exchanges, 143
  convenience, 146
  depression period, 142
  leverage, 145–46
  margins, 143
  pricing, 147
  quotations, 143–44
  reasons for use of, 145–48
  trading in, 122
  trading price limits, 147
Gold market machinations, 2
Gold pool dealers, 177
Gold refiners' hallmarks, 134–35

Gold standard
  suspension of, 119
  switch to, 118–19
Gold veins, 108–9
Goodman, George J. W. (Jerry),
  8–9, 179
Government banks, 53
Grace, W. R., & Company, New
  York, 92
Great Money Game, 2, 6, 17, 23,
  68–100
  American, 68–81
  British, 82–87
  business favorites, 97–100
  floating currency rates, 190–93
  giants playing by legal rules, 68–
    69
  illegalities, 69–81
  individual dodger and illegalities,
    68–69
  Italian, 87–97
  legal playing of, 97–100
  media coverage, 68–69
Greek gold, 113
Green, Timothy, 108 n
Greenback period, 126
Grossmunster Protestant Church,
  39
Growth of industry, 47–48, 51, 54
Growth of Swiss banks, 7
Guild industries, 47–48
Guisan, Henri, 61–63
Gurus, 7, 15, 18, 20–21, 23–25

H

Habeas corpus, absence of, 9–10
Hambros Bank, 128
"Hand payments," 93–97
Handling charges, 248
Hapsburg Empire
  independence from, 45
  tyranny of, 42
Harrison, George, 117
Harry Schultz Letter, The (HSL),
  16–20
Hegetschweiler, chief counsel of
  Swiss Credit Bank, 13
Helvetic Republic, 48–50
Hentsch & Co., 52

Herstatt Bank of Cologne, Ger-
  many, 265
Hirsch, Fred, 27 n
Historical influence, 39–67
Hitler, 62–63
Hoadford Securities, 83–84
"Hot money," 30, 34–38
Housing construction, 211
*How to Profit from the Coming De-
  valuation*, 21
Hughes, Helga R., 11–13
Hughes, Howard, 10–13
Hyperinflation, avoidance of, 233

I

Ilkle, Max, 245 n
Illegal money, 30, 34–38
Illegalities, 69–81
Image of Swiss banks, 218
Immutability, 2
Import of money, 46–47
Inconvenience of Swiss account,
  246
Individual freedom, belief in, 41
Industrial capacity, emergence of,
  50
Industrial capitalism, formation of,
  55
Inflation, 21–22, 25, 233
  gold as hedge against, 123–27
Inflation/recession prospects, 190
Informal collective guidance sys-
  tem, 249
Insider trading case, 74–75
Institutional Investor, 26, 32
Insurance firms, founding of, 53
Interest Equalization Tax (U.S.),
  268–69
  removal of, 239, 243
Interest payments; *see* Current ac-
  counts *and* Savings accounts
International commerce, 50
International Credit Bank of
  Geneva, 27
International finance, 238
International Harry Schultz Letter,
  15
International Monetary Seminars,
  16, 244, 268

International outlook, 238
International trade, 51, 55
Interol Bank, 84
Investment currency (British), 82
Investment diversification, 156
Investment funds, 174–76
Investment management function, 237–44
Investment portfolios, 6
  management of, 31–34
Irving, Clifford, 7, 10–13, 194–95
Irving, Edith, 7, 10–13, 194–95, 204
Italian banking schemes, 87–97

J

"Jeremiahs," 15, 25
Johnson, Matthey (Bankers), Ltd., 128, 134
Judicial assistance, 224–28

K

Kassenobligationen, 164
Keller, Pierre, 173
Kemmerer, D. L., 102 n
Keynes, John Maynard, 102
Khider, Mohammed, 28
Kimberley diamond mines, 117
Kleinwort, Benson, Lonsdale, Ltd., 128
Kruger Rand, 101, 148
Kummerli, Rudolph, 9

L

Lansky, Meyer, 74
La Roche & Co. of Basle, 52
Lauchli, M., 91, 94
League of Nations, 59–60
Legal departments, availability of, 180–81
Legal system, Roman law as basis of, 9
Legal tax avoidance efforts, 97–100
Leu & Compt., 51
Lewis, Arthur, 86–87
Liberalism, trend of, 57
Liechtenstein, 97
Liechtenstein Anstalts, 83
  securities frauds involving, 75–76
Limited liability status, 172–73

Liquid investment alternatives, 153
Little, Stanley, 85–87
Lloyd-Jacob, David, 109–11, 140
Lloyd's Bank
  branches of, 214
  Swiss unit, 27
Lombard, Odier & Co., 52, 173, 230, 236
London *Sunday Observer,* 21 n, 23
Lugano banks, 87–93
L'Unita, 88–89, 91–93
Lure for money, 1, 3, 38

M

McGraw-Hill Book Company of New York, 10–13
Machines for textile trade, manufacture of, 49–50
Magnavox, 83
Margin credit violations, 76–77
Marriage dissolution, 227–28
Marshall, John, 115
Marx, Karl, 57
Mass media coverage, 26–27
Mast, Hans, 35–36, 194, 205
Me Too Corporation case, 77–78
Media coverage in Great Money Game, 68–69
Media intervention, 26–27
Medium-term bond, 164
Mercenary soldiers, 40, 44–47
  ending of use of, 51
Merrill Lynch, Pierce, Fenner & Smith, 143
Mexico, privacy in, 220–21
Middlemen's activity, stories about, 94
Midland Bank Group, 128
Miller, Arthur R., 219
"Millionaire's Conference, The," 16, 25
Misappropriation of funds, 8
Mocatta, Goldsmid, 101, 128
Monetary privacy, 219–21
Money
  avoiding taxation by another country, 35
  import of, 46–47
  illegally obtained in another country, 35

Money—*Cont.*
state of disarray, 54
Money Game, 8
Money-management success, 1
Money market funds, 153
Montagu, Samuel, 116
Montagu, Samuel, & Co., 128
Moratorium on foreign payments (Germany), 231
Morgenthau, Henry, 119
Morgenthau, Robert M., 29, 71, 74–79, 157
Mortgage banks, 53
Multi-currency checkbooks, 267
disadvantage of, 198
handiness of, 186, 197
Multinational corporations, 179
Multiple currency availability, 156
Munoz, Julio, 9–10
Mutual Assistance Treaty between Switzerland and United States, 36, 41, 225, 259–60
summary of, 226–27
Mutual funds, 174–76, 238–42
Myths, 3–4, 184–212
persistence of, 5

N

Names of more than one person for account, 261
Napoleon Bonaparte, 48–50
National Westminster, branches of, 214
Nationally guaranteed currency, 54
Nazi Germany
flight of capital from, 59, 221–22
threat of, 60–61
Negative interest rate, 187–88, 191, 215, 233
Neutrality, 45, 54, 58–64, 229
New state, 50–51
New York Stock Exchange, 166, 177
News reports, 26–27
Newsweek magazine, 15
Nidwalden, canton of, 42
Nonresident purchases of Swiss securities, 243
Normal aspects of a banking relationship, 214–45

Numbered accounts, 4, 180
advantages of, 208–9
defined, 203
honesty of banks, 205
Mafia/underworld use of, 204–5
minimum size, 206–7
misconceptions about, 202–10
multiple payment inconvenience, 208
myth shroud, 185
numbers used, 209
references for, 207
refusal of, 207
regular accounts distinguished, 203
skepticism of Americans' opening of, 206
spies' use of, 204
where available, 221
Numbers game; *see* Numbered accounts

O

Offler, H. S., 45 n, 64 n
Oil drilling programs, 153
Olympics-style timing devices, 196
Orelli Im Thalhof, 52
Orwitz, Max, case, 74–75

P

Paper money, 54
Paperwork for accounts, 158–62
Past history of Switzerland, 39–67
Patman committee, 71
Patman hearings, 73–74
Peasant textile industries, 47
Peasant uprisings, 46
Penn Central, 31–32
Personal accounts, tax evasion on, 80–81
Personal independence, belief, in, 41
Personal relationship, 215–16
Persons who own Swiss bank accounts, 14–25
Phoenician gold, 112
Pictet & Co., 52, 230
Pillars of Swiss banking, 41–43
Pixley & Able, 116

Political asylum from persecution, 221
Political neutrality, 41
Political process, pattern of, 58
Political stability, 232
Popularity of Swiss banks, 216–18
  increase in, 25
  media intervention affecting, 26–27
Portugese counter-coup, 220
Potter, G. R., 45 n, 64 n
Pound sterling, devaluation of, 6, 68, 119, 233
Predictions; *see* Gurus
Press reporting, 26–27
Privacy, 2, 4, 38, 219–24
Private banks, 51–52
  establishment of, 230
  public bank, trend to become, 172–73
  securities portfolio management, role in, 171–74
  services rendered by, 173
Private transfers of money, 94–97
Promotional activities, 210–12
Protection, 2
Protestant reformation, 44
Publications by Swiss banks, 211, 253

R

Racketeer money, tax evasion on, 79–80
Rahn & Bodmer, 51
Railway enterprises, financing of, 52–53
Rate of return, 195–96
Real estate
  investment trusts, 153
  management services, 181
  mutual funds, 270
  syndicates, 153
Realty Equities Corp., 74
Reception rooms in banks, 149–52
Recession, 25, 153, 191–92
Recession shield, 264–71
Reformation, 43–45
Regular accounts, 4
  numbered accounts distinguished, 203

Religious strife, 40, 43–46
  moderation of, 51
Remoteness of Swiss accounts, 246–47
Reserve Bank of South Africa, 109
Reserves of large liquid deposits, 262–63
Revolution, cry of, 48–50
Rhodes, Cecil, 117
Roman gold, 113–15
Roosevelt, Franklin D., 103, 119
Rosenkranz, Hanna, 11–13
Rothschild, N. M., & Sons, 52, 128–29
Rousseau, Jean Jacques, 48
Rudd, Charles, 117
Runaway inflation, 22
Russian gold, 115
Rütli Meadow conference, 62
Rütli Meadow principles, 42, 46, 48

S

Safit, 176
Sample account form, 158–59
San Diego First National and Franklin Bank, demise of, 27
Sarasin, A., & Co., 52
Savings accounts, 153, 162–66
  basic, 162–63
  deposit, 162–63
  interest payments, 162–63
  interest rate changes, 164
  investment type, 163
  minimum account size, 235
  notice of withdrawal requirements, 162
  special, 163
Savings banks, 53
Schellenberg, Walter, 63
Schlesinger, Arthur, 232 n
Schulthess, Felix W., 30, 254–61
Schultz, Harry, 15–20, 24–25, 110 n, 218, 244, 268
Schweis as name of empire, 45
Schweizerische Spar und Kreditbank, 27
Schweizerische Volksbank, 53
Schwyz, canton of, 42
Secrecy, 1, 4, 7, 10–12, 14, 30, 38, 66–67, 254–57

Secrecy—*Cont.*
  abuses of, 70–71
  criminal penalties for violations
    of, 60, 222–23
  effects of, 185
Securities and Exchange Commission, 75
Securities frauds, 74–77
  investigations of, 2
Securities gains, tax on, 262
Securities portfolio management,
    166–71, 237–44
  brokerage commissions, 239,
    261–62
  fees and charges for, 167–69
  managers' handling, 170
  nonfee basis, 168–69
  personal attention, 170
  physical form of securities, 169–
    70
  private banks, role of, 171–74
  registration of securities, forms
    of, 169
  size variations, 168–69
  stock brokerage affiliates in
    United States, 170–71
Seesaw analogy, 190–93
Services offered by Swiss banks,
    152–81, 234–39, 243–44
Sharps, Pixley, 116, 128
Silver backing to dollar notes, withdrawal of, 18
Single accounts
  penalty regulations governing,
    188–89
  prohibition against interest payments for, 186
Sitzimmers, 150
Small amount deposits, 157–58
"Smith, Adam," 8
Social Contract, 48
Socialist thought, 57
SoGen, New York, 171
Solzhenitsyn, Alexander, 221
Sonderbund, 56
South African gold mines, 108–9,
    117–18
Spinning jenny spinning machines,
    exports of, 50
Stability, 228–34

Stanley, John Charles, 82–84
Stock brokerage affiliates in United
    States, 170–71
Stock exchanges, 176–77
Stock market collapse in United
    States, 152–53
Stock purchase margin rules,
    abuses of, 76–77
Stucki, Lorenz, 46 n
Supermoney, 8–9
Sutherland, C. V. H., 108 n, 112,
    114 n
Swiss-American Corporation, New
    York, 171
Swiss army, 40, 232–33
Swiss bank accounts
  lack of knowledge about, 1–2
  number of Americans holding, 3,
    6
  persons who own, 14–25
  profitability of holding, 3
Swiss Bank Corporation, 53, 171,
    211, 265
  branches in United States, 215
  mutual funds, 241
  securities portfolio management
    procedures, 167–68
Swiss Bankers Association, 77
Swiss bankers talk, 253–61
Swiss Banking Commission, 38
Swiss banks; *see specific topics*
Swiss corporation, establishment
    of, 181
Swiss Credit and Bank Corp.,
    175
Swiss Credit Bank, 30, 35, 171, 194,
    204–5, 211, 230, 254, 265
  launching of, 53
  mutual funds, 242
  securities portfolio management,
    169
Swiss Credit Bank on Paradeplatz
    in Zurich, 166
  Helga R. Hughes' account at,
    11–13
Swiss currency, devaluation of, 233
Swiss franc
  gold backing of, 199–202
  interest-bearing deposits, 189
  record of, 155

Swiss National Bank, 54, 186, 188, 191, 199
Swiss Re-Insurance, 53
Swiss union, formation of, 41–42
Switzerland and Other Financial Havens, 15

T

Tax avoidance, 225–26
Tax collection dodging, 81
Tax evasion schemes, 79–81
   investigations of, 2
Tax fraud, 225–26
Tax havens outside of Switzerland, 97
Tax return preparation, 181
Tax shelter investment advantages, 153
Technicalities, 261–63
Tell, William, legend of, 41–43, 48
Textile industry, 47
   cheap English machine-spun cotton, introduction of, 49
Those Swiss Money Men, 250
Thrower, Randolph W., 79–81
Thürer, George, 44 n, 61 n
Ticino bank growth, 87–88
Toggenburg Bank merger, 53
Trade Bill of January 1975, 269
Trading currencies, 235–36
Treasury bills, 153
Trusts, establishment of, 181
Truth About Swiss Banking, The, 224
Tyranny, 48

U

UCB, Basle, A. G., 244, 247, 249
   scandal, 8–9
Ufitec, Zurich, 31
Union Bank of Switzerland, 23, 25, 27, 53, 75, 89, 171, 199, 211, 230, 250, 253
   branches in United States, 215
   deposits in, 6
   mutual funds, 240

Union Bank of Switzerland—*Cont.*
   reception area in Lugano branch, 149–52
   reorganization of, 232, 265
   securities portfolio management, 168–69
United California Bank, 8
U.S. Bank Secrecy Act of 1970, 2, 219–20
U.S. Mint, gold coins minted by, 115–16
Unitex Capital Fund (U.K.), Ltd., 83–84
Uri, canton of, 42

V

Vicker, Ray, 32 n, 250
Vienna, Congress of, 50–51
Villmergen wars of 1656 and 1712, 46
Vontobel, J., 52

W

"Walk away" money transfers, 94–96
Wall Street Journal, The, 8, 26, 29, 33, 201, 217
   gold futures, 144
Waller, Leslie, 74 n
War for money, 45–47
Watergate scandals, 217, 219
Western Bancorporation of Los Angeles, 8
Western Union, 83
Westphalia, Peace of, 45
White-House directed IRS audits, 220
White, Weld, Inc., New York, 171
Wills, drafting and notarizing of, 181
Winterthur Bank merger, 53
Withholding tax on interest payments, 165–66
Wojnilower, Albert, 154, 156
Worker/capitalist dichotomies
World War I, 58–59, 119, 231
World War II, 41
Wormser, R. A., 102 n

Y

You Can Profit From a Monetary
Crisis, 21, 23, 217
Yukon gold rush, 108, 118

Z

Zurich, canton of, 43

Zurich, Canton of—*Cont.*
constitutional revision, 57
Zurich Accident, 53
Zurich Bankverein merger, 53
Zurich Bourse, 166, 169, 175–77